THE ADAM BROTHERS IN ROME

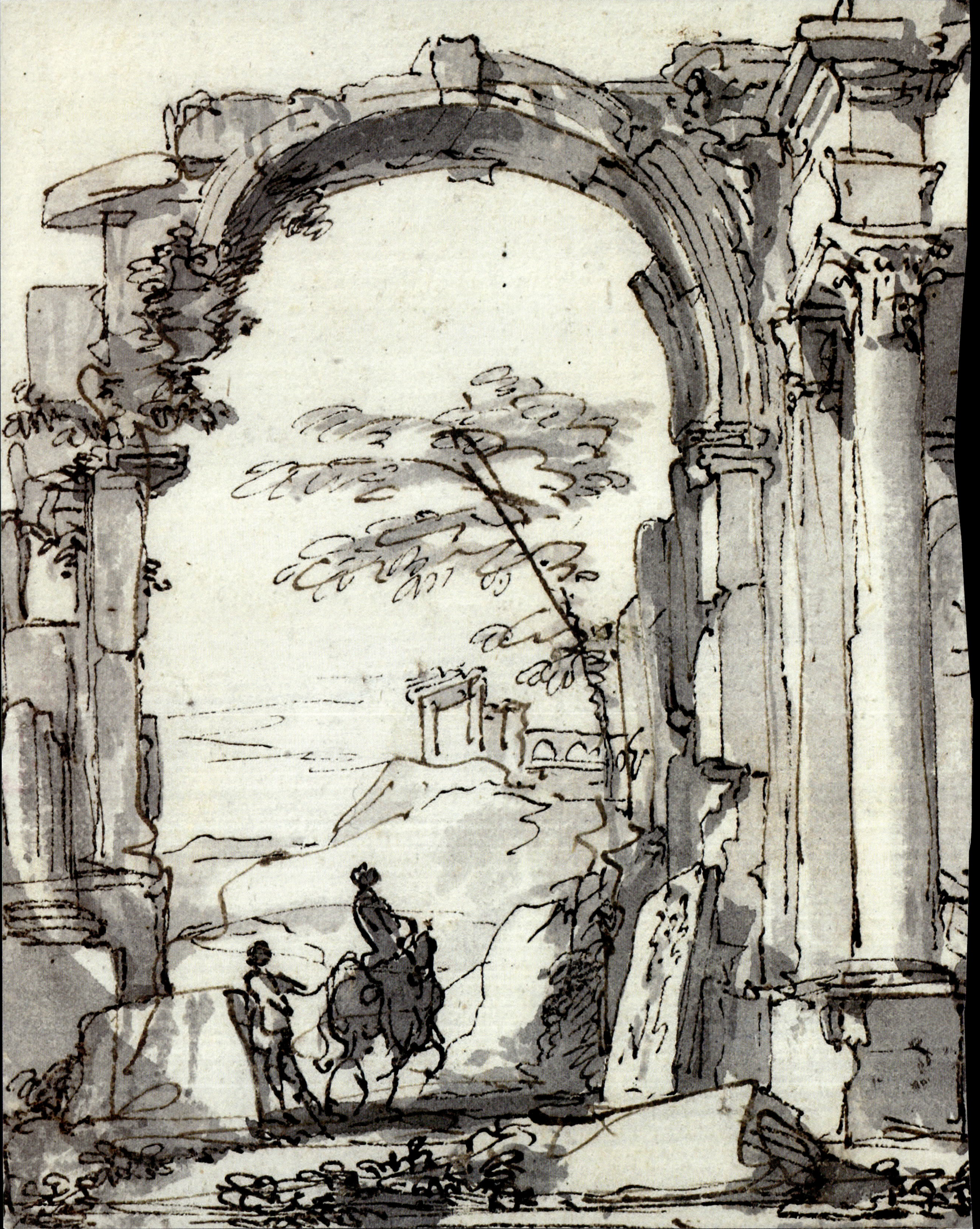

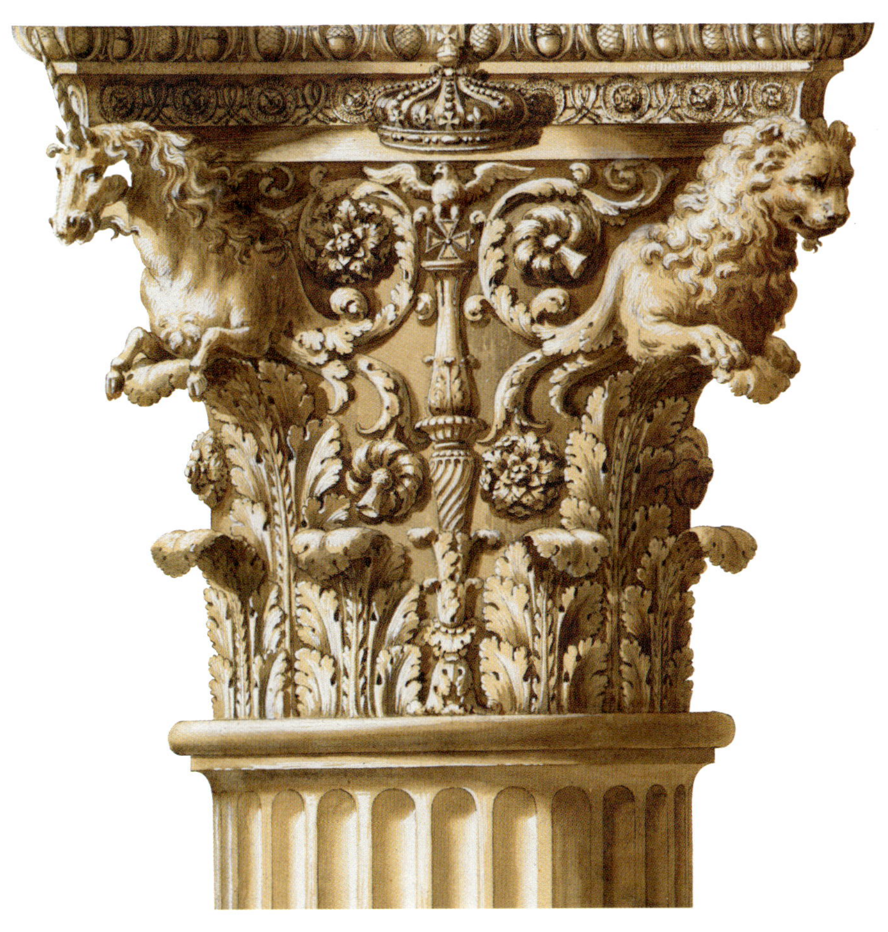

THE ADAM BROTHERS IN ROME

Drawings from the Grand Tour

A. A. TAIT

SCALA

First published in 2008 by
Scala Publishers Ltd
Northburgh House
10 Northburgh Street
London ECIV OAT, UK
www.scalapublishers.com

In association with
Sir John Soane's Museum
13 Lincoln's Inn Fields
London WC2A 3BP
www.soane.org

ISBN 978 1 85759 574 1

Edited by Sandra Pisano
Designed by Nigel Soper
Printed in Spain

10 9 8 7 6 5 4 3 2 1

Page 2: Robert Adam *Attributed to*
Architectural capriccio of a ruined arch with two figures below, 1756–67, pen and grey wash, 132 x 112 mm, Adam vol. 56/79.

Page 6: Robert Adam
Landscape study of young deciduous trees in a park-like landscape, after 1755, pen and watercolour, 290 x 214 mm, Adam vol. 56/156.

Page 8: Charles-Louis Clérisseau *Attributed to*
Architectural capriccio with a boat sarcophagus in the foreground, 1756, pencil, pen, grey and brown washes and watercolour, 202 x 264 mm, Adam vol. 56/102.

ACKNOWLEDGEMENTS

There are around 1,000 drawings that can be connected with the Grand Tours of Robert and James Adam. They are in seven of the fifty-five volumes of Adam drawings purchased by Sir John Soane from the Clerk (Adam) family in 1833. In working with them, I have had the help and advice of many people both within Sir John Soane's Museum and outside. From the inside I should like to thank the former Director, Margaret Richardson and the current Director, Tim Knox; also Sue Palmer, Margaret Schuelein, Stephen Astley and Jerzy Kierkuc-Bielinski. From outside the Museum particular thanks are due to Amanda Claridge, Jill Lever, Michael Snodin and Shaun Cole at the Victoria and Albert Museum, and last but not least to the editor at Scala Publishers, Sandra Pisano.

Of the books that I have consulted, I must happily emphasise that John Fleming's *Robert Adam and his Circle in Edinburgh and Rome* was of great value and indeed inspiration; many of the quotations used in this book are taken from this source. Once again, I have used extensively the Clerk of Penicuik manuscripts and I am grateful to the late Sir John Clerk for permission to quote from the Adam letters.

A.A. TAIT
London, May 2008

PHOTOGRAPHIC CREDITS

All images by courtesy of the Trustees of Sir John Soane's Museum.

Photo: Hugh Kelly (back cover, pp 2, 6, 8, 13, 21 [bottom], 23, 27-33, 36-39, 48, 50-55, 60, 61, 66, 67, 70, 77-81, 84-91, 96, 97, 100-103, 108-112, 118-122, 128-134, 136, 137, 140, 141, 144, 148, 149, 152-157).

Photo: Geremy Butler (front cover, map shown on pp 5, 10, 14, 24, 44, 62, 104 and 124, pp 17 [right], 18-20, 21 [top], 22, 34, 35, 40-43, 49, 56-59, 68, 69, 71-76, 82, 83, 92-95, 98, 99, 113-117, 123, 135, 138, 139, 142, 143, 145-147, 150, 151).

CONTENTS

Foreword
6

Introduction
8

The Collection
10

A Showcase for the Collection
14

Scotland
24

Robert Adam's Grand Tour

Naples
44

Rome
62

Collecting
104

James Adam's Grand Tour

Rome
124

BIBLIOGRAPHY
158

INDEX
159

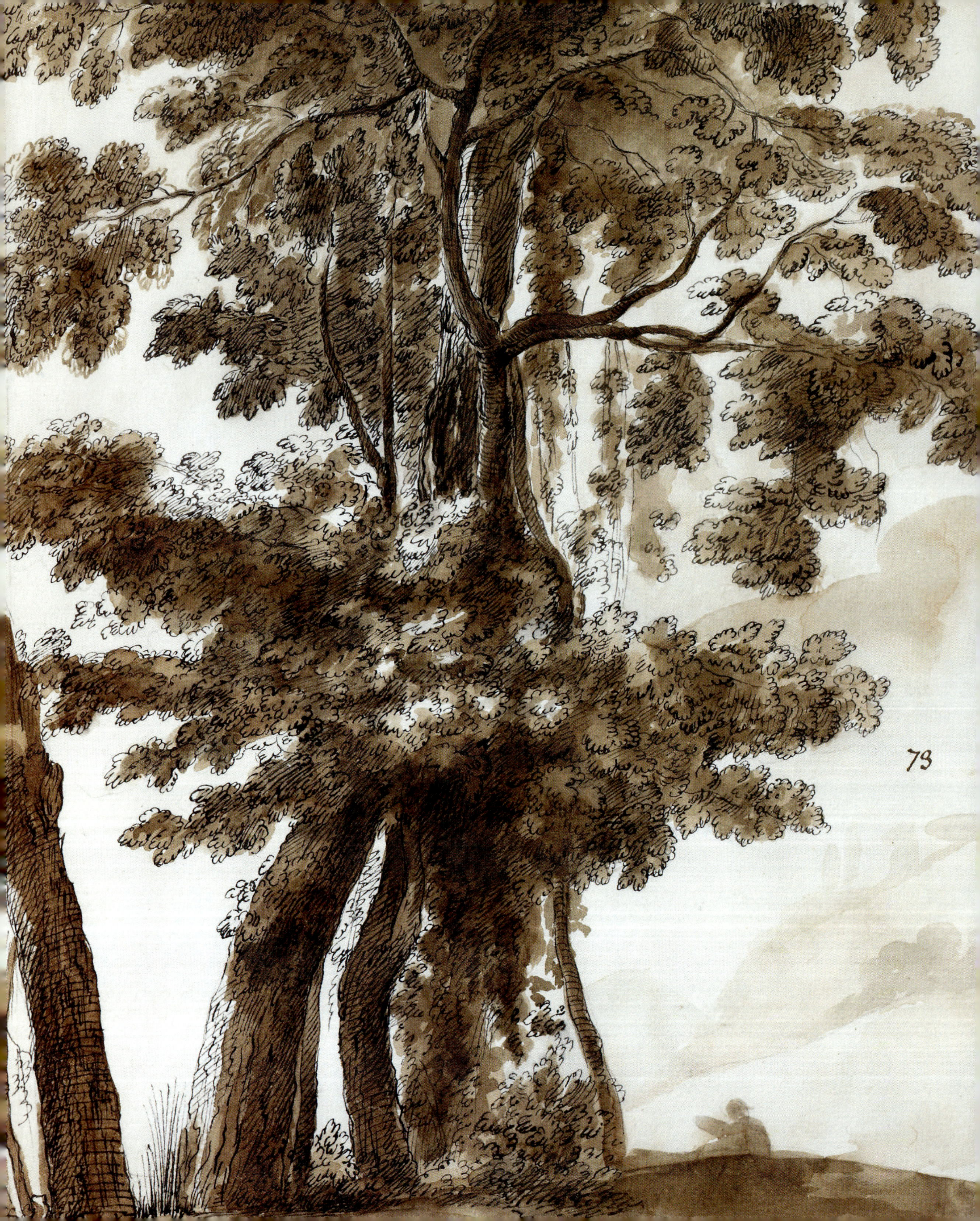
78

Foreword

THIS BOOK, the first of a series of five illustrated books on the work of Robert and James Adam planned with Scala Publishers, celebrates the completion of the first stage of an ambitious project to catalogue all the drawings by the Adam office in the collection of Sir John Soane's Museum in London. The 1,000 or so drawings executed by Robert and James Adam on their respective Grand Tours of Italy in 1754–57 and 1761–63, as well as those by the other draughtsmen in their entourage – significant figures in their own right, artists of the calibre of Charles-Louis Clérisseau, Jean-Baptiste Lallemand, Laurent-Benoît Dewez, Agostino Brunias, Antonio Zucchi and Giuseppe Manocchi – are among the most beautiful and interesting as any in the 57 albums that comprise the Adam Collection in the Research Library of Sir John Soane's Museum. Ranging from Robert Adam's amateurish early attempts at topographical drawing at the elbow of his mentor Clérisseau, to the peerless wash renderings of details of James Adam's impossibly grandiose scheme for a new Houses of Parliament by the professional draughtsmen Zucchi and Manocchi, this is just a foretaste of the riches of the Adam office archive.

Professor A.A. Tait has devoted many years to studying and cataloguing these little-known drawings, unravelling their complicated chronology and authorship, as well as their purpose and – in many cases for the first time – pin-pointing their exact topographical location. *The Adam Brothers in Rome: Drawings from the Grand Tour* is the culmination of this valuable work and we thank him for his patience, his determination, and for his support of the Museum in so many ways. Thanks are also due to my predecessor Margaret Richardson, Curator of Sir John Soane's Museum between 1995 and 2005, whose idea it was to commission Alan to embark upon this very worthwhile project. Over the years he has been supported by Soane Museum staff, most notably by Stephen Astley, Curator of Drawings, who has an unrivalled knowledge of the Adam Collection at the Soane. Thanks are also due to Susan Palmer, Soane Museum Archivist, who has taken on much of the work of preparing this volume for publication, and to Helen Dorey, Gordon Higgott, Eileen Harris, Jill Lever and Mike Nicholson for their advice and support. Outside the Museum, thanks are due to John Harris and Frank Salmon, to Sally Williams who edited the online catalogue entries, to Amanda Claridge who checked the catalogue descriptions for topographical drawings relating to classical archaeology, and made many helpful suggestions and identifications, and to Hugh Kelly who took the admirable new digital photographs that illustrate this work. We are grateful to Selina Fellows for introducing us to Jenny McKinley and her efficient team at Scala Publishers, who have been such a pleasure to work with. Finally, this book, the photography and much of the recent work of editing the online catalogue would not have been possible without the generous and constant financial support of Mrs Gisela Gledhill, who dedicates this work to the memory of her late husband, Richard Harris. His love of the art and architecture of the eighteenth century is fittingly commemorated in this celebration of the Adam Brothers' Grand Tour.

TIM KNOX, JUNE 2008

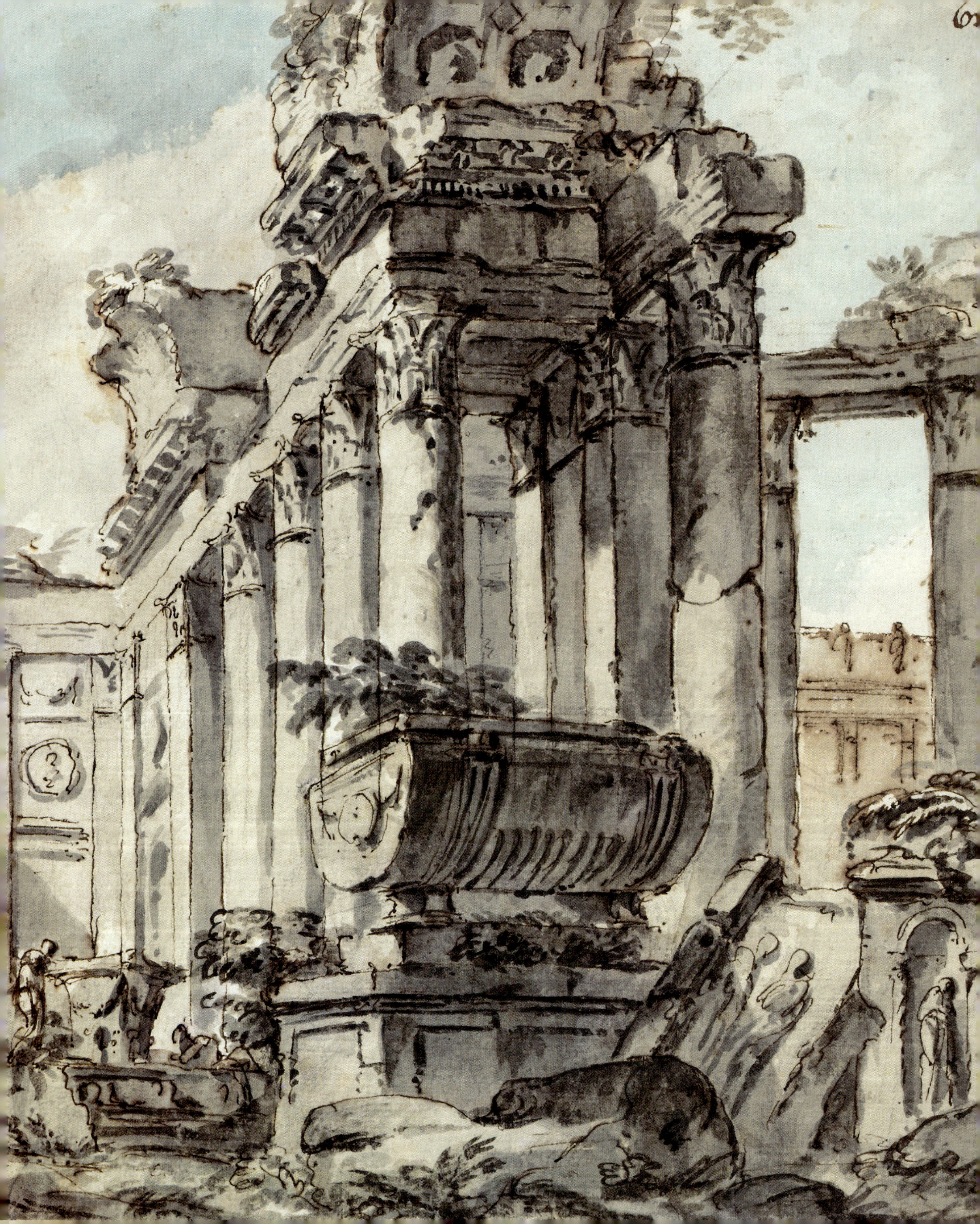

Introduction

The Grand Tour, like such cultural phenomena, was all things to all men. For Robert and James Adam, Italy offered a world of intense intellectual, professional and social development. Their limited Scottish education had equipped all four brothers (the eldest was John Adam and the youngest, William Adam) to practise architecture in Scotland and had given them a fine understanding of the Scottish system of patronage, but little else. To attain greater things, they needed the space to branch out and break with tradition. This meant travel abroad – that is, beyond England. For anyone interested in extending or developing their understanding of the visual arts in the eighteenth century, this certainly meant Italy, regarded as the cradle of antiquity and centre of the classical world. To that end, and with money enough, the Grand Tour was the most agreeable route to take.

For Robert and James Adam, the purpose of their tours was never in doubt. It was to provide them with a clear understanding of classical architecture, root and branch, and enable them to effectively express that understanding pictorially. Such was the bedrock of the Adam style and the basis of their later triumph in London.

Beyond this was the part the brothers played as collectors, in the traditional role of the Grand Tourist, though here both means and end were different. While it was true that the collection of drawings made on a heroic scale by Robert Adam, and on a lesser by James, had a practical purpose more than an aesthetic one – of value as future inspiration for 'we modern devils' – this was hardly the whole story. A collection so assiduously and expensively formed was intended for higher and better things than mere copying and training of the eye. These drawings were more an ambitious attempt to form a history of drawing and draughtsmanship, from the Renaissance through the seventeenth century to the contemporary manner of Clérisseau, Piranesi and Lallemand. Such a collection was intended as much to illustrate drawing styles and architectural composition as the broader artistic development of the times.

The counterpart of such a paper collection was the less restricted one of painting and sculpture. It was in the brothers' Jekyll-and-Hyde role as scholar-connoisseurs that they scoured Rome hand-in-glove with the city's dealers, ready to take advantage of every opportunity in typical Adam fashion. The acquisitions they made, virtually all between 1755 and 1764, were, however, viewed with a sharp and calculating eye, and the brothers were at all times ready to sell should the right opportunity present itself. The whole range of paintings, drawings and antiquities were there to support both taste and income, as well as to lend prestige to their names in Rome and London.

The Co

llection

THE DRAWINGS that are reproduced here are all taken from the collection of 57 volumes of Adam drawings purchased by Sir John Soane. They are almost exclusively drawn from those volumes that relate to the brothers' time in Rome. The collection itself had come from 13 Albemarle Street, the house and office of the brothers until its sale in 1821. Robert and James had left the collection to their unmarried sisters and then to their niece, Susan Clerk, and their youngest brother, William. It was Miss Clerk who arranged the sale to Soane after a series of disappointing negotiations with the British Museum and the Edinburgh Board of Manufactures and an abortive and somewhat farcical auction in Edinburgh in 1833 during which the floor collapsed. Soane bought the collection for £200, explaining that 'I entertain so high a regard for the memory of Mr Robert Adam that I should regret the dispersion of such a collection of his works and as in the event of my becoming possessed of these Volumes they will be permanently secured with the rest of my Library & Collection for the use and advantage of Students in architecture and the artists of Great Britain in general.' Included in the list of the drawings, made by the somewhat slap-happy Edinburgh lawyers, Gibson Craig, Wardlaw and Dalziel, there was a note that described what was termed the third and final series as 'XII volumes folio of Mr Adam's architectural studies while in Rome'. It is largely the contents of these volumes that are dealt with here.

There are in fact seven rather than twelve volumes of what may be termed those of the Adam brothers' Grand Tours. The arrangement of the drawings within the volumes is of some interest in itself, appearing to reflect a sense of historical awareness, or at least perspective, of their contents as a remarkable record of time and taste. Six of the volumes candidly reveal the roots of the Adam style, both through the brothers' drawings as well as the works they collected. And a case can be made that some of the volumes, such as Volume 7 and Volume 55, were arranged by the brothers themselves, with the drawings numbered in ink in a late eighteenth-century hand, possibly also by them. The lawyers also recorded 'two volumes bound in parchment, containing J Adam's studies at Rome', of which one is certainly Volume 7, held at the Soane Museum. Its companion is now at Penicuik House, Edinburgh, the family home of Miss Clerk, and was probably left there by accident during the general confusion of the sale. It is bound in parchment and the topographical nature of its content would suit 'studies at Rome', although the hand is largely Robert Adam's.

Two volumes, Volume 9 and Volume 55, offer a particularly vivid insight into Robert's academic studies in Rome. They carry a typical Italian watermark for the period – a circled fleur-de-lis – and the drawings themselves came from a variety of portfolios and sketchbooks and were pasted in at some later date and numbered in ink. There is a note, probably in William Adam's hand, beside the first drawing in Volume 55, that 'All the Sketches that follow were drawn abroad', with the same statement repeated in an eighteenth-century hand on the flyleaf. The 71 drawings in Volume 9 are almost exclusively plans showing Robert at work composing endless variations on various set themes, such as the centralised villa, with subjects either suggested or reviewed by his architectural instructor, Laurent-Benoît Dewez. They reveal the other side of his ambiguous role as the scholar-connoisseur, something that marked both him and James out from the conventional 'milordi' as much as from the indigent artists gathered in Rome. Both Robert and James were assiduous and voracious collectors, whose geese were always swans in their own eyes. Their collecting leavened the rigours of three years of studying in Robert's case, and four in that of James, and made more meaningful their architectural tours the length of Italy, from Baiae to Venice.

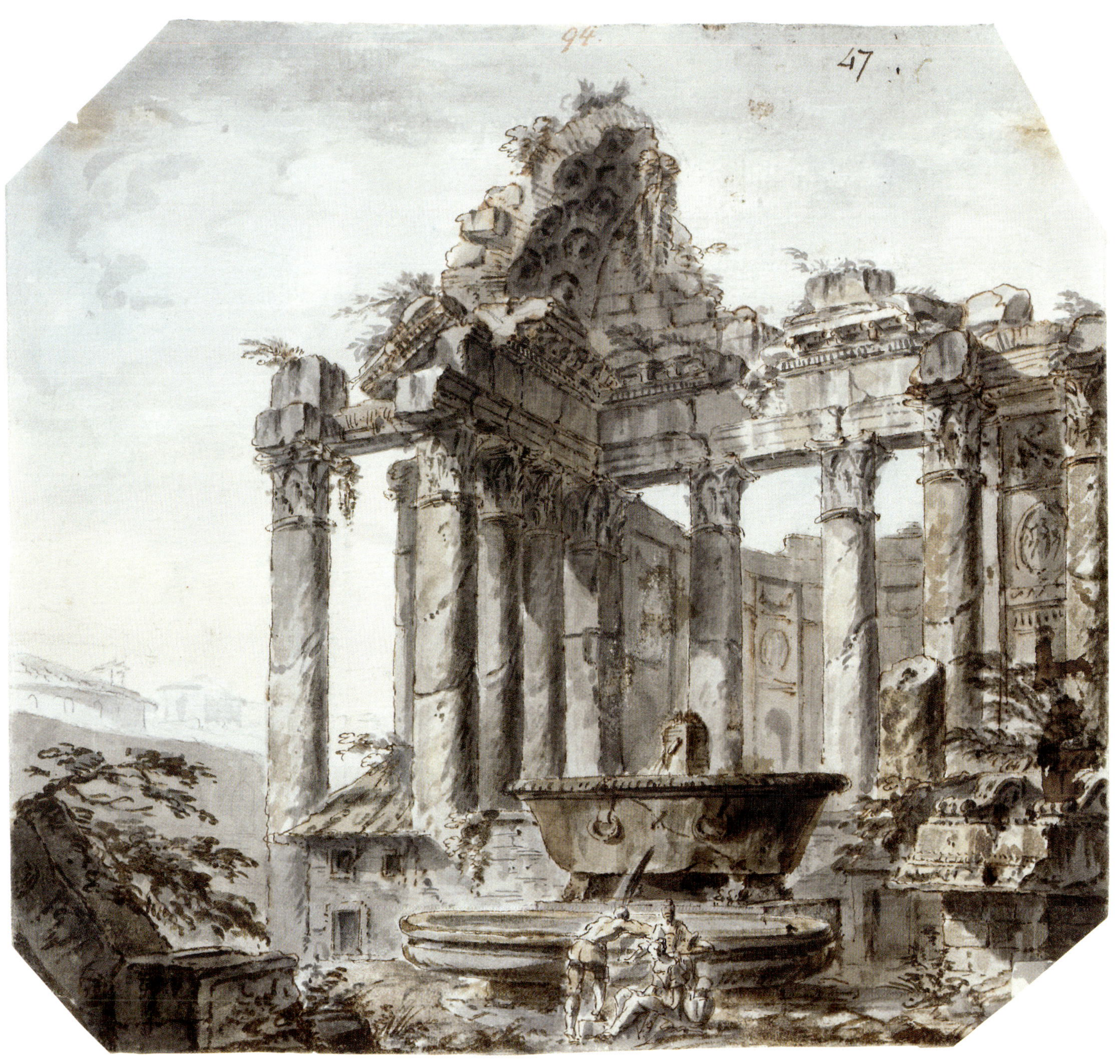

1. Charles-Louis Clérisseau (1721–1820)
Architectural capriccio showing a ruined temple with a curved apse seen through a screen of columns

1756
Pencil, pen, and brown and grey washes
204 x 223 mm
Adam vol. 56/94

This drawing illustrates Clérisseau's mastery of light, which is captured in the liveliness of the brown and grey washes.

A Showcase
the Co

for llection

THERE IS PERHAPS no more direct and fitting monument to the Adam brothers as Grand Tourists than the Casino (Italian for little house) – probably built for the garden of their London house at 75 Lower Grosvenor Street in 1764 [fig.2]. It was a simple octagon with a coffered dome, 27 feet in diameter, with sculpture set in niches beside a Renaissance-style chimney-piece [fig.4]. The idea was a simple one as well: to provide a showcase for what they had acquired in Italy – paintings, sculpture and drawings, all rubbing shoulders one with another and revealing the sources and discrimination of the brothers' taste. Similar to Robert Adam's Birthday Pavilion of 1762 for George III, the canvas and wood Casino was an intimate essay, and probably a temporary one, for the garden was small and the house on a leasehold. Its small portico led into a central room with four large niches for antique sculpture on plinths set between pilasters. These were decorated with grotesque work in the style of the Vatican *stanze* that the brothers knew well, and of which copies had been made for them by Volpato and Lhuillier around 1763 [fig.5]. Robert also owned two similar panels 'of Antique & cinque cento design' that Sir John Soane bought later at the Adam sale of 1818, and these may originally have been set up in the Casino [fig.6]. A drawing by Robert from before 1764, annotated as a 'Sketch of the Manner of placing Ancient Marbles under the room in my area', showed how the smaller fragments were to be displayed in a symmetrical fashion on the wall, with the inscriptions 'Roma' and 'R.A' [fig.7]. A handsome drawing of a sarcophagus front, annotated 'Ex Museo JA' by James Adam, was probably set up there too and sold in 1773 to the Adam plasterer, Joseph Rose [fig.8].

Similar displays were continued throughout the public rooms of the house, though probably not as densely. The Adam parlour, the street-facing room of the terraced house, contained paintings: at least two by Jacopo Amigoni, two landscapes by Teniers, Guido Reni's *St Francis* and a picture described as 'figures riding through the Colosseum'. The dining room had Robert's large Domenichino, *Allegory of Time*, which was acquired in Bologna in 1757 and sold for 10 guineas in 1785. Also, Carlo Maratta's *Holy Family* on copper, bought at auction in Rome, and Guido Reni's small *St Catherine.* In addition to these was the display of architectural and topographical drawings that had struck Robert's future client, Sir Nathaniel Curzon of Kedleston, 'all of a heap with wonder and amaze'. Sadly, little can now be traced of such riches apart from some of the antique sculpture and architectural fragments bought by Soane at the 1818 sale [fig.9]. To such a loss must be added the missing collection of drawings for the revision and expansion of Antoine Desgodetz's publication, *Les Edifices Antiques de Rome*, finished in Rome in 1757 and described by Robert as 'all completed and to be sure it has cost me a great deal of trouble and plague', a hint of its scale and magnificence [fig.10].

The Casino, ephemeral as it was, succeeded in what it set out to do – to put the Adam brothers and the Adam style on the map. It explained visually and physically what they had accomplished during the long Italian years of their Grand Tours and the critical standards they now imposed on their new architecture. It suggested the new Adam style in its interpretation of both past and present themes. More generally, the Casino showed the Grand Tour was not so much a journey as a state of mind, and the objects it housed represented, as it were, the milestones along the road. It did not last long as such a beacon, its blaze doused by the first Adam sale of 1765, which reduced the collection. And its purpose was over by 1772, when the brothers moved themselves and their office to the newly built Royal Terrace in The Adelphi. What remained of the collection went on sale a year later, on the other side of the Strand in Catherine Street, yet the ghost of the Casino still lingered in the Adam imagination. After the brothers' removal to 13 Albemarle Street and the deaths of Robert and James in 1792 and 1794, respectively, William Adam, the youngest and surviving brother, proposed 'to close in the backyard of this house & fit it up properly & make a sale of them there', of the 'Antique Sculpture of Greek and Roman workmanship'.

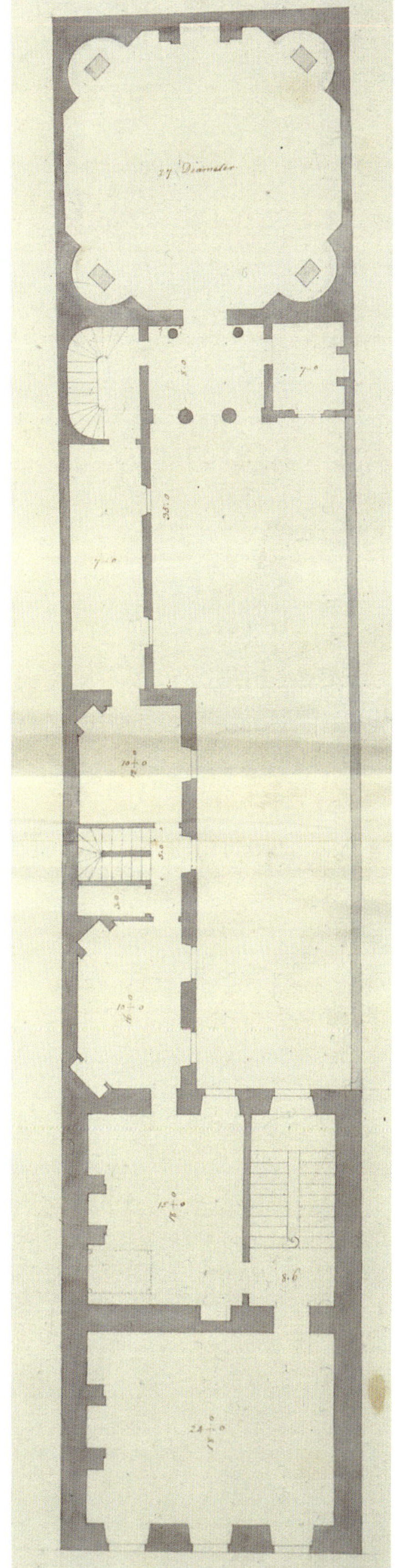

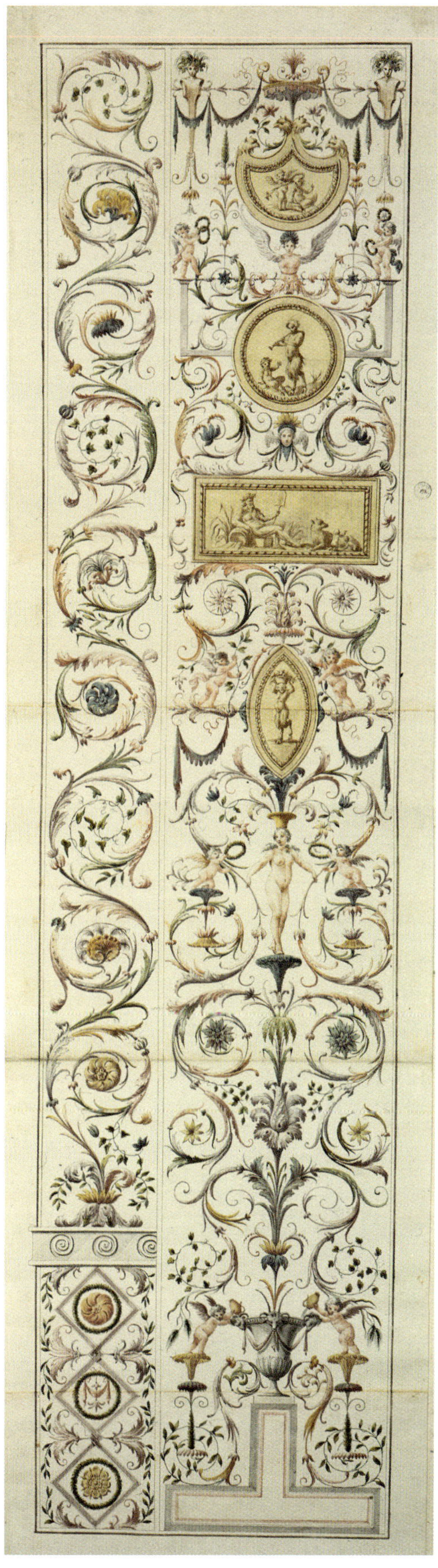

2. Adam office

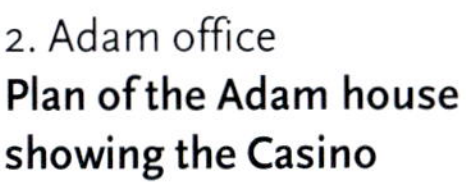

Plan of the Adam house showing the Casino

1764
Pencil, pen and grey washes
203 x 182 mm
Adam vol. 7/227

In January 1758, Robert Adam returned from Italy and soon after took a lease on 75 Lower Grosvenor Street, London. With the intention that his house should 'blind the world by dazzling their eyesight with vain pomp', he planned a covered passageway from the house leading to a casino at the end of the garden, elaborately decorated and displaying the sculpture he and his brother, James, had acquired in Italy.

3. Giuseppe Manocchi (*c*.1731–82)
Attributed to
Study of a decorated pilaster

c.1756
Pen, watercolour and bodycolour
1240 x 354 mm
Adam vol. 26/192

This is one of a series of studies that James Adam commissioned, of the Vatican *Loggie*. He later used versions of them in the proposed decoration of the Adam house at 75 Lower Grosvenor Street.

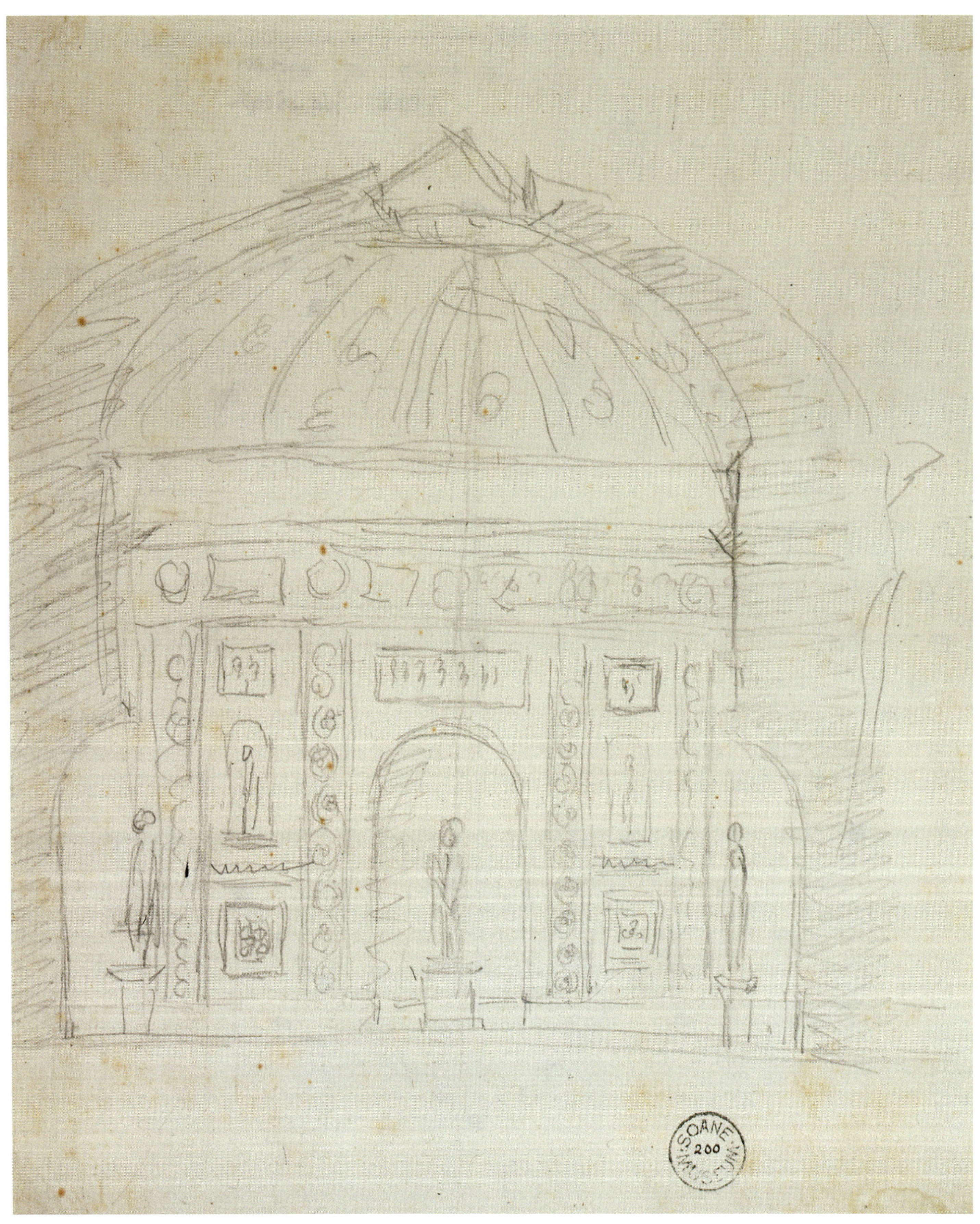
SOANE
200
MUSEUM

4. Robert Adam (1728–92)
Sketch section of the Casino

1764
Pencil
242 x 182 mm
Adam vol. 7/200

This sketch shows Robert Adam's design for the domed Casino, lit by an oculus, as a miniature Pantheon. It also shows sculpture on plinths standing in niches, and an elaborate decorative scheme based on prototypes he had seen in Italy.

5. Robert Adam
Design for the decoration of the Casino

1764
Pencil and pen
320 x 205 mm
Adam vol. 7/223

This detail of the decoration proposed for the Casino shows one of the niches. All is highly decorated, and there is space for a painting. The plinth for the sculpture is also ornamented and the pilasters emulate those Robert Adam had seen and copied in the Vatican *Loggie*.

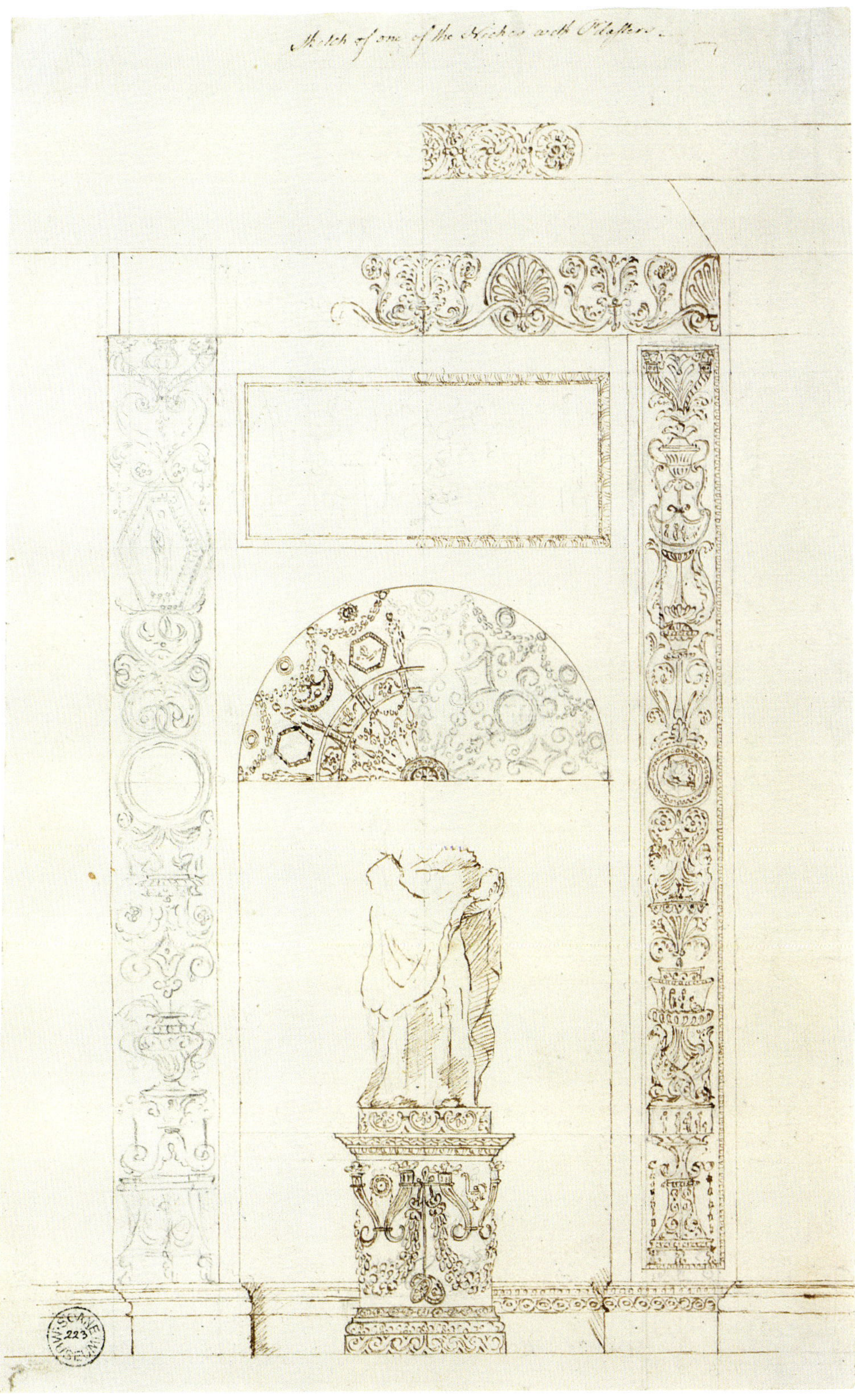

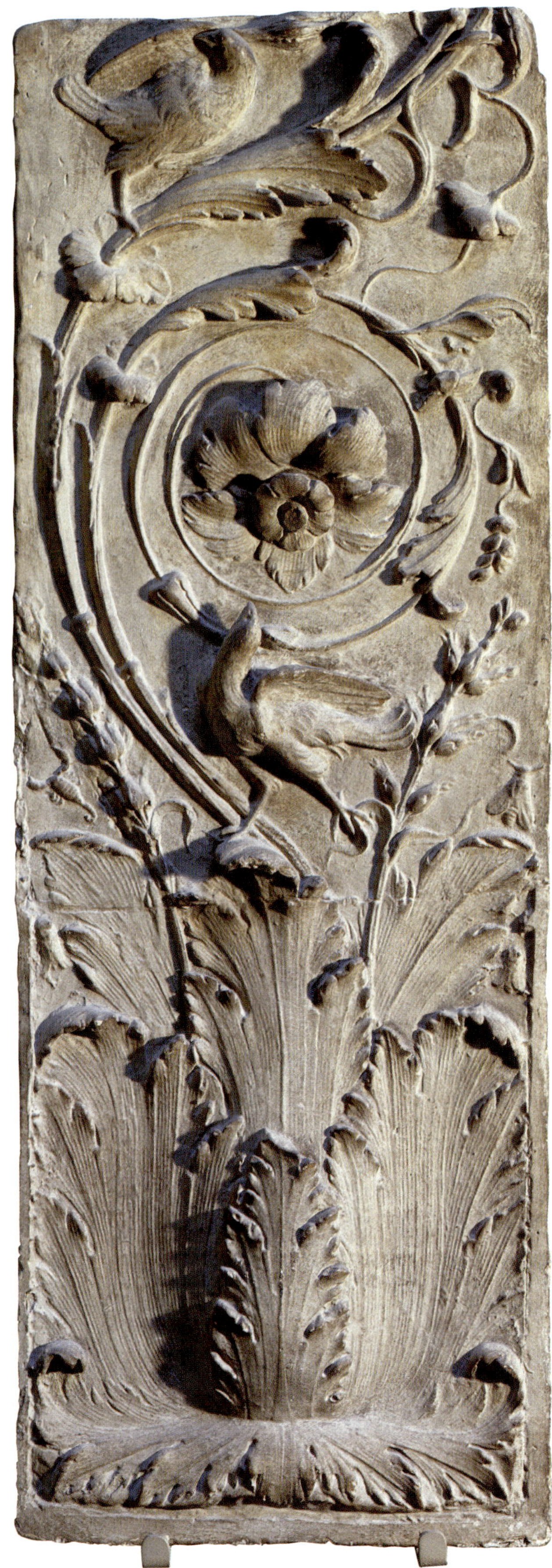

6.
Plaster cast of a decorative panel or pilaster

Late 18th century
Plaster
763 x 233 x 40 mm
Soane Museum A3

This was possibly part of Lot 40 in the 1818 Adam sale, which was purchased by Sir John Soane for 10s 6d. Such casts were made in Italy for tourists and architects. Robert Adam brought it back to London to include as part of the repertoire of Renaissance ornament available to him in his collection.

7. Robert Adam
Sketch for arranging sculpture at 75 Lower Grosvenor Street

*c.*1758–60
Pen
196 x 232 mm
Adam vol. 54 / Series 3/28

Some of the sculpture Robert Adam brought back from Italy was to be displayed in the area at the rear of the Adams' house at Lower Grosvenor Street. It was a statement about what the brothers had seen and acquired in Italy, and much was discreetly for sale.

8. Unidentified 18th-century architect
Study of front panel of antique sarcophagus

*c.*1762
Pencil, black chalk, black wash and white heightening
150 x 553 mm
Adam vol. 26/55

This panel has been identified as that described as Lot 20 in the 1773 Adam sale. It does not match any of the sources given in James Adam's list of 'good Antiquitys' of 1762, and was probably acquired from a Roman dealer.

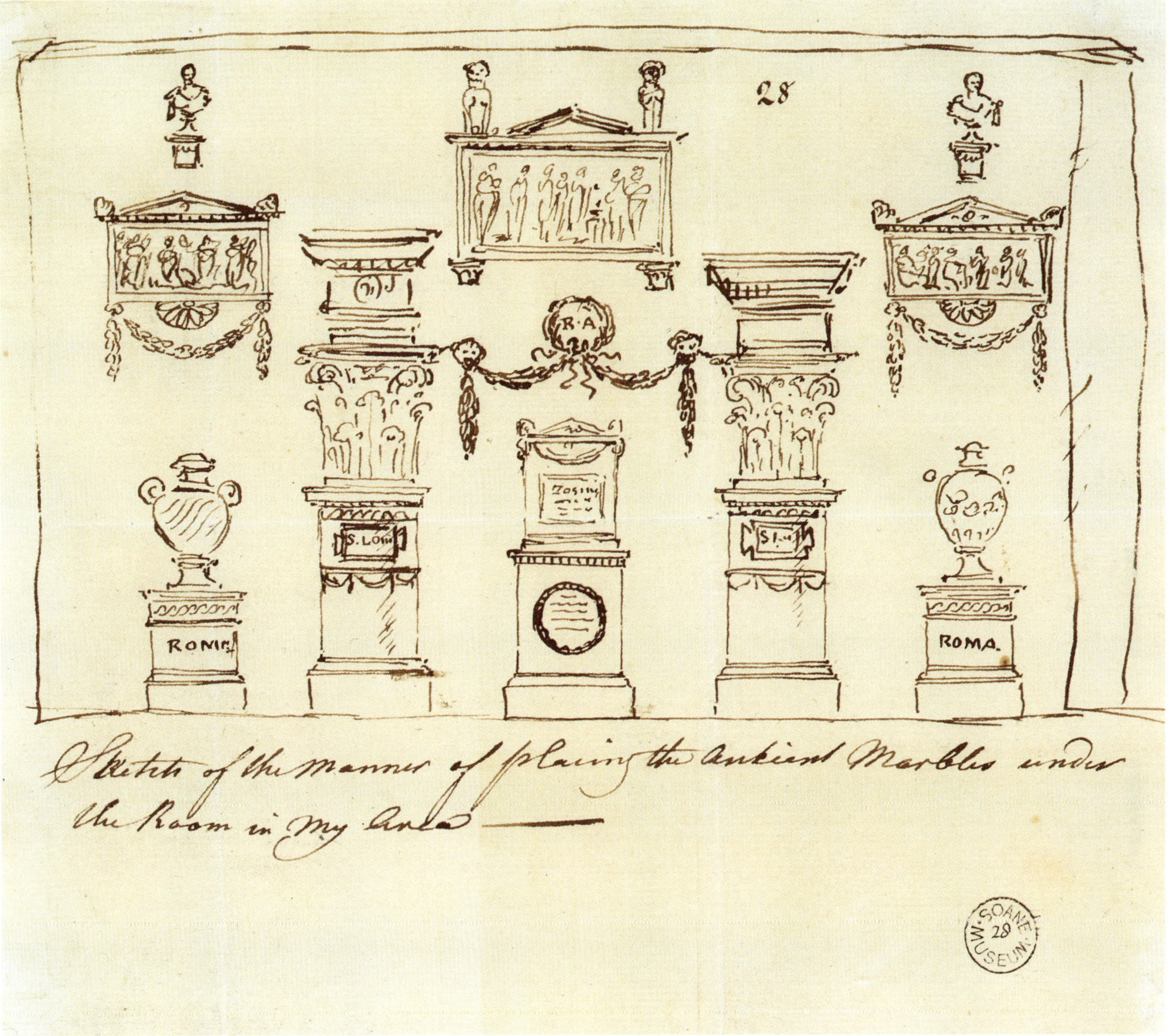

Sketch of the Manner of placing the Antient Marbles under the Room in My Area

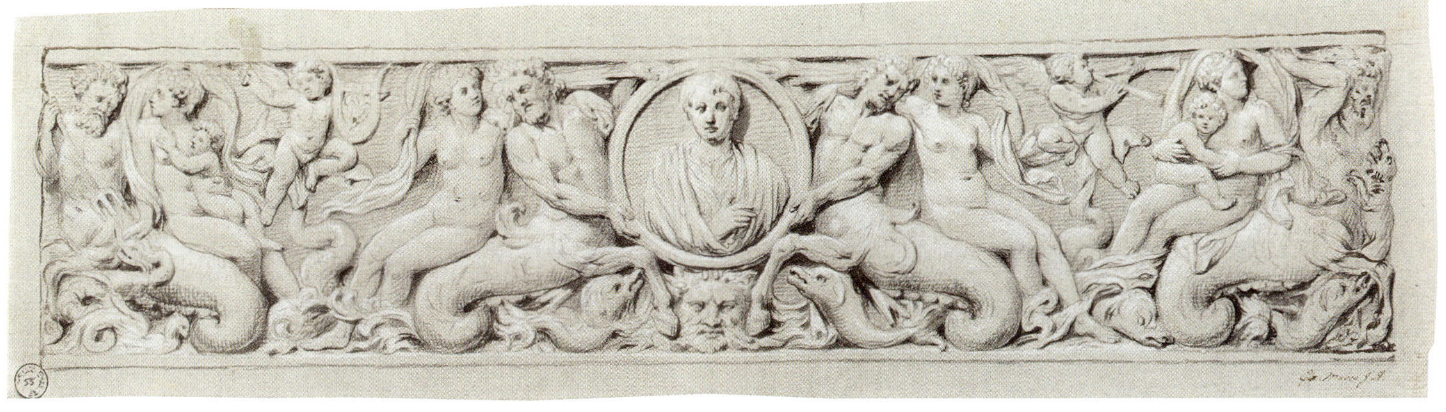

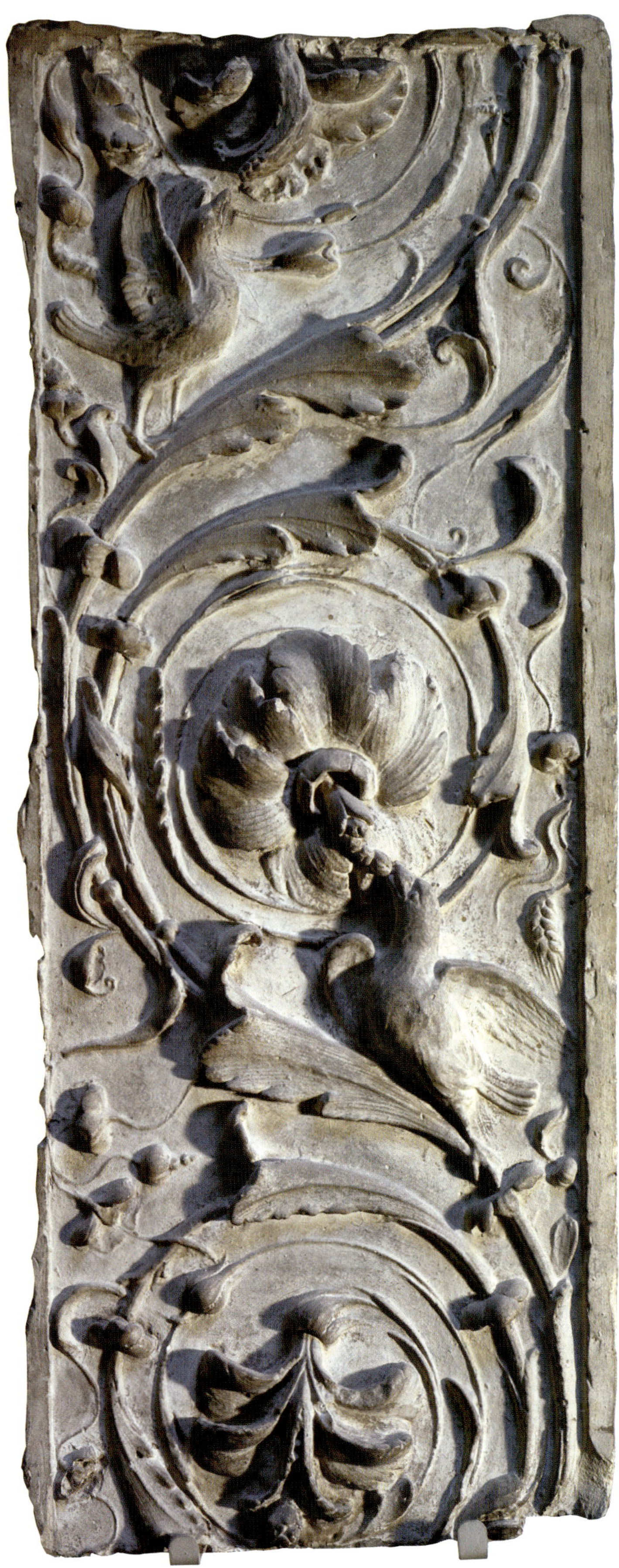

9.
Plaster cast of a decorative panel or pilaster
Mid-18th century
Plaster
716 x 290 x 30 mm
Soane Museum A2

As with fig.6, this was probably purchased by Sir John Soane at the 1818 Adam sale. It is a cast of a panel of sixteenth-century ornament, of a type described as 'Arabesque', and was brought back from Italy by Robert Adam to act as an exemplar of such ornament, for use in his architectural practice.

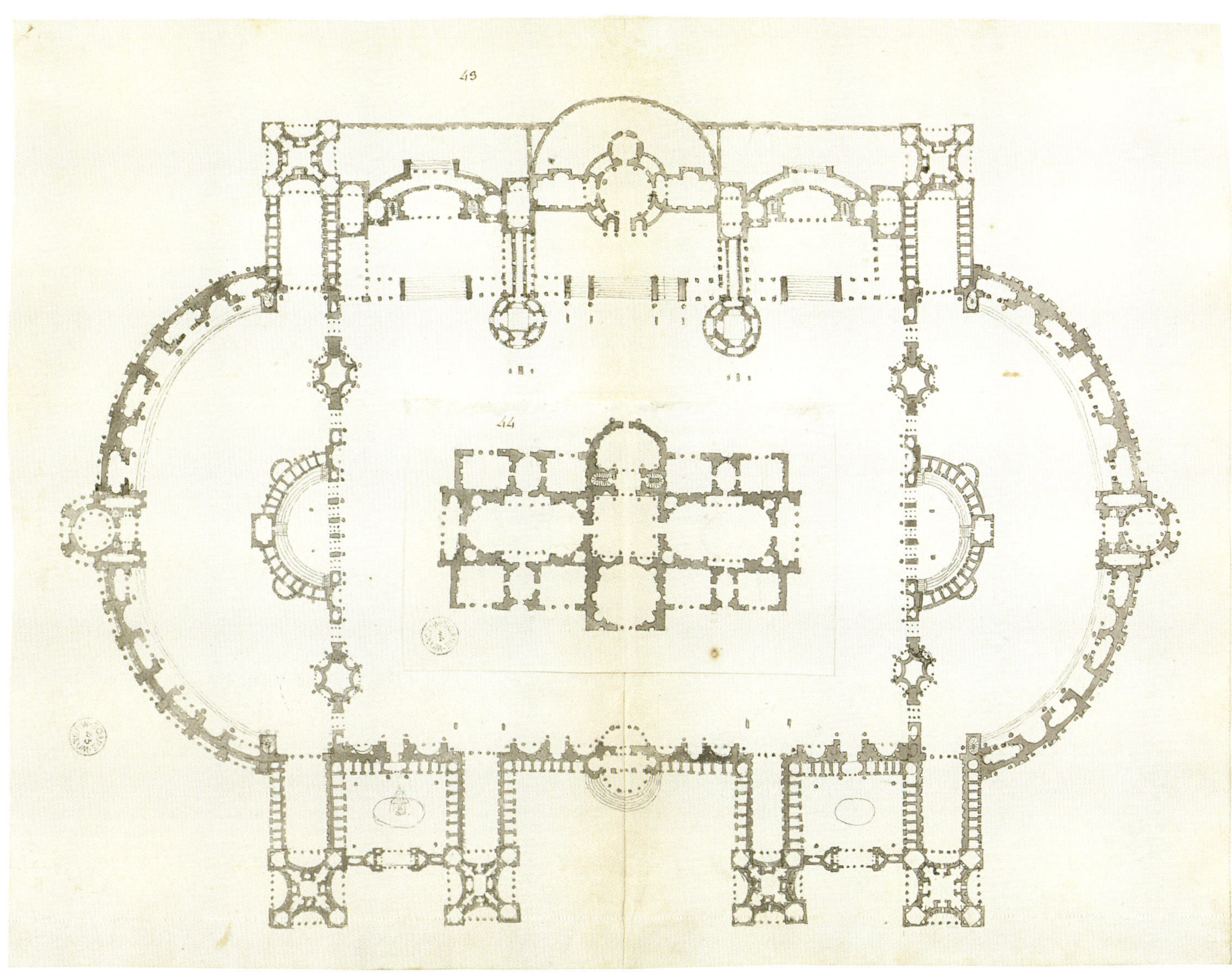

10. Robert Adam
Study of the plans of two large public buildings, one superimposed on the other

*c.*1756
Pencil, pen and grey wash
450 x 343 mm
Adam vol. 9/43 & 44

One of several such compositions, this plan of a monumental structure is derived from various ancient buildings, notably the Baths in Rome, which Robert Adam had studied in detail. Although not fully finished, it is possible that drawings such as this were amongst those that caught the public eye when displayed in his London house at Lower Grosvenor Street in 1758.

Sco

tland

IT IS SURPRISING that Robert and James Adam waited so long to undertake their tours of Italy. When he left for Rome in October 1754, Robert was 26 and had worked in the office of his father, William Adam, and later that of his brothers in Edinburgh, for eight years. His early taste in drawing was for landscape with an architectural bent, so much so that at some point he had toyed with the notion of becoming a painter. His brother-in-law, John Clerk of Eldin, went further and claimed that no sooner could Robert's 'infant fingers hold a pencil when he discovered by his childish productions with what in a riper season he would charm the world'. A pen drawing Robert made in 1744 when he was sixteen, of a partially ruined tower on an island, supports such an interest, though it is not perhaps outstanding [fig.11]. Rather more impressive were his red chalk drawings after prints such as those of Vivares, which he studied in the library at home at Blair Adam [fig.13], or his adaptation of a Salvador Rosa engraving of St William of Maleval. The compositions he directly copied, like those after Marco Ricci or Gaspar Poussin, set out a world filled with peasants and brigands and their cottages and castles, evoking an idealised Italy in contrast to a humdrum Scotland [fig.12]. His architectural designs of this time were of the pavilion and villa sort, set in the informal landscape of boating parties and frivolous picnics, equally removed from the grey world of Presbyterian Edinburgh [fig.14]. In many ways, these watercolours and pen sketches provided an escape, even relief, from the practical drudgery of the building of Fort George in the Highlands, the family's largest public commission. The endless journeys through the dull Highlands and the boredom of barrack lodgings at the Fort were tolerated by the Adam brothers, for the income the Fort produced would ultimately pay for Robert and James' Grand Tours, providing each of them with £5,000.

Yet no building held greater importance for the brothers than this fort beside the sea, outside Inverness; almost within sight of the Culloden battlefield, and built as much to threaten as to defend Scotland, or North Britain as it had become. For all its great size, it was a fairly standard design of the sort found in the nascent empire, and exercised the brothers' building rather than their design skills. The commission also provided an opportunity for study and reflection, a safe haven for the brothers when marooned beside the North Sea and surrounded by the limited, military mind, all of which may well have encouraged ideas of escape to Italy. In some ways, too, Edinburgh and the Adam office cannot have been much better, for it was clear that Scotland was on the fringes of fashionable taste (which was centred upon London) and the patronage that went with it. Outside influences were important to the brothers, and the Edinburgh circle probably included the English architect, Roger Morris, building Inveraray Castle with the Adams, and certainly the Sandby brothers, Paul and Thomas. Paul Sandby was a draughtsman to the Board of Ordnance, principally involved with surveying the various Scottish forts and castles and with an enthusiasm for their picturesque qualities and settings, such as that at Hawthornden, in a wooded gorge above the river North Esk [fig.15]. It was a taste he shared with and helped develop in Robert, and both of them drew views, such as the ruins of Elgin Cathedral, with varying success [fig.16]. Robert pursued this interest throughout his tour of England in 1749–50 when he visited the informal garden that William Kent had created for the Queen in Richmond Park. He collected a sheet of Kent's drawings for the Hermitage there, possibly around the same time [fig.18]. Without doubt, the influence of both Sandby and Kent on Robert was a profound one: all were, to an extent, architect-artists who saw the informal and picturesque landscape as the ideal architectural setting, one where the balance of gardens and buildings was in harmony. As Robert wrote in 1754, just before his departure to Italy: 'romantic rocks, trees, bridges and spires, form a scene which would delight and even charm one that had no taste in landscape' [fig.17].

Robert struggled to find this freedom in his drawing style. Both he and his brother, James, were wedded to the practical clarity of the office style, with its black ink margins and rather careful, old-fashioned draughtsmanship, especially when compared with the landscape drawings they made [fig.19]. To escape from this restrictive tradition, the brothers needed a fresh view of their subject that would challenge the familiar pattern of plan and elevation and bring into play the perspective of painting with light, shade, colour and movement – what James described later in *The Works in Architecture* as 'the rise and fall, advance and recess, with other diversity of form, in the different parts of a building'. The pen drawing Robert made when his boat was becalmed outside Porto Fino in January 1755, carefully worked up from a pencil underdrawing, reveals the typical care and caution hidden beneath his seemingly spontaneous draughtsmanship, all of which was to change irrevocably a few months later [fig.21].

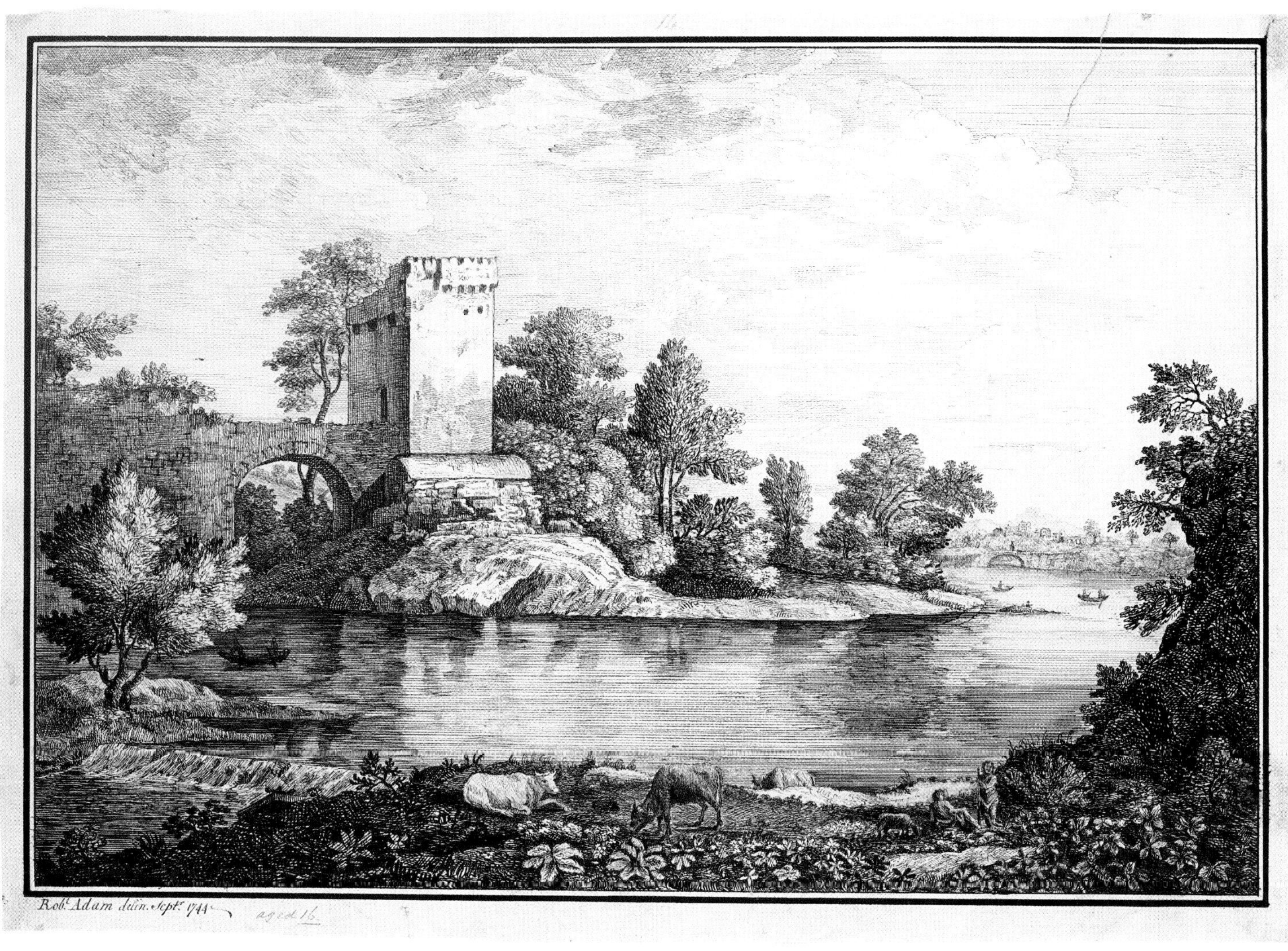

11. Robert Adam
Composition showing a partially ruined tower on a small island, or isthmus

1744
Pen, with ink framing lines
303 x 432 mm
Adam vol. 56/14

The earliest dated drawing by Robert Adam in Sir John Soane's collection is signed and dated 1744, when Robert was just 16. The ruined and battlemented tower is certainly Scottish and medieval, though the landscape setting, especially with the figures in boats and the distant bridge, seems invented.

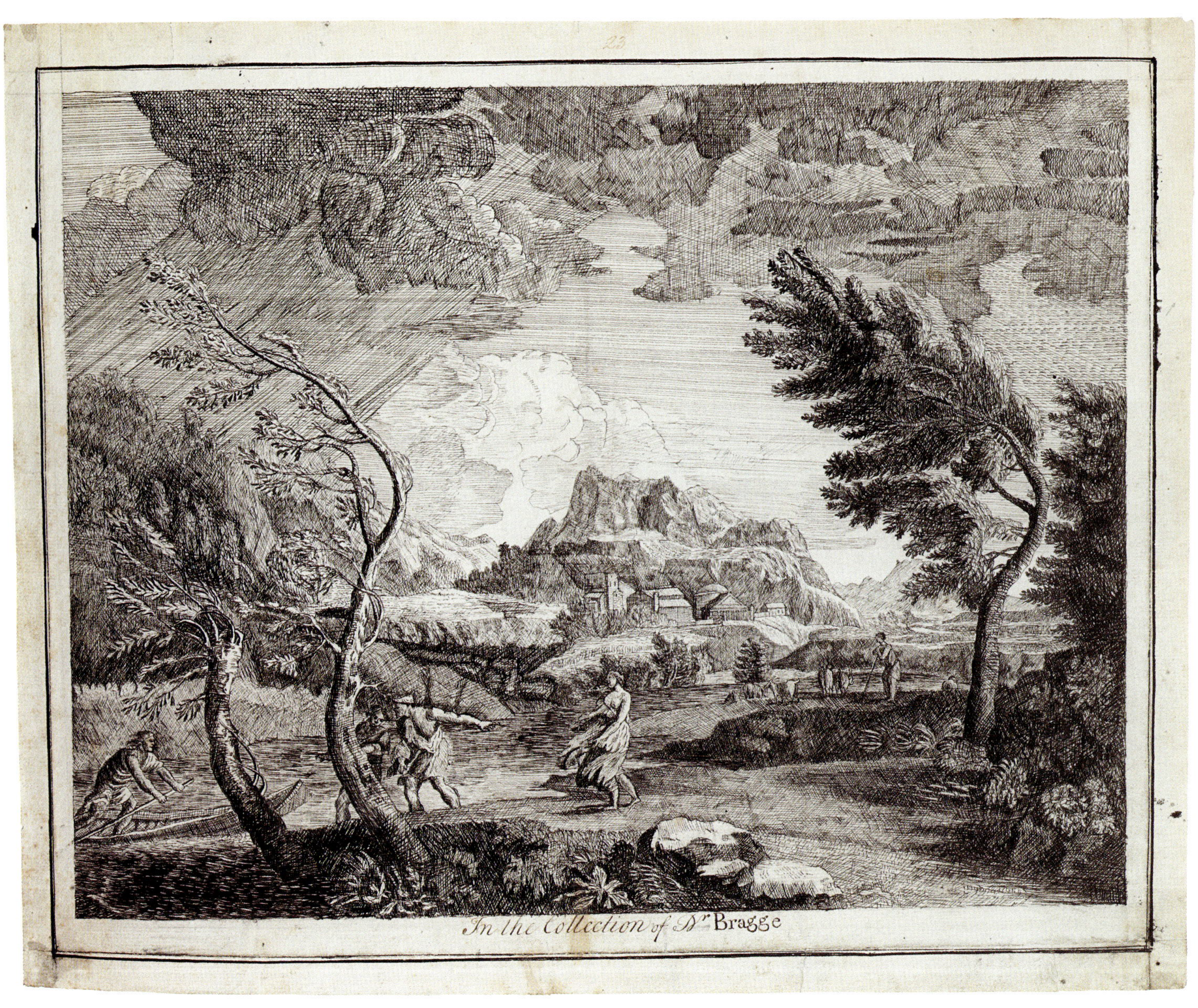

12. Robert Adam
Copy of a print after a painting by Gaspard Dughet

*c.*1744
Pen, with ink framing lines
342 x 430 mm
Adam vol. 56/23

This is a painstaking copy of the print by J.-B.-C. Chatelain, published in 1742 after Gaspard Dughet's painting *Batelier sous l'Orage*, which was then in the collection of Dr Bragge. The study and copying of prints in the library of their home at Blair Adam was an aspect of both Robert and James Adam's artistic education.

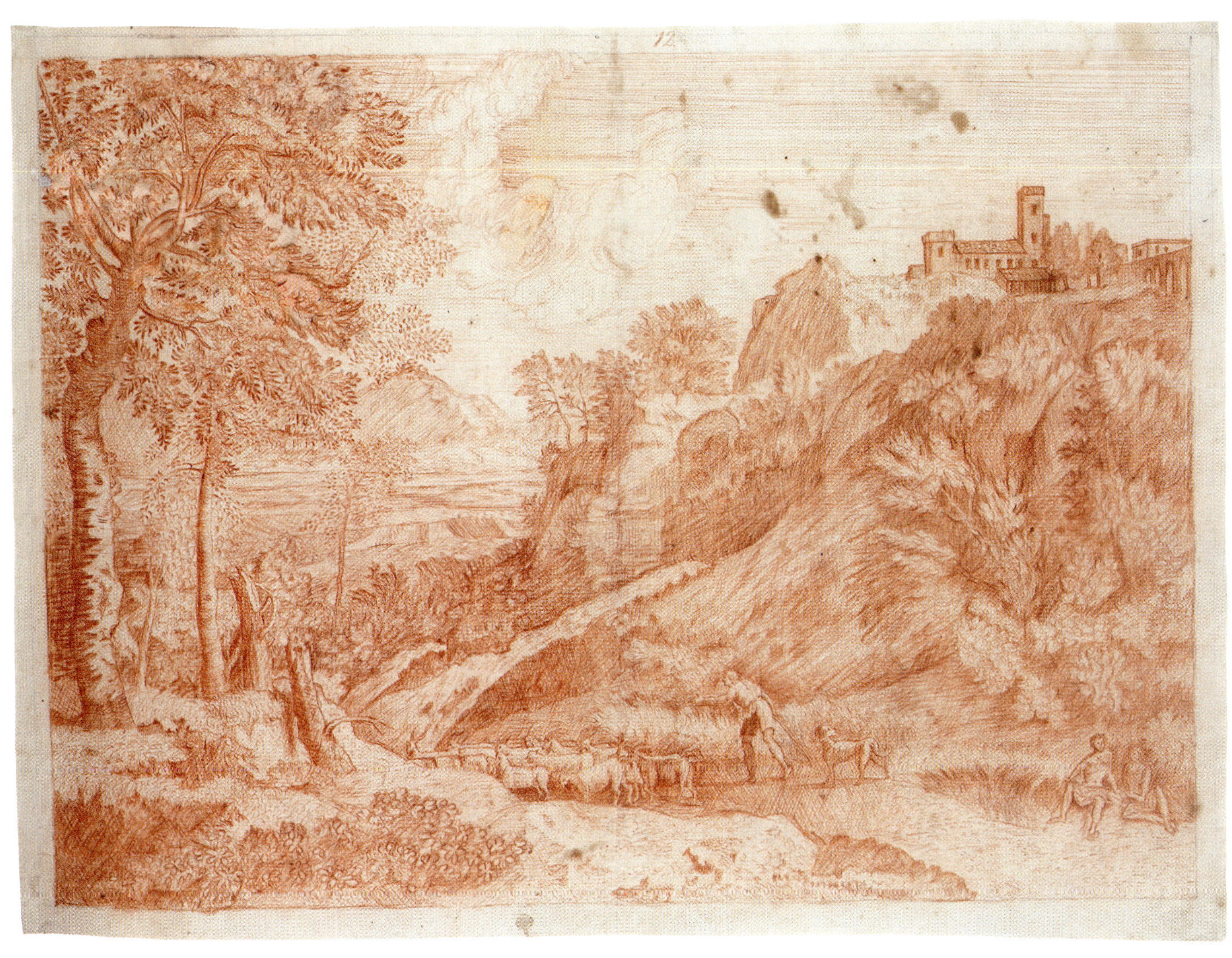

13. Robert Adam
Copy of a print after a painting by Gaspard Dughet

*c.*1746
Red chalk, with pencil framing lines
300 x 413 mm
Adam vol. 56/12

This drawing is copied from a print by Vivares, which was published in 1741 and was in the library at Blair Adam. Vivares' source was Gaspard Dughet, *La Cascade*, now in the Hermitage, but at Houghton Hall, Norfolk, from 1740 to 1779. The choice of subject and use of red chalk may reflect the friendship between Robert Adam and the young artist, Paul Sandby, who was working in Scotland from 1745.

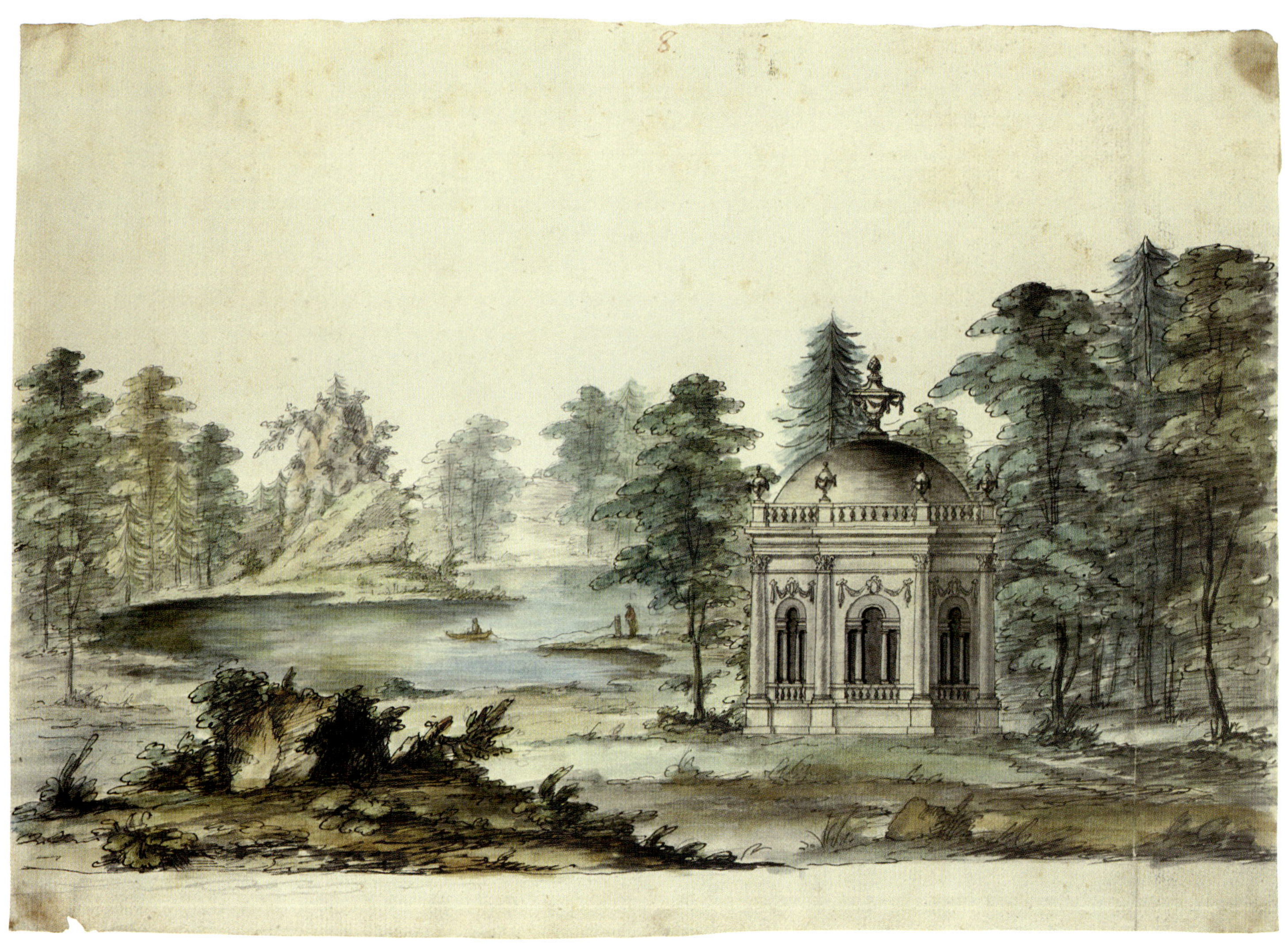

14. Robert Adam
Capriccio showing a pavilion in a landscape

*c.*1755
Pencil, pen and watercolour
253 x 367 mm
Adam vol. 56/8

The pavilion is typical of Robert and James Adam's compositions of the mid-1750s. The informal landscape reflects Robert's taste during the 1750s and is based on prints rather than topographic observation.

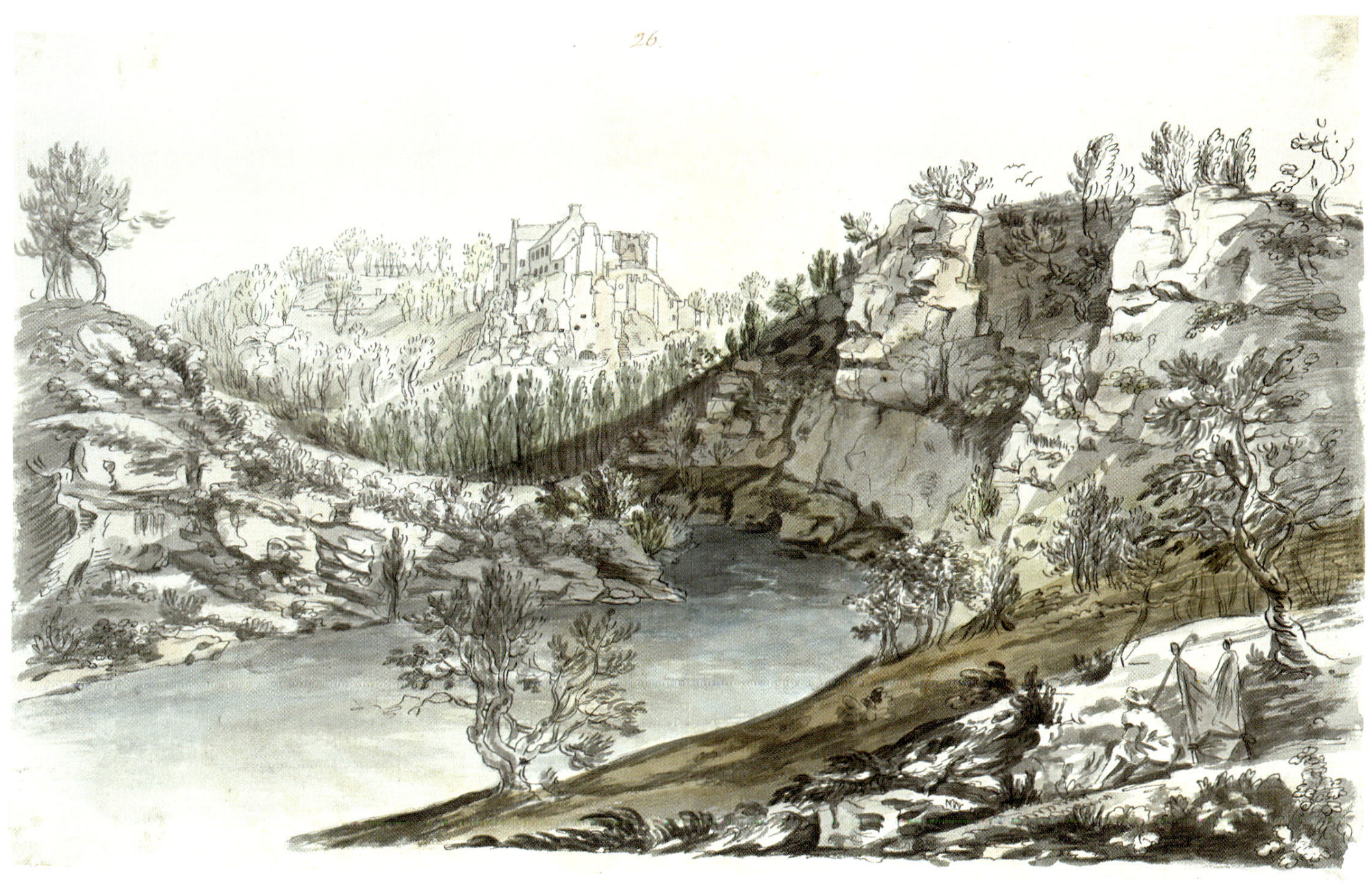

15. Paul Sandby (1725–1809)
View of Hawthornden Castle, Midlothian

*c.*1748
Pen, and brown and grey washes
240 x 388 mm
Adam vol. 56/26

The ruined castle of Hawthornden, on its cliff-top setting above the wooded gorge of the river North Esk, was within easy reach of Edinburgh and a favourite subject for artists in the eighteenth century. This drawing presumably belongs to Sandby's Scottish period of the late 1740s.

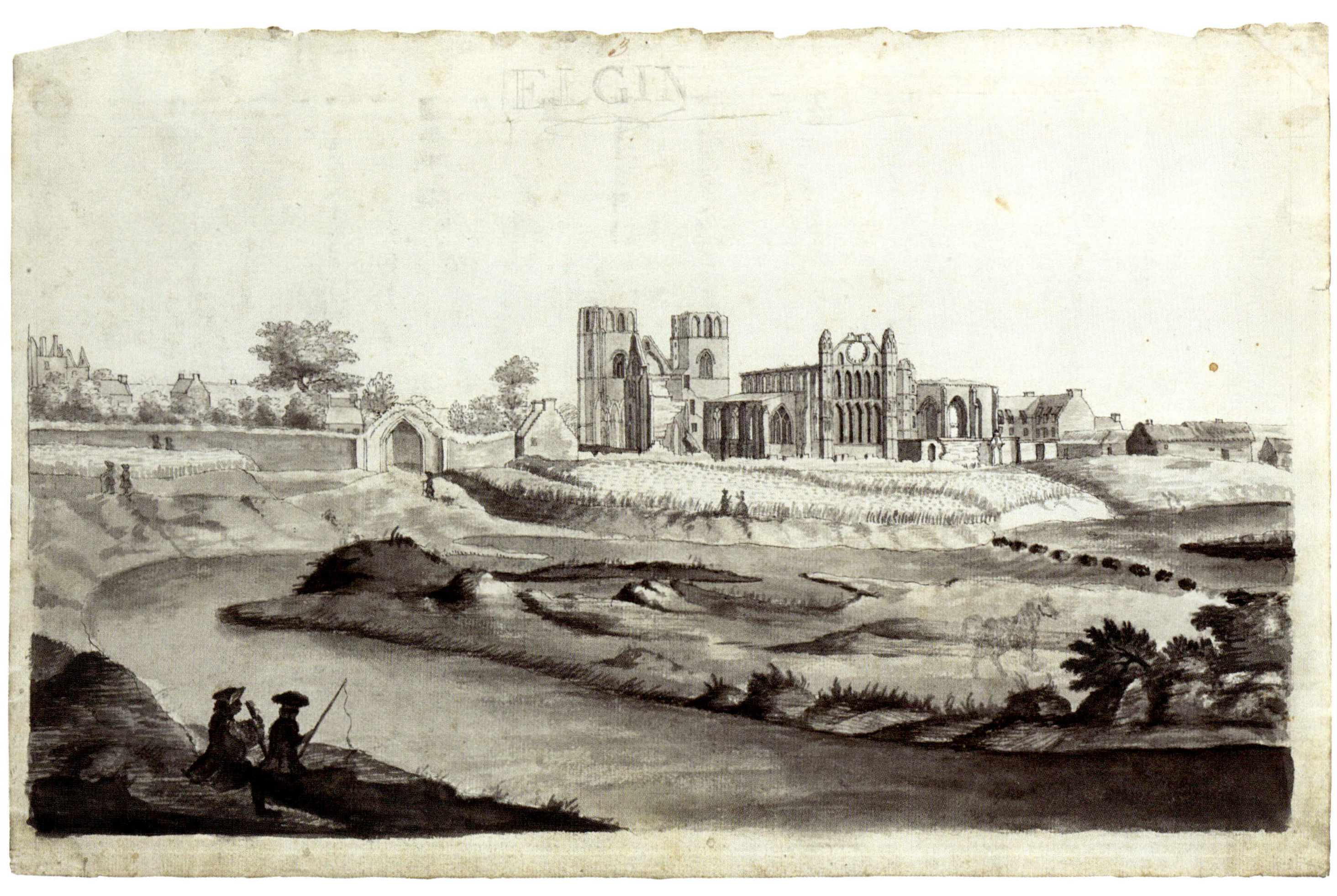

16. Robert Adam
View of the ruins of Elgin Cathedral seen from across the River Lossie

*c.*1746
Pencil, pen and grey wash
240 x 382 mm
Adam vol. 56/3

This is a version by Robert Adam of a *c.*1746 drawing by Paul Sandby, now in the National Galleries of Scotland. Apart from the inferior quality of the Adam copy, it has additional figures in the foreground. The large and unfinished pencil caption 'Elgin', at the top of the sheet, suggests that the drawing was intended for engraving at some point.

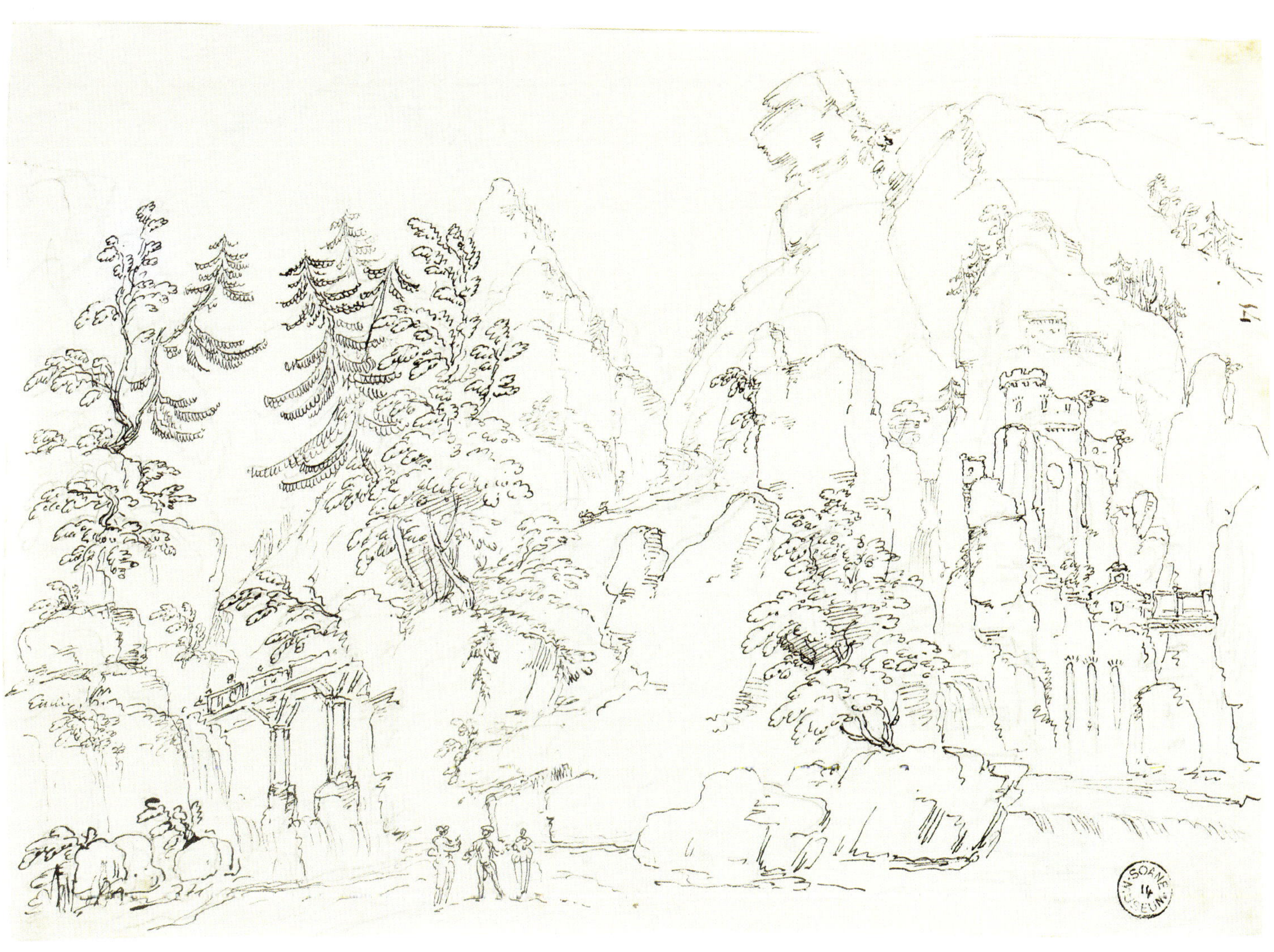

17. Robert Adam
Capriccio showing mountainous country with a road passing over an alpine bridge

*c.*1750
Pencil and pen
220 x 311 mm
Adam vol. 54 / Series 5/14

The composition of this drawing is in the strong picturesque style of the painter, Salvator Rosa, and may have been taken from one of his prints. In Italy in 1760, James Adam bought what he described as '... 2 landscapes by Poussin and one by S. Rosa - all clever and I'm sure will please Bob'.

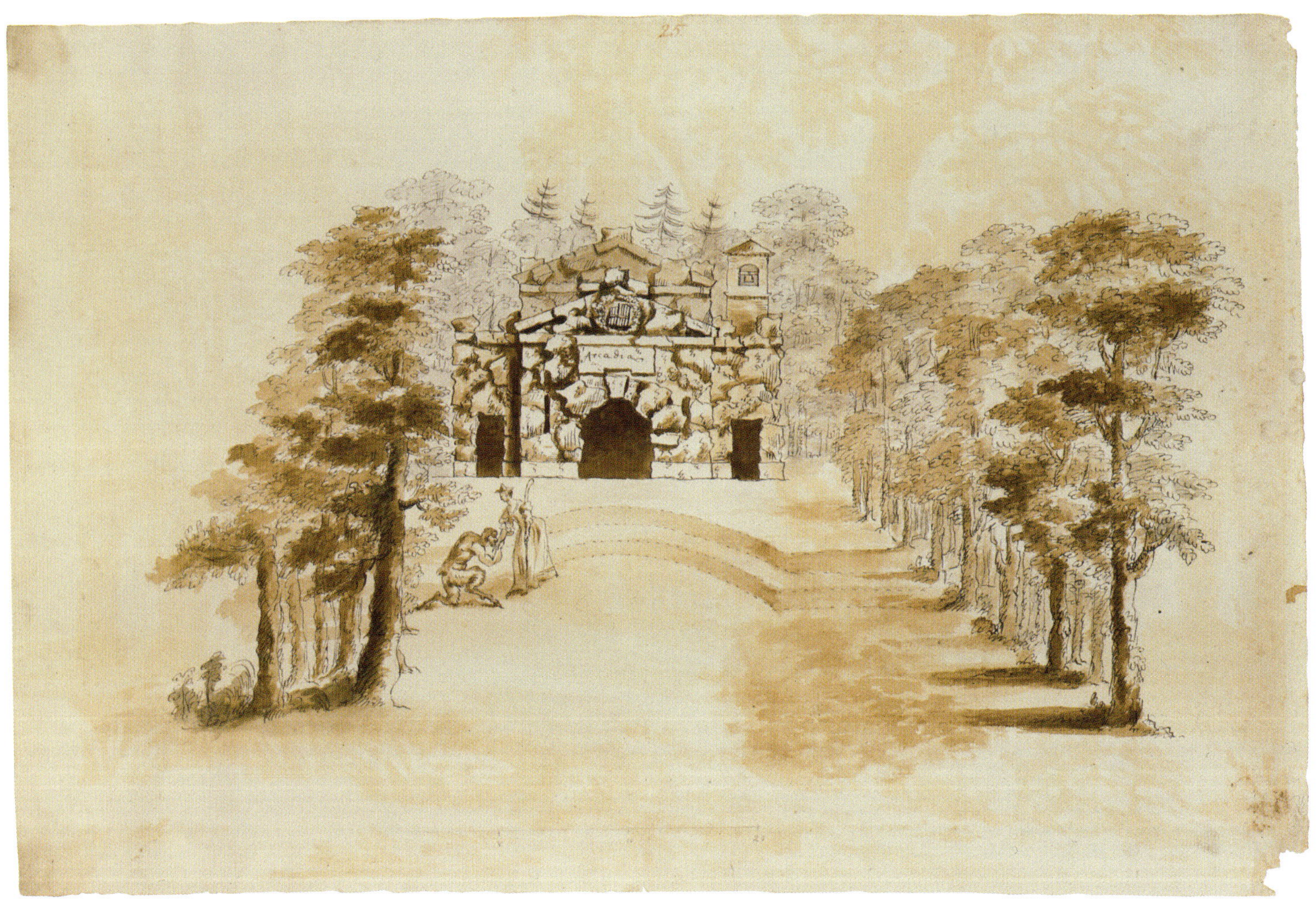

18. William Kent (1685–1748)
Design for Queen Caroline's grotto in Richmond Park

*c.*1737
Pencil, pen, and brown and grey washes
304 x 462 mm
Adam vol. 56/25

This is a scheme for the grotto, or hermitage, designed by William Kent for Queen Caroline. Robert Adam visited Richmond Gardens in 1750 and drew the Hermitage. He may have acquired this drawing then, or when he became Royal Architect in 1761 and had access to the drawings for royal buildings.

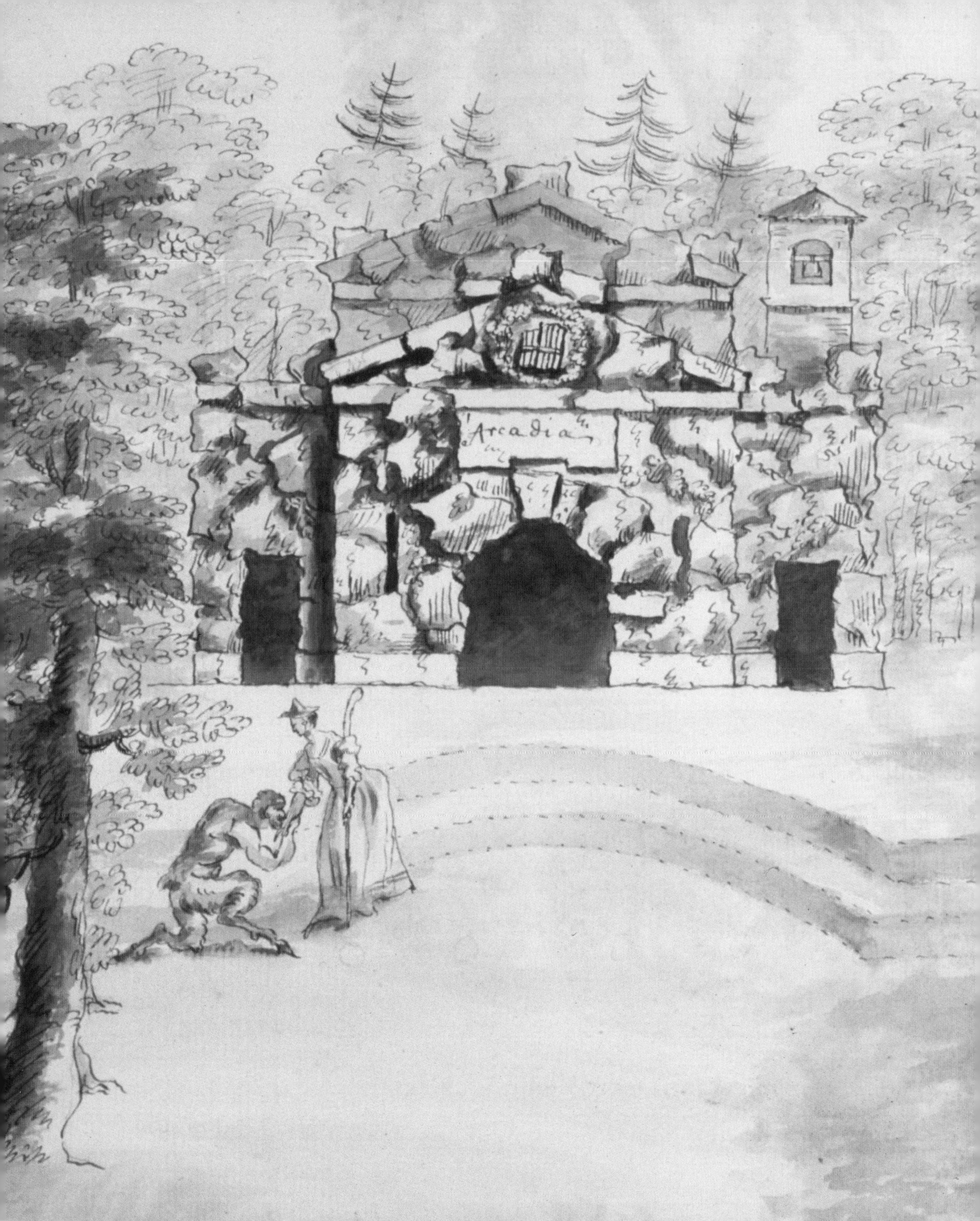
Arcadia

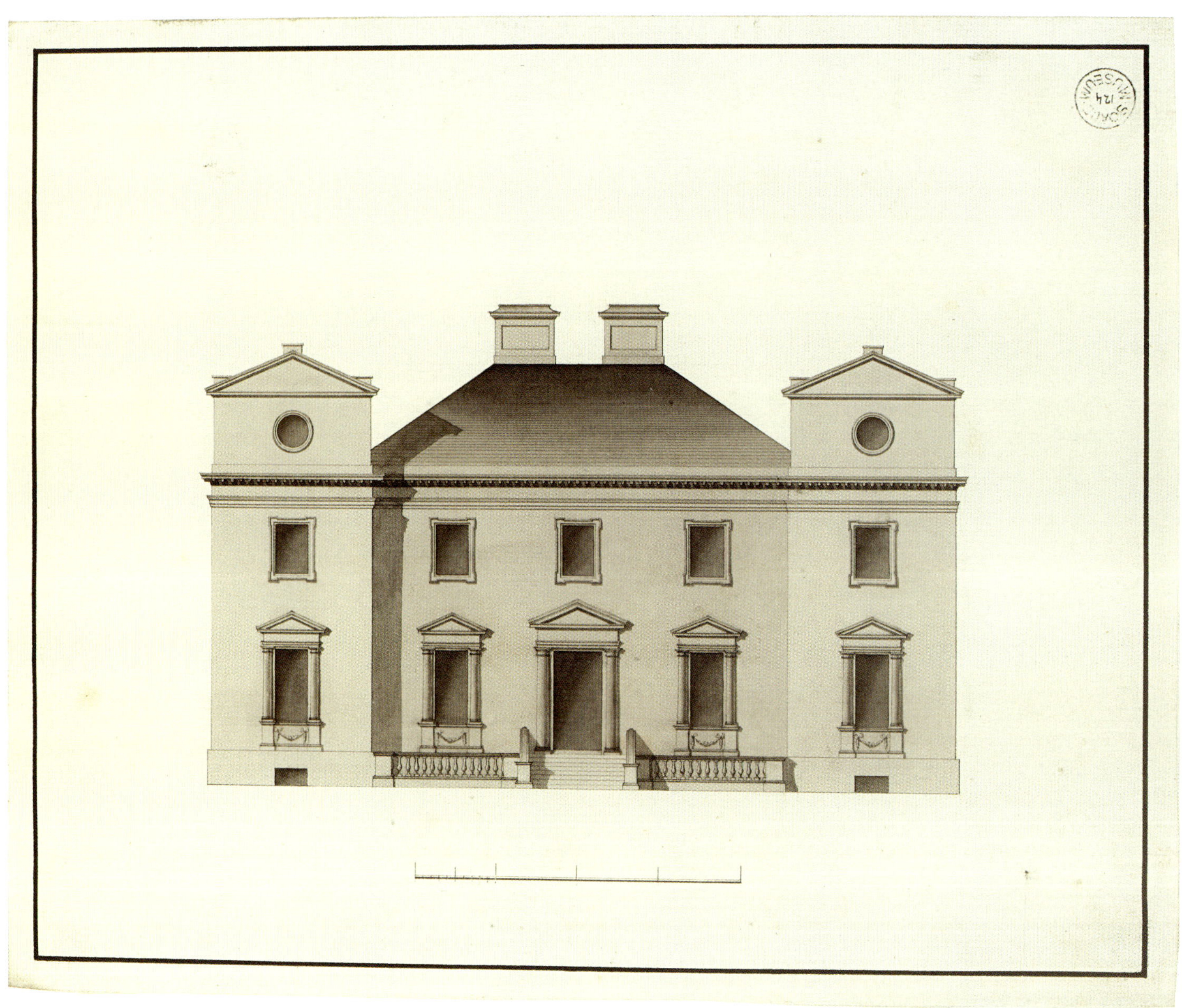

19. Adam Scottish office
Design for a house with four corner towers

*c.*1755
Pen and grey wash, with black margins
219 x 273 mm
Adam vol. 7/124

The composition with corner towers was a familiar one in the Scottish practice of William Adam, the Adam brothers' father, for example at Duff House of 1735–41. The draughtsmanship is typical of the Scottish office in the 1750s. Like many such schemes, this drawing is probably an academic exercise and is associated with James Adam.

20. Robert Adam
View of the Adam Mausoleum in Greyfriars Churchyard, Edinburgh, with Heriot's Hospital in the background

1753
Pencil, pen and grey wash, with trimmed ink margins
473 x 378 mm
Adam vol. 56/2

The Greyfriars Mausoleum was designed by Robert and John Adam (the eldest of the four Adam brothers) in 1753 to incorporate the tomb of their father, William Adam, who had died in 1748. It was completed in October 1755. A more fanciful scheme by Robert was devised in Rome around 1755 (fig.41).

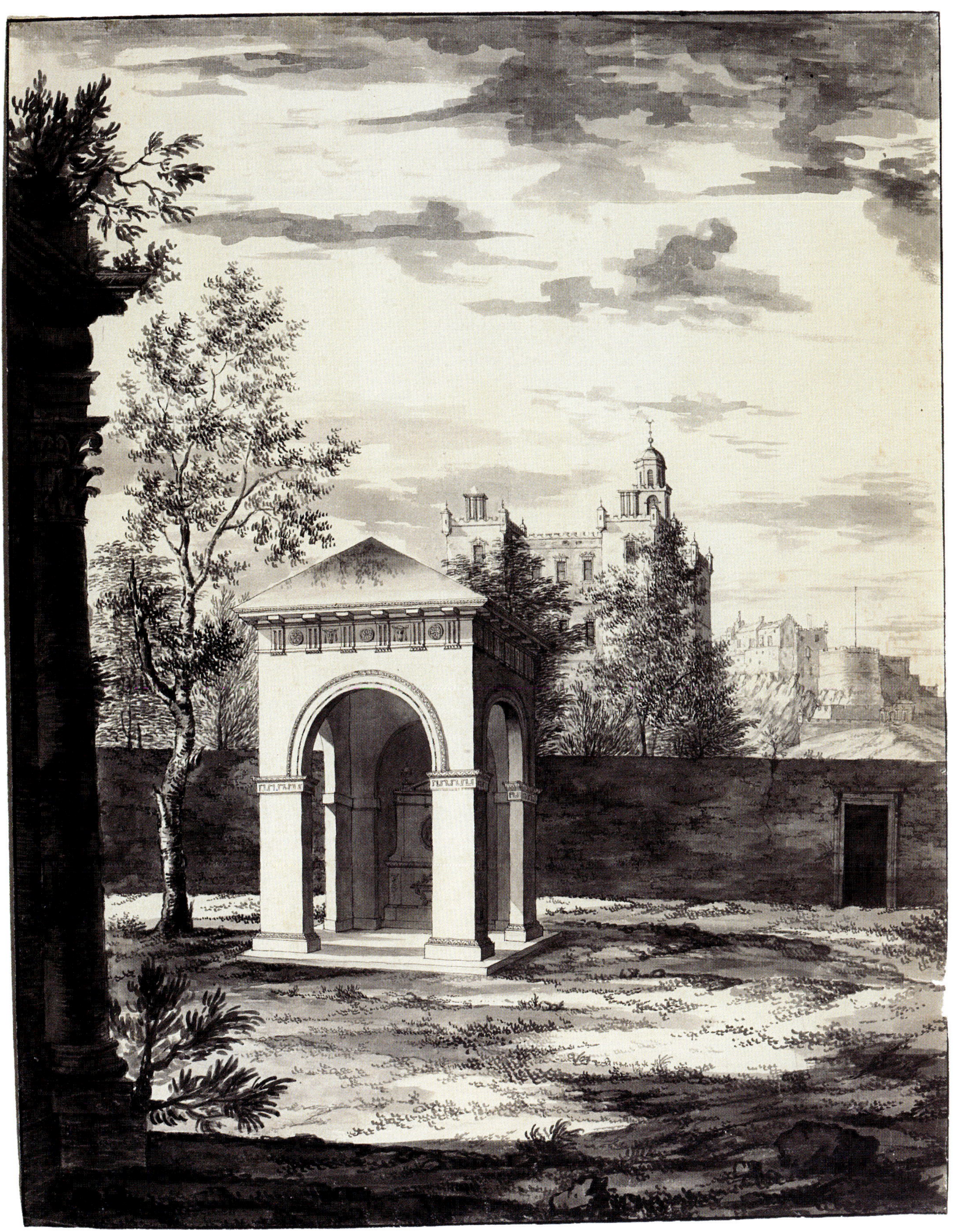

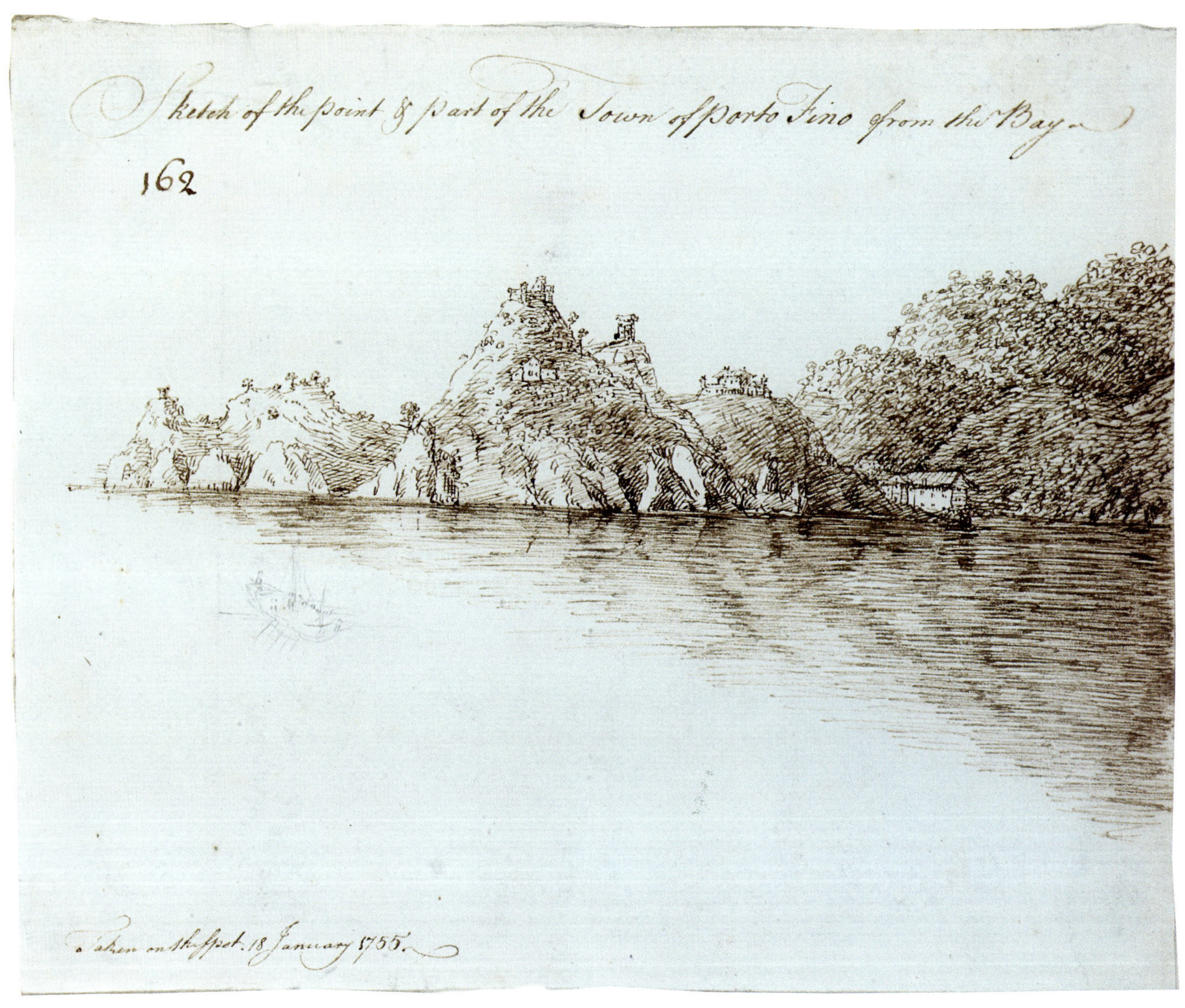

21. Robert Adam
View of Porto Fino on the gulf of Genoa

18 January 1755
Pencil and pen
186 x 229 mm
Adam vol. 57/162

This view was made after Robert Adam sailed from Genoa to Sestri Levante on 18 January, disembarking at '...Lerici the next night after rowing the whole day along the coast with a sea as smooth as glass and no wind'. The boat with oars and a mast, shown in pencil in the middle distance, may be the one to which he refers. This drawing parallels in intimacy and immediacy that sketched from Robert's window at the Casa Guarnieri in Rome (fig.37).

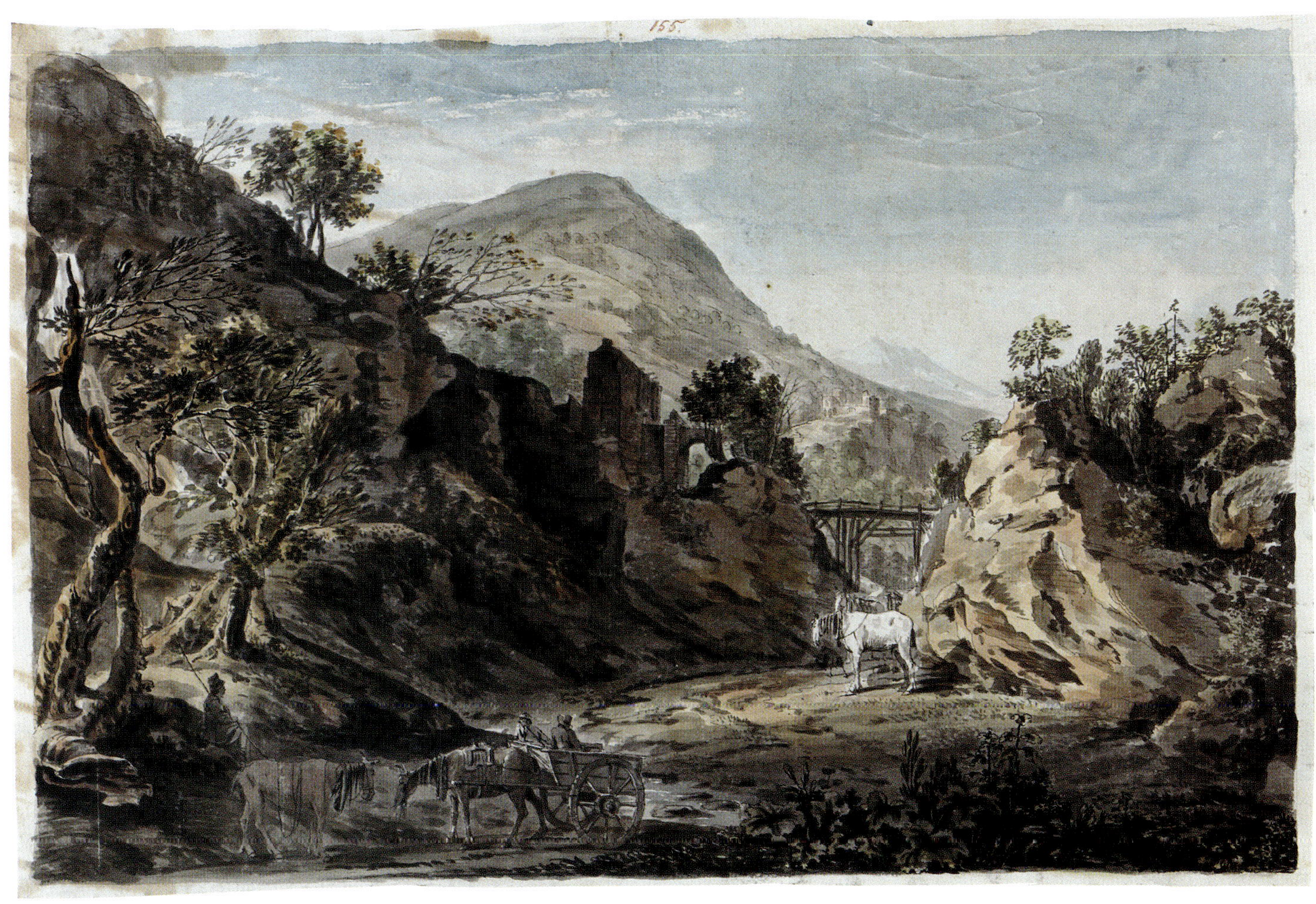

22. Paul Sandby
A Scottish scene showing a river gorge in rocky landscape spanned by a simple wooden bridge

*c.*1750
Pen and watercolour
292 x 446 mm
Adam vol. 56/155

This view is typical of Paul Sandby's work of around 1750. The scene is probably on the North Esk, and the building shown in outline may be Roslin Castle or, possibly, a further view of Hawthornden (fig.15).

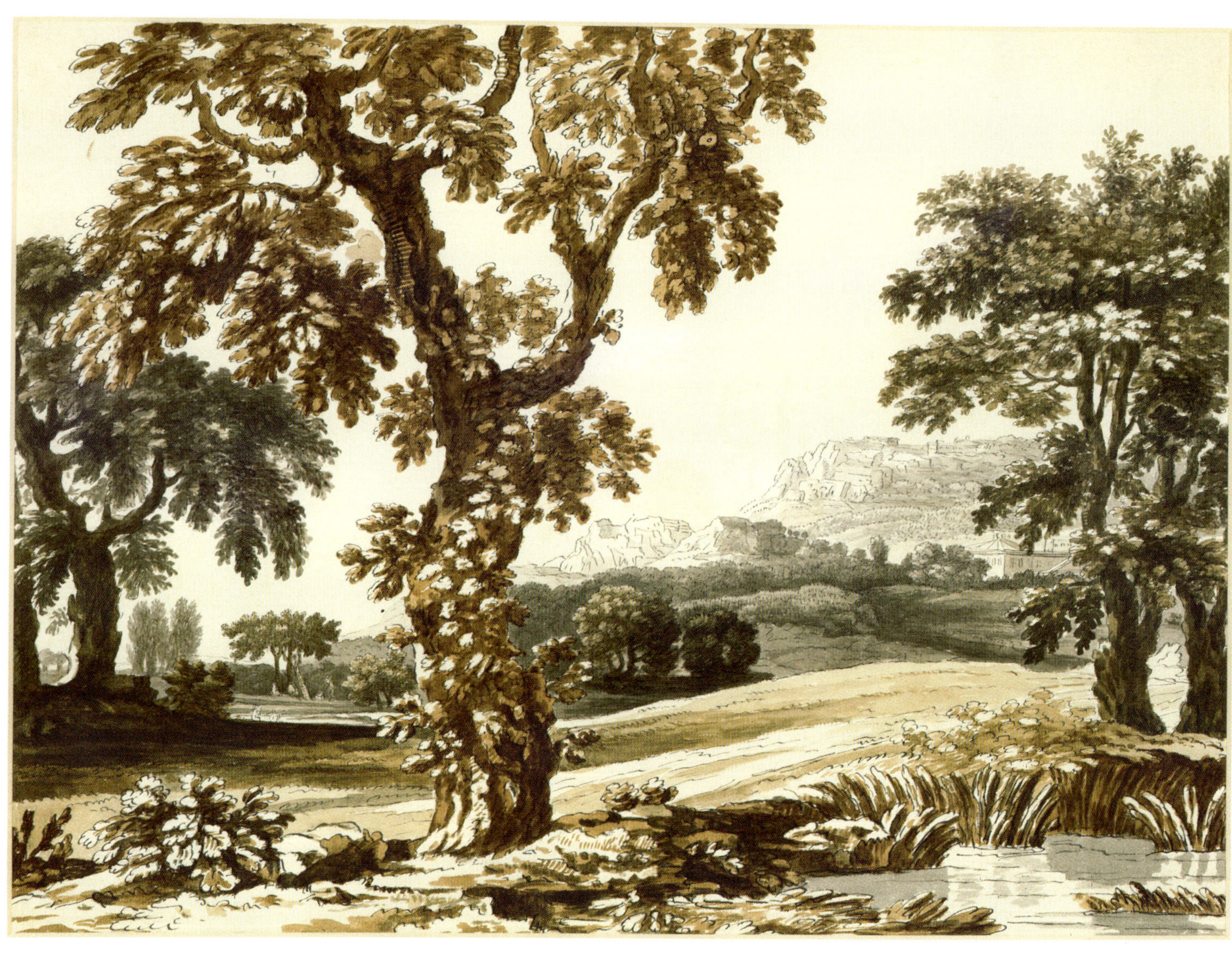

23. Paul Sandby *Attributed to*
Landscape study of an expansive flat and wooded scene with large deciduous trees in the foreground

*c.*1750
Pencil, pen, and brown and grey washes
347 x 460 mm
Adam vol. 56/27

The pen and wash drawing is typical of Paul Sandby's work and particularly his Scottish views. Both Paul and Thomas Sandby were associated with the Adam family from around 1746 and Paul Sandby worked for Robert Adam on the plates for the *Ruins of the Palace of the Emperor Diocletian at Spalatro* of 1764.

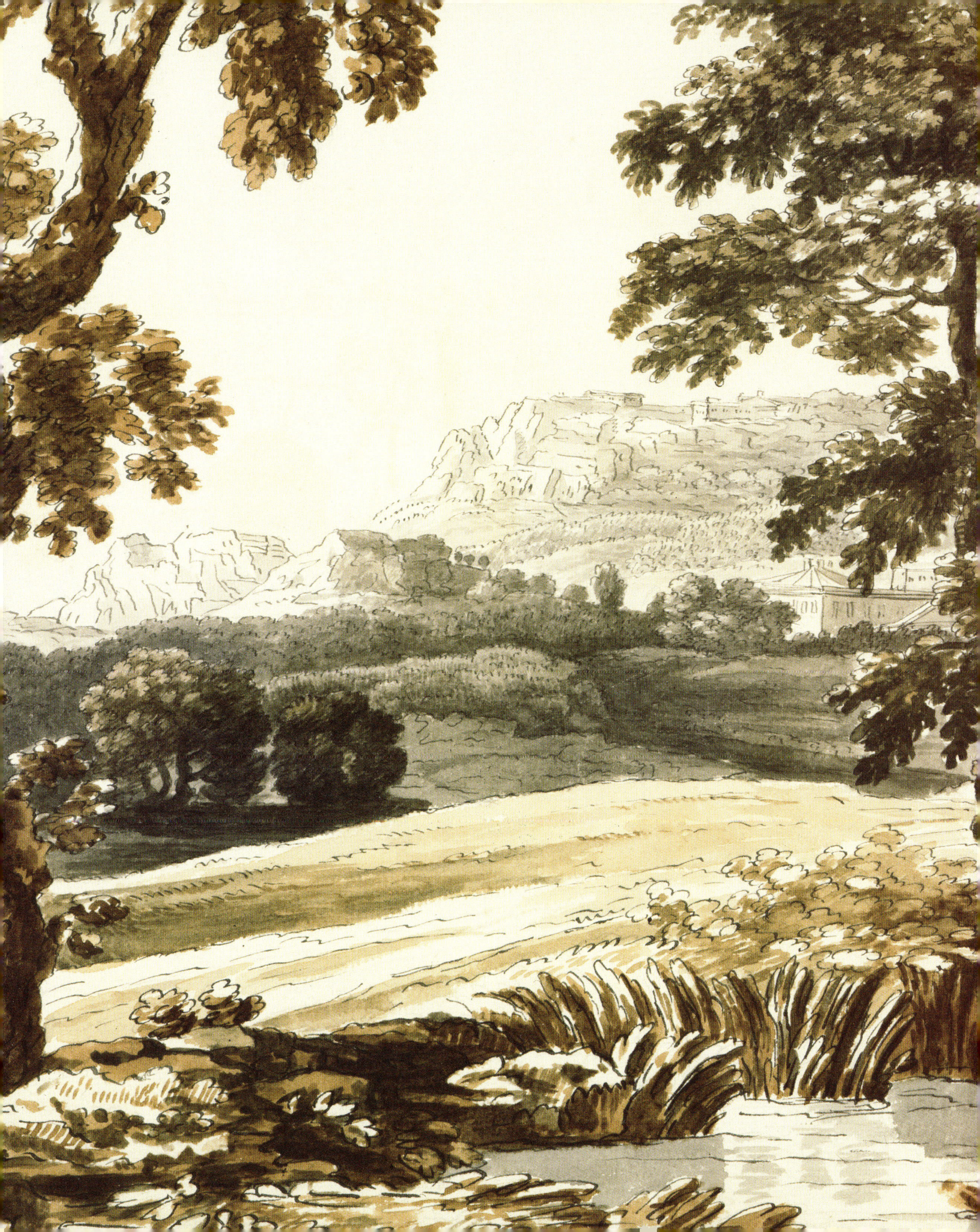

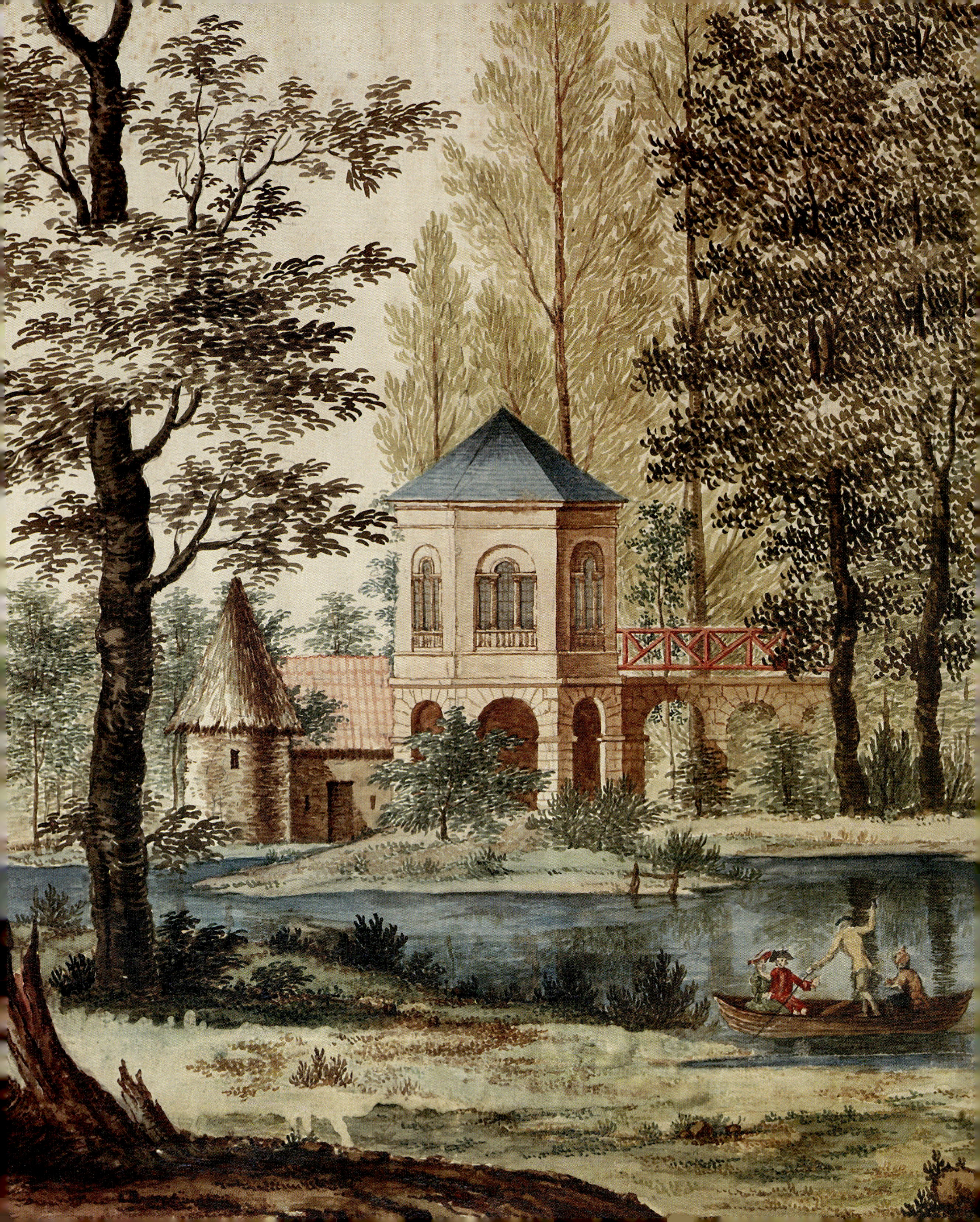

24. Robert Adam
Study for an octagon pavilion on a rusticated arcaded basement with Venetian windows

*c.*1752
Pencil, water and bodycolour
560 x 385 mm
Adam vol. 56/5

The assured hand is that of Robert Adam and the landscape is typical of his various watercolours of the early 1750s. It may be compared with his later and more accomplished Italian compositions of around 1756. There are a number of similar Adam compositions that have remained in the Blair Adam collection.

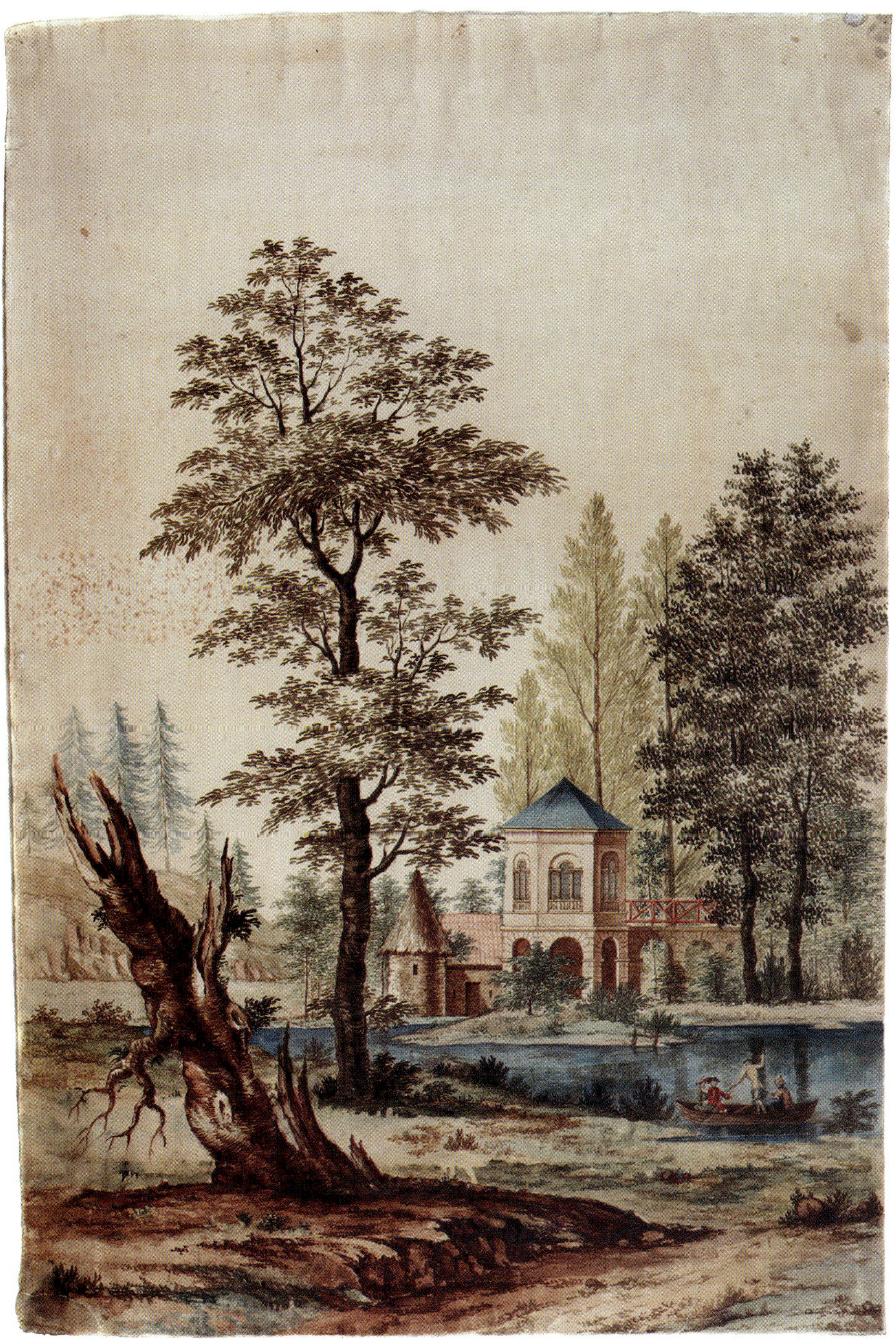

Robert Adam's

Grand Tour Naples

In 1754, Robert Adam set off for France, travelling down the Rhône valley from Paris, sketching and examining antiquities such as those at Nîmes and the Pont du Gard [fig.25]. He continued in chill weather along the coast to Genoa, by sea to Lerici, then overland to Florence and Rome, arriving there in January 1755. He was then almost immediately ill with a form of nervous breakdown – later diagnosed as rheumatic fever – that haunted him throughout his career and struck at particular times of acute strain and crisis. To recover from this and so that he might relax in a warm spot, he left in April for the south and Naples with his artistic cicerone, Charles-Louis Clérisseau, by his side. It was a somewhat strange relationship, for both sought to gain from the other – Clérisseau to take advantage of Robert's patronage, Robert to capture and emulate Clérisseau's insight into the Antique and his ability to translate it onto paper. Each was making a name at the other's expense and both were, in every sense, testing each other.

Their goal was Antiquity, and modern Naples interested them very little. They were much keener on the partially excavated cities of Pompeii and Herculaneum, and the scattering of sites along the bay west of Pozzuoli and Naples. Through the fortunate survival of Robert's disbound sketchbook, it is possible to follow the path he and Clérisseau took from major to minor sites, and to discover what engaged their attention. Their 46 drawings show the positive way in which each approached the problem of composition and the meaning they wrought from the picturesque ruins they encountered. They were not, of course, the first, and some sort of visual education had already been set out in the contemporary prints made by Giovanni

Battista Natali and later published in Paoli's *Avanzi delle antichita esistenti a Pozzuoli Cuma e Baia* of 1768 [fig.26]. They can be seen, one standing in front of the other, drawing a domed ruin, illustrated by Natali, of what was then accepted as Virgil's tomb at Mergellina. Robert candidly noted that 'it is now quite ruinous and is only beautiful from its antiquity' and that this 'induced me to make several sketches of it' [fig.27]. Of the two, as might be expected, Robert's drawing was honest though prosaic, and to give his drawing depth and interest he cut from his composition the distant view over the bay at Posilippo that Clérisseau made much of [fig.28]. This pattern is repeated in the two drawings they made further along the bay, of the temple of Diana at Baiae. Once again, Robert's drawing was a fairly straightforward record of what was there, while that of Clérisseau, done on grey paper with white heightening, showed the view dramatically through a deepened foreground [fig.29].

The Naples tour was a crowded one and the pace set by Clérisseau brisk. Robert wrote with satisfaction that, 'In one days jaunt we visited the Ancient town of Puteoli now called Pozzuoli, The Infernal Lake, the Grotto of Sybille...The temple of Apollo... From that we went to ancient Baiae, where Nero had a palace the Ruins of which are yet conspicuous. The consequence of this town may be judg'd by the Many Ruins of Temples which are yet to be seen, such as the Temples of Diana, Mercury & Venus, of which my friend Clerisseau [sic] & I took sketches to enable our friends to partake of our pleasures' [fig.30]. They moved onwards, and on 7 April, Robert saw the buried city of Herculaneum 'with great pleasure & much astonishment'. While there, he watched the staged uncovering of several earthenware vases and a marble pavement, and was shown 'some feet of tables in marble which were dug out the day before we were there' [fig.31]. This small table may be one of the objects that Robert studied and drew, and the original is possibly in the museum at Portici. This more scholarly aspect of the tour manifests itself in the studies he and Clérisseau made at Pozzuoli and Capua, where Clérisseau composed an outstanding bird's-eye view of the market place showing its plan with great clarity, a study which he renewed on his visit there with James [fig.33]. Clérisseau's large perspective was balanced by several detailed, academic studies, roughly drawn to scale, of the capital and cornice from the amphitheatre in Capua [fig.32]. The lesson for Robert was clear: there should always be a scholarly underpinning to the grandest and most inventive of classical compositions.

A good part of this education was repeated when Clérisseau took James on much the same tour in 1761. However, their tour had a very different purpose, for Naples was intended to be the starting point for a journey to Sicily. Whilst waiting there for his passport to be issued by the British ambassador to the Neapolitan court, James made several excursions with Clérisseau to the antiquities that his brother had seen in 1755, including Herculaneum. None of his drawings survived, though his cooler and more detached account of the excavation at Herculaneum and of the other sites did, and was published in 1831, ironically as Robert Adam's. James' deadpan account of the excavations is fairly typical of the journal as a whole: 'I went and visited the Subterranean City of which one sees only the Theatre distinctly, where the gradini are perfectly entire: but one cannot form any idea of the scena and proscenium, which are most at a loss about. The rest of the passages are an underground maze, that one can form no idea of, only that one sees here and there fragments of houses, incrustation of marble, and mosaic pavements. This serves, however, to give an idea of the height of the larva, which is immense, having been no less than a perpendicular body about 130 feet thick.' James reckoned on having 'about 18 or 20 very interesting views of classical monuments, together with two most curious plans', but none survived to complement his detailed journal. Perhaps the only surviving drawing of James' tour is Clérisseau's view of the interior of the temple of Mercury at Baiae, now in the Pierpont Morgan Library, New York, which shows what may be Adam seated and sketching.

It took Robert five days to travel from Rome to Naples, following what he termed the 'Appian Ways and Classic Plains', through Velletri and Terracina. To make his return to Rome, he went through Old Capua and then took the hill road to Cassino, which he described as 'by a Famous & beautiful Mountain called Mount Cassina and … through a Most Glorious Country'. His fetching view of the Isola di Liri at Sora gives some idea of his response to the picturesque landscape of the 'Glorious Country' [fig.34]. After Monte Cassino, he probably took the lower road to Frascati and then on to Rome itself.

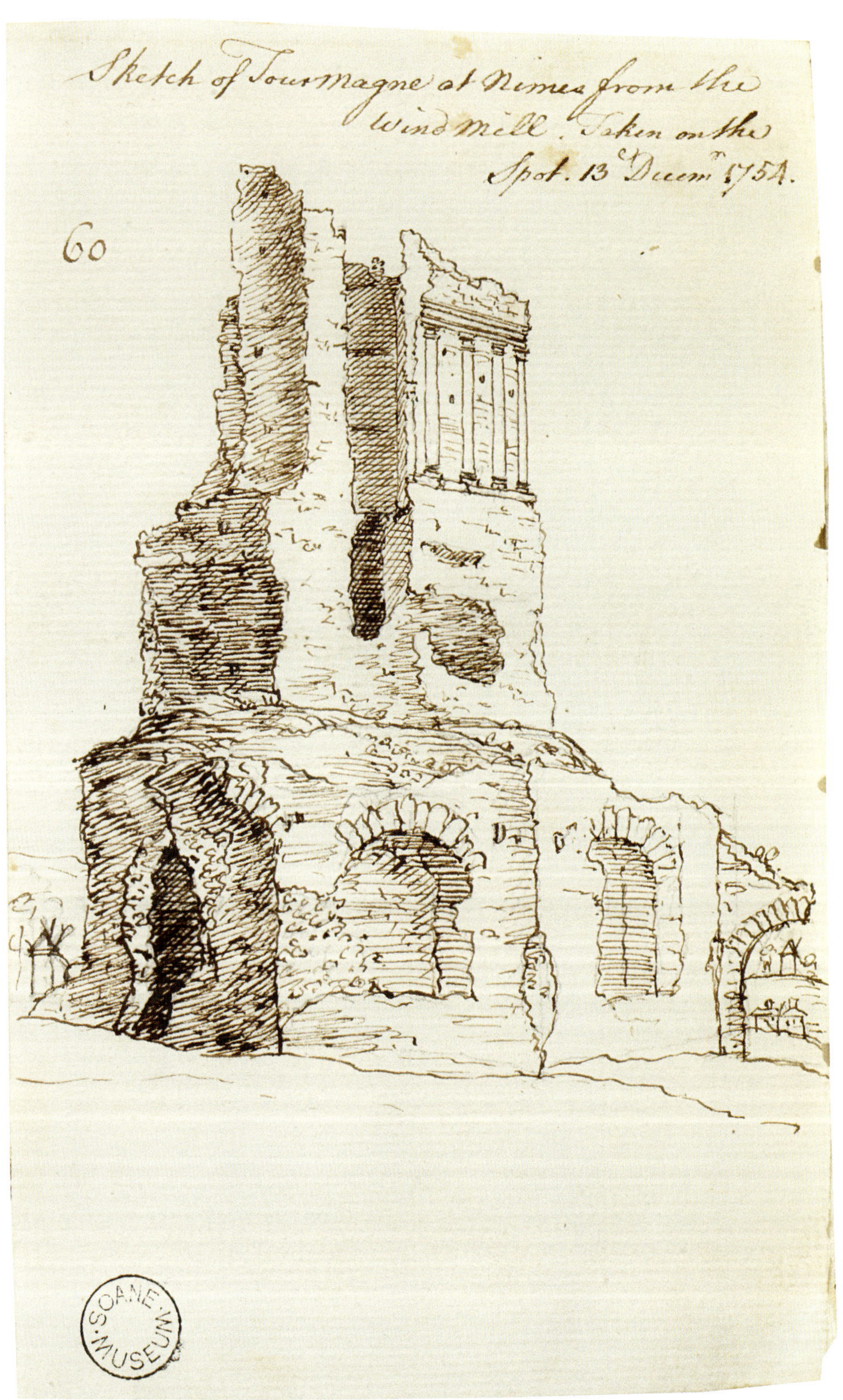

25. Robert Adam
View of the Tour Magne at Nîmes

13 December 1754
Pencil and pen
181 x 117 mm
Adam vol. 55/60

On his way through France, Robert Adam drew several of the antiquities around Nîmes. In a letter home of 5 December he wrote: 'We proceeded to Avignon by way of Bagnol, to which place I fancy we must return in order to get upon the post road to Pont du Guard [sic] (another Antiquity) & to Nimes where we will remain 2 or 3 days.' This untrimmed drawing is a complete page taken from a small notebook.

26. Antonio Paolo Paoli (*fl.*1768–84)
Avanzi delle antichita esistenti a Pozzuoli Cuma e Baia

Naples, 1768, plate 8
Soane Museum Library

Paoli's view of Cicero's tomb was taken from the then entrance above the original structure. His book was up-to-date and took advantage of the work of what he termed '*Professori di Pittura di Architettura di Scultura*'.

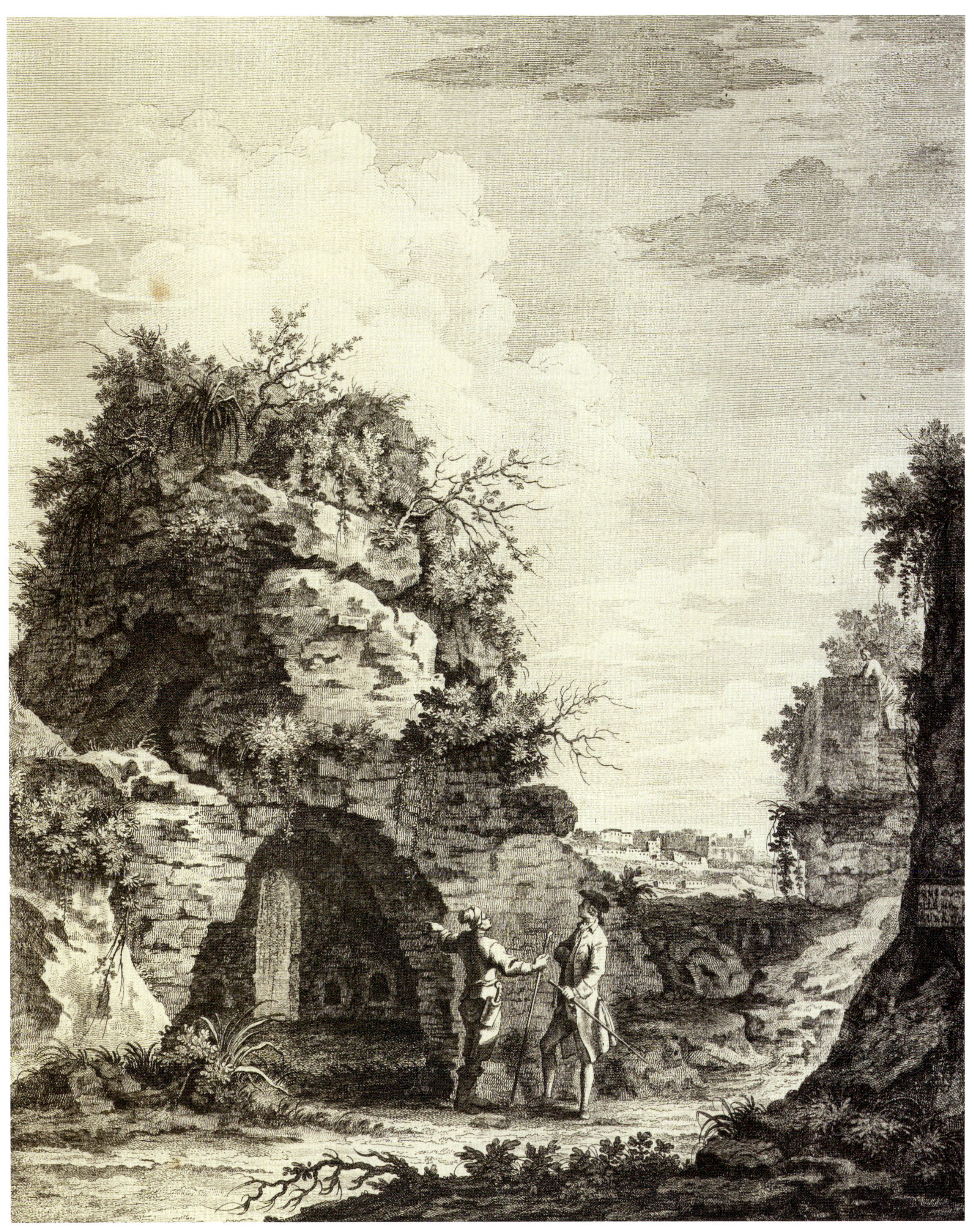

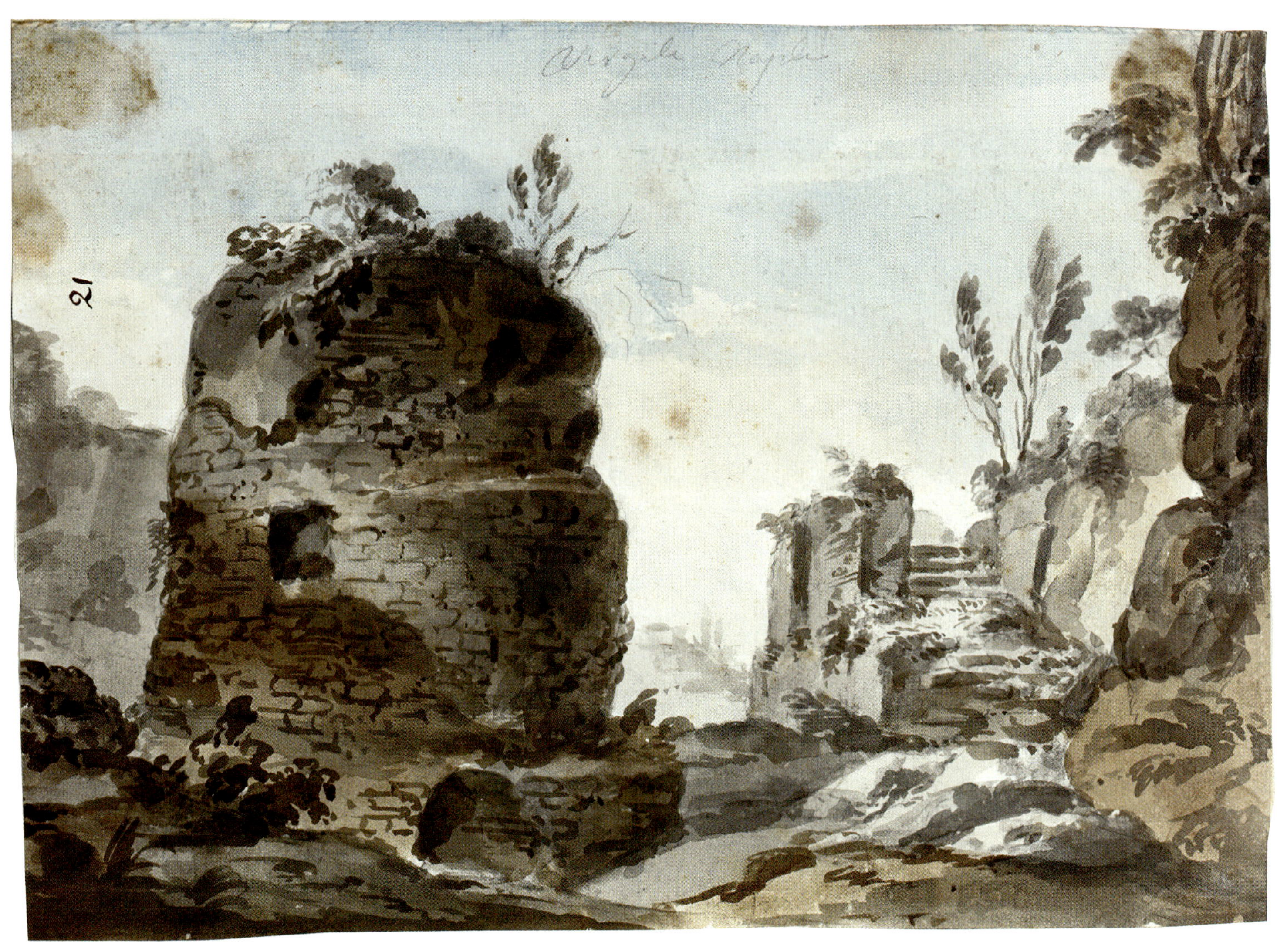

27. Robert Adam
View of 'Virgil's Tomb' at Mergellina

April 1755
Pencil, and brown, blue and grey washes
205 x 293 mm
Adam vol. 57/21

This is Robert Adam's version of the scene drawn by Clérisseau (fig.28). The Adam view is the more prosaic, though honest, as Robert limited the distant prospect over the bay at Posilippo that gave Clérisseau's drawing both depth and greater interest. Robert wrote on 8 April 1755 from Naples that he had seen the 'Tomb of Virgil' and that its antiquity 'induced me to make several sketches of it', of which this is probably one.

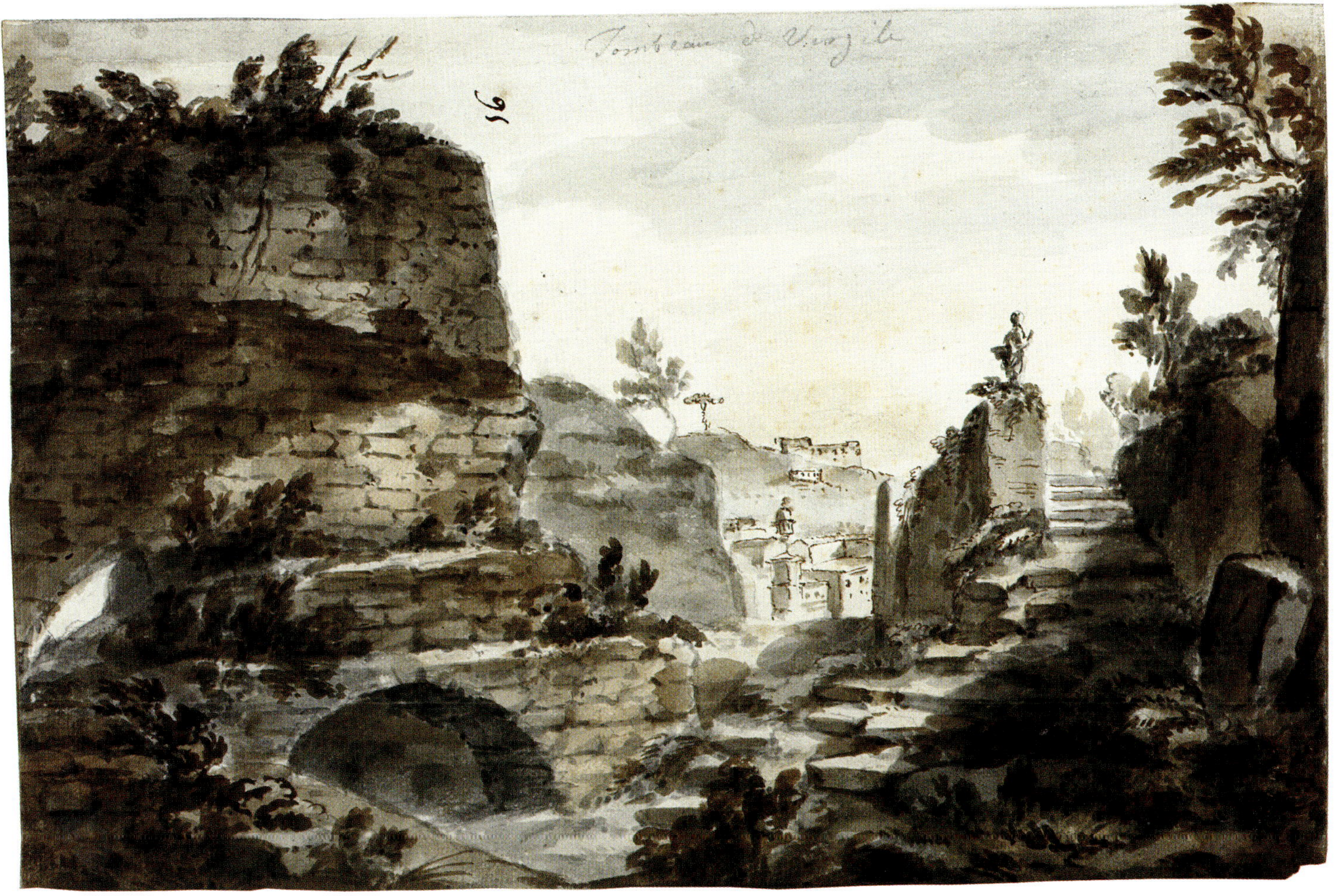

28. Charles-Louis Clérisseau
View of 'Virgil's Tomb' at Mergellina and a distant view of Posilippo

April 1755
Pencil, pen, and grey and brown washes
198 x 304 mm
Adam vol. 57/16

Robert Adam's drawing (fig.27) is taken from virtually the same spot but lacks the depth given by Clérisseau's introduction of the distant view over Posilippo. There are also none of Robert's adjustments of scale and detail which serve to strengthen the architectural form of the mausoleum.

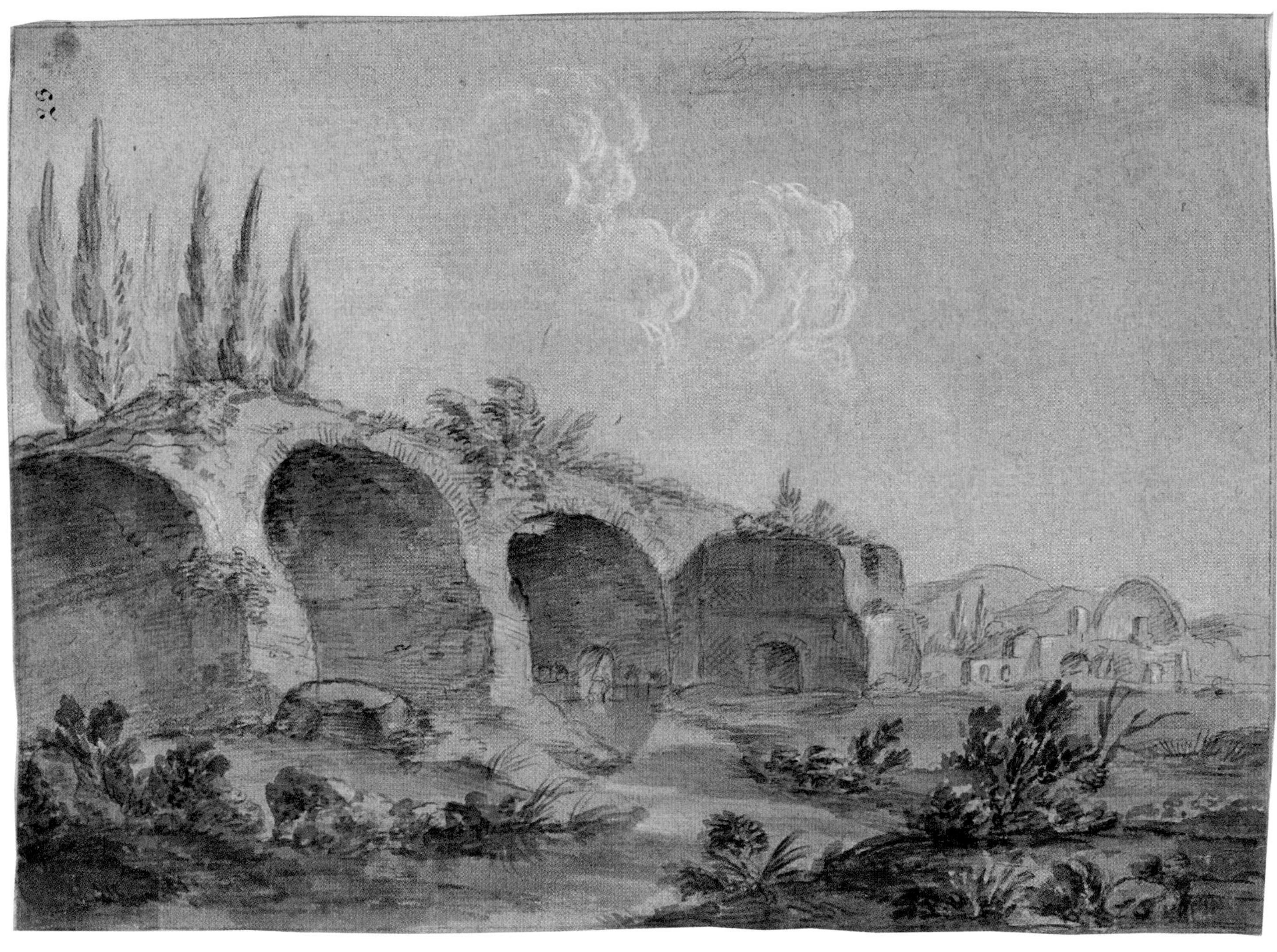

29. Charles-Louis Clérisseau *Attributed to*
View over the ruins of the imperial villa at Baiae and the temple of Diana or Venus in the distance

1755
Pencil, with brown and grey washes, white and white chalk heightening on grey paper, pencil margins, trimmed
228 x 319 mm
Adam vol. 57/23

This drawing is one of several views made of this thermal complex by both Robert Adam and Clérisseau. The use of white chalk and the delicate cloud forms is unlike Robert and closer to Clérisseau. The drawing effectively depicts the scattering of ruins of the original thermal establishments, of which the temples of Venus, Diana and Mercury were part.

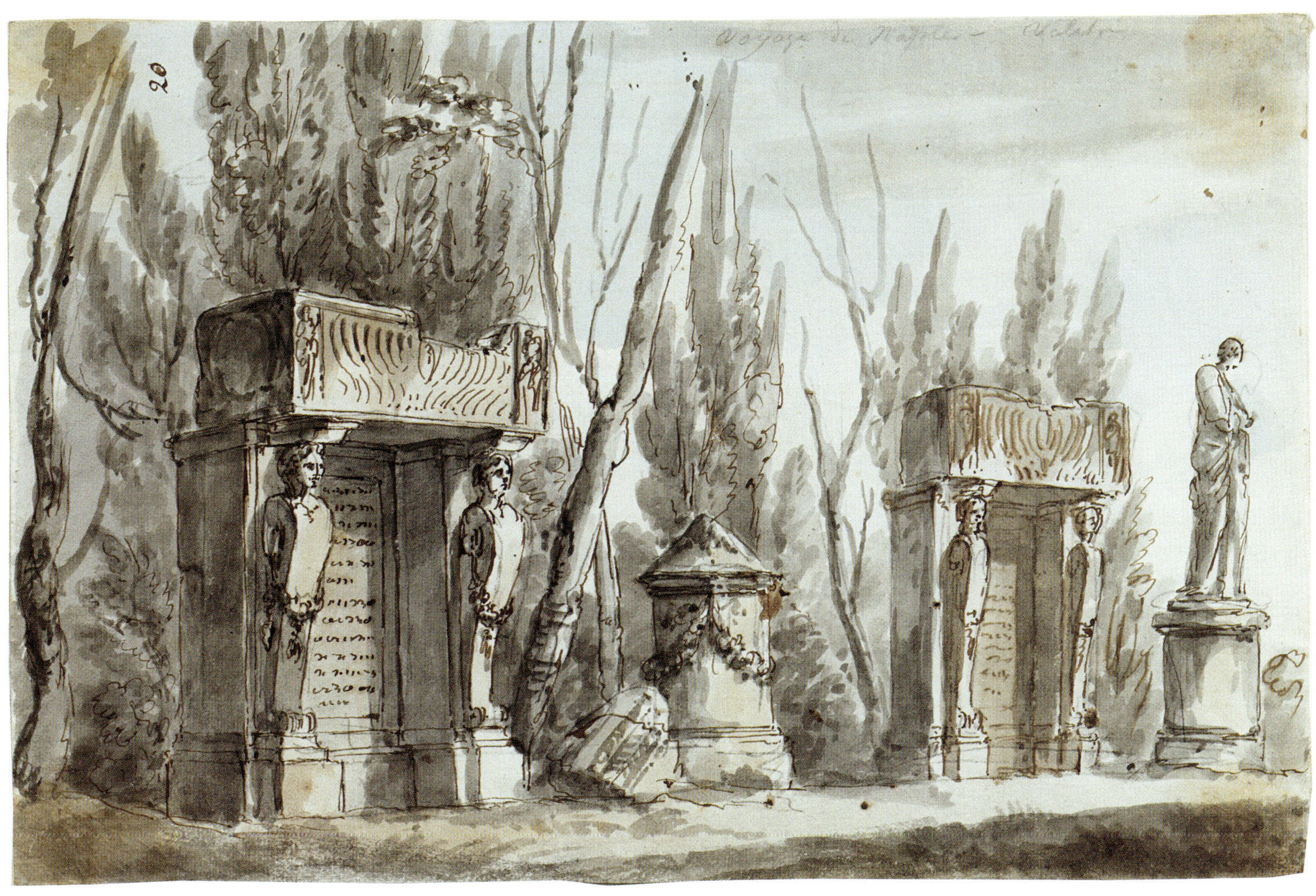

30. Charles-Louis Clérisseau
View of three tombs beside a path in a woodland setting

1755
Pencil, pen, and brown and grey washes
204 x 312 mm
Adam vol. 57/20

This may either be an imaginary composition or a version of some monuments near Velletri, south of Rome and on the Via Appia. If the latter, then these funerary monuments may be those found near Civita Lavinia and Velletri, which were later admired by James Adam in 1761. The bold and lively drawing style, with the effective use of light, is typical of Clérisseau's work.

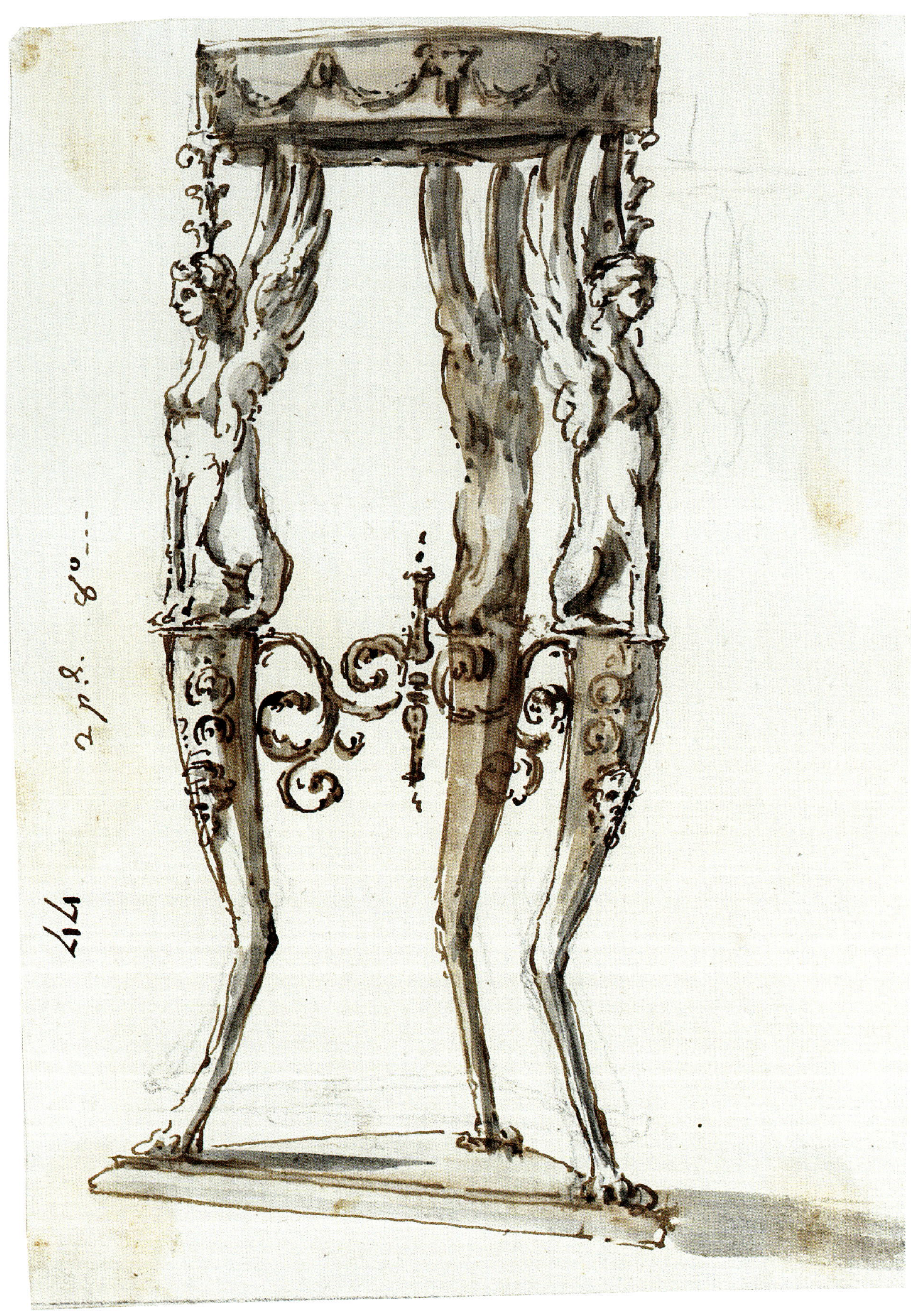

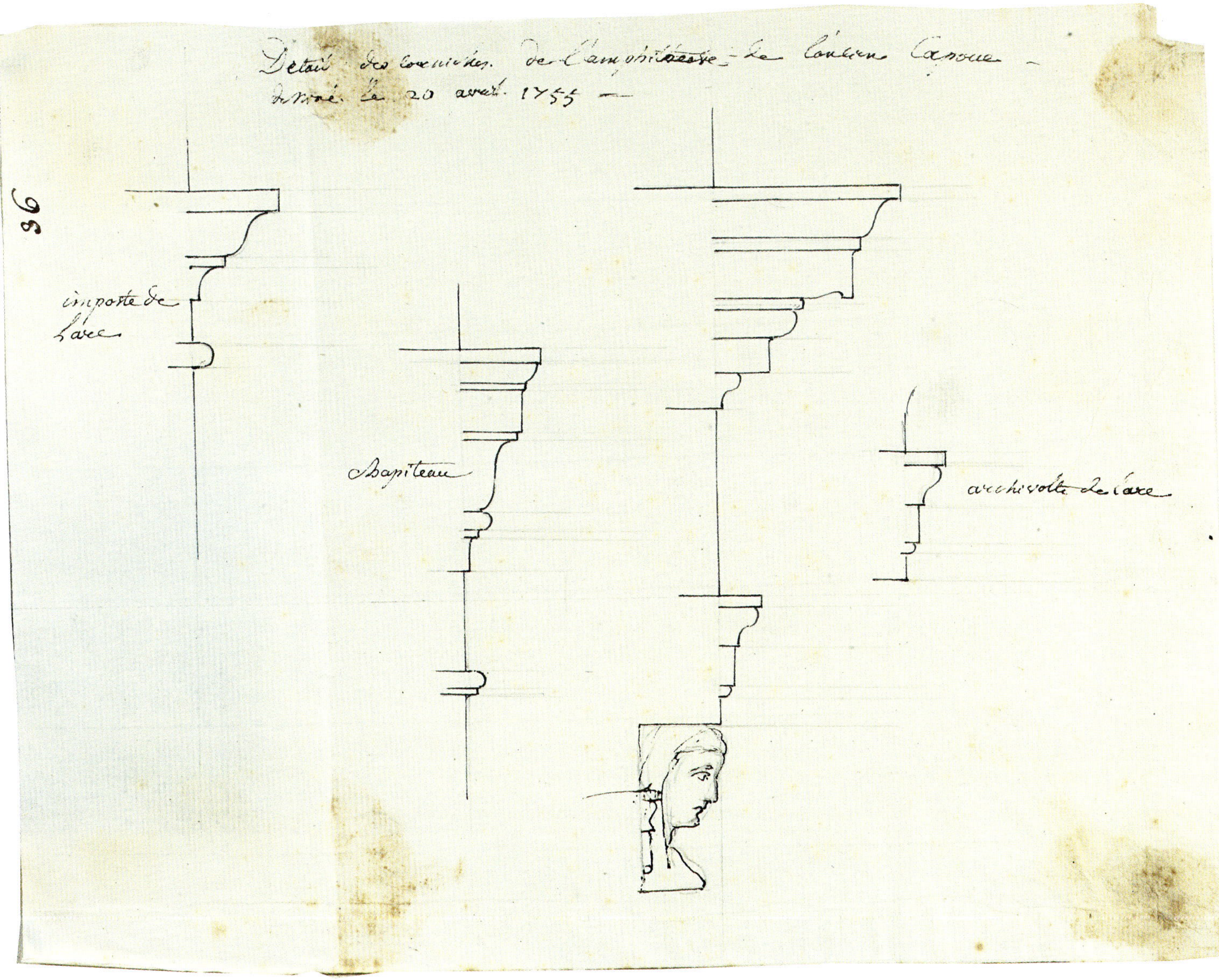

31. Robert Adam
Study of a tripod table

1755
Pencil and brown wash
179 x 129 mm
Adam vol. 57/44

On 7 April 1755, Robert Adam saw at Herculaneum '...earthen vases and marble pavements just discovered while we were on the spot and were shown some feet of tables in marble which were dug out the day before we were there'. This small table may be one of such objects that he studied and drew, and the original is probably in the Museum at Portici. It was later engraved by Piranesi in his *Vasi, Candelabri, Cippi, Sarcofagi* of 1778.

32. Charles-Louis Clérisseau
Details of cornices from the amphitheatre at Capua

20 April 1755
Pencil and pen
217 x 282 mm
Adam vol. 57/36

Robert Adam wrote that he and Clérisseau returned to Rome from the south of Italy via 'Old Capua', and this drawing fits that chronology. Robert also drew the amphitheatre, which had survived well and is second in size only to the Colosseum in Rome.

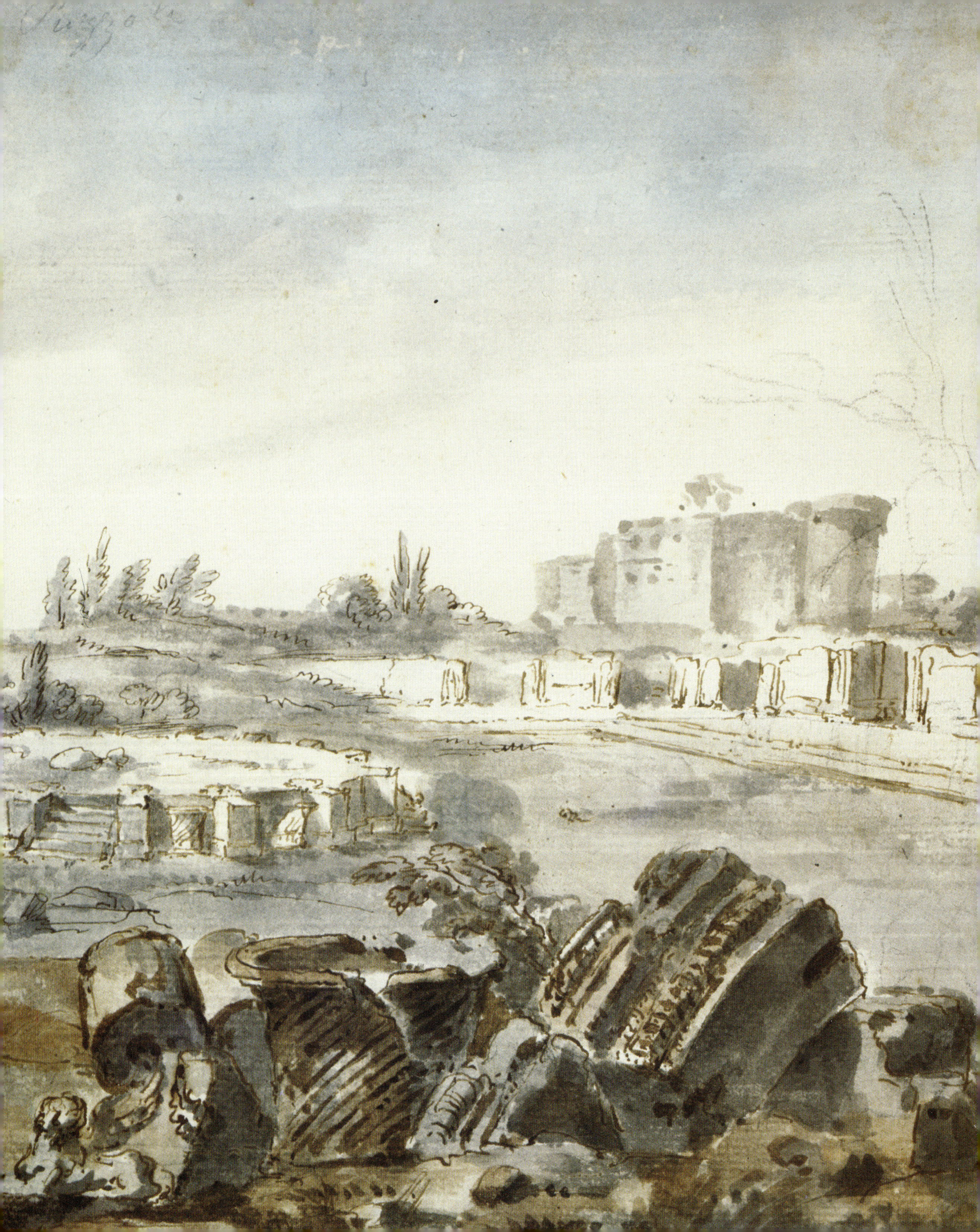

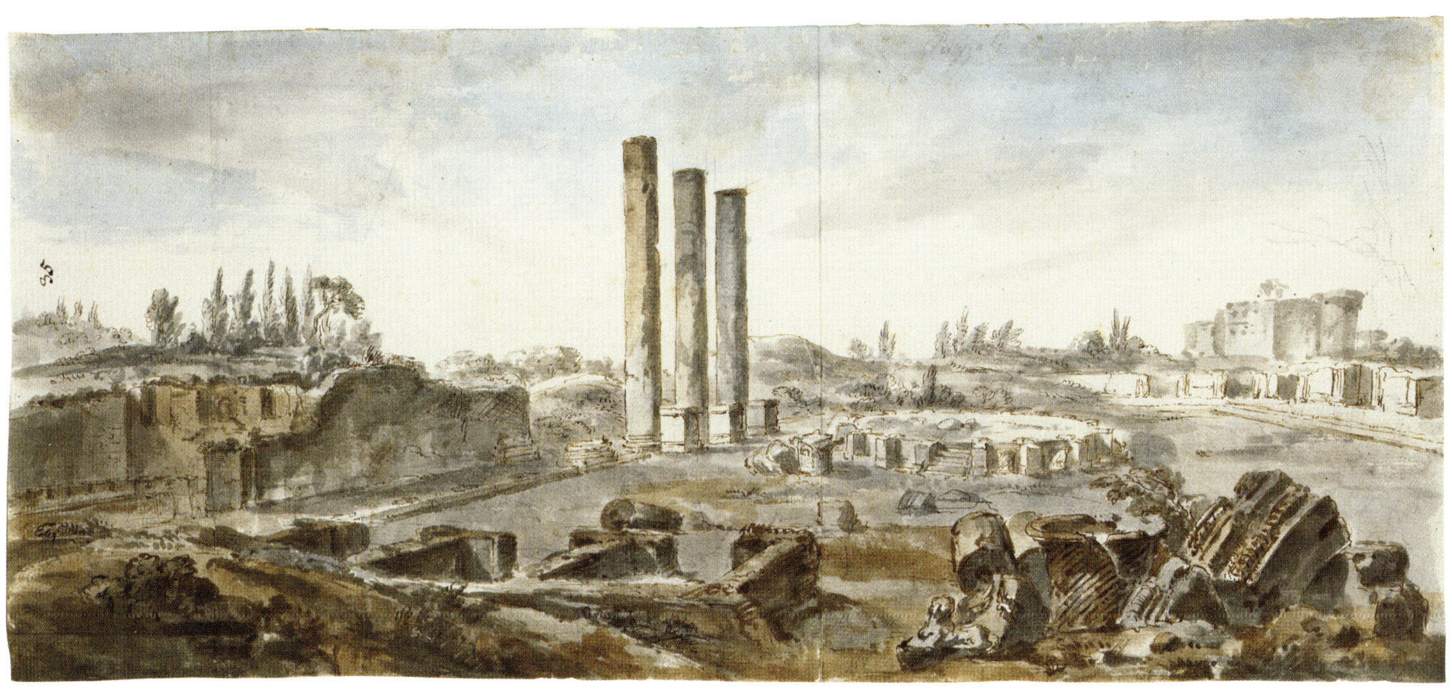

33. Charles-Louis Clérisseau
View of the ruins of the market building at Pozzuoli

1755
Pencil, pen, and brown, grey and blue washes
228 x 513
Adam vol. 57/35

This is a view of the new excavations and reconstruction of the market area, dating from the first half of the second century AD. It is a successful attempt to make what is largely an archaeological drawing stimulating and attractive in the style of Piranesi's similar drawings, and was later issued by Clérisseau as a print in London in 1766.

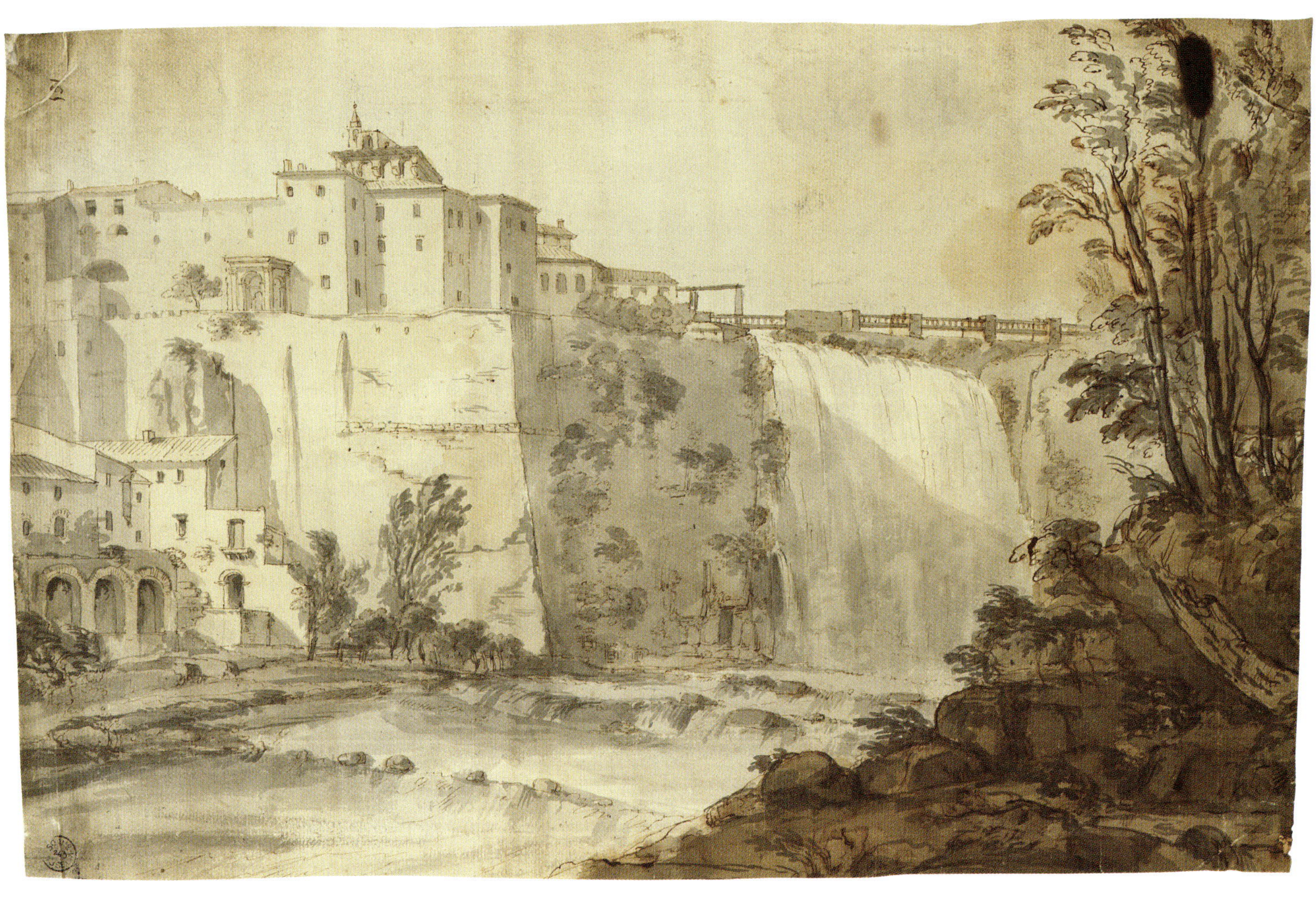

34. Robert Adam
View of Isola di Liri at Sora

1756
Pencil, pen, and brown and grey washes
323 x 505 mm
Adam vol. 1/243

Robert Adam and Clérisseau visited the Falls of Liri at Isola di Liri again in June 1756, on their tour to Sora. The tour to the area 60 miles south of Rome was not thought to be the most profitable or productive of their travels in Italy.

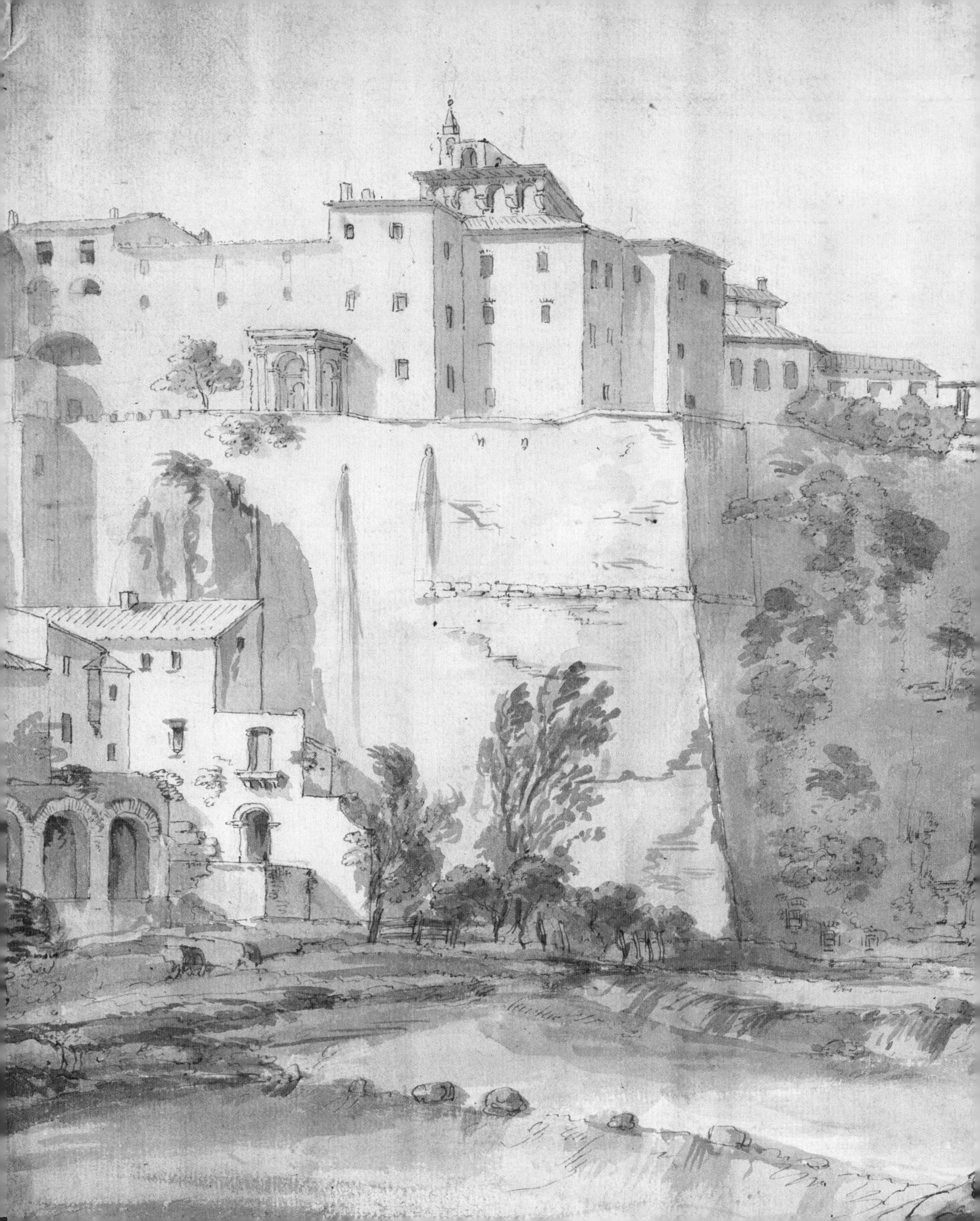

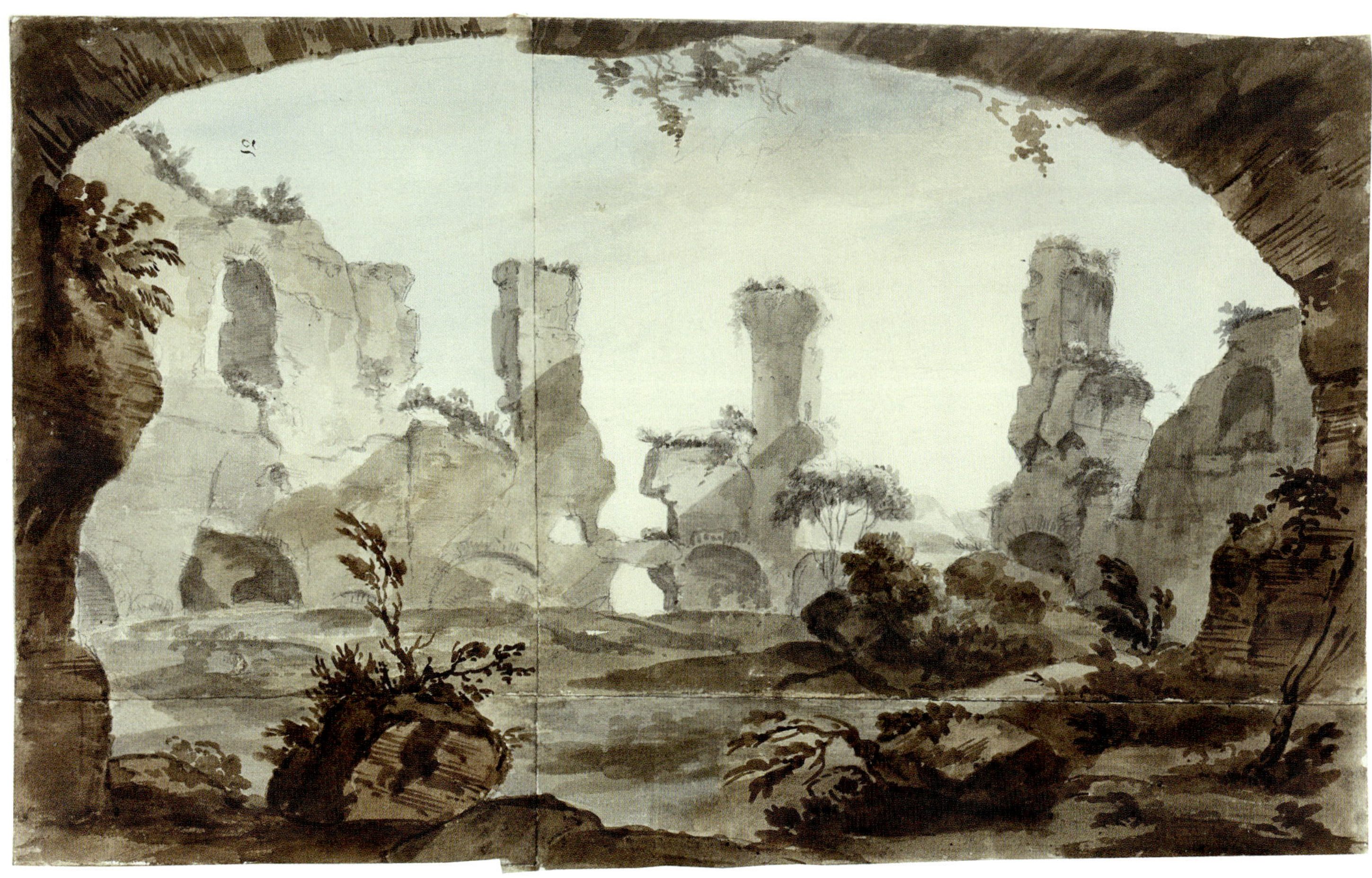

35. Charles-Louis Clérisseau
View of a ruined and overgrown circular building as seen through an arch showing the broken walls

1755
Pencil, pen, and brown, grey and blue washes
303 x 508
Adam vol. 57/12

This is an accomplished view by Clérisseau on four pieces of paper joined together, like the drawing of the market at Pozzuoli (fig.33). The note 'Naples' possibly refers to the city itself and not to the antiquities at Baiae or Pozzuoli. However, nowhere in Naples itself provided a ruin of this form in the mid-eighteenth century, whereas the amphitheatre at Pozzuoli did.

36. Jean-Baptiste Lallemand (1710–*c*.1803) *Attributed to*
View of two ruined vaults composed of large blocks of stone, leading up steps to further vaulting with vegetation in the foreground

c.1756
Black chalk on grey paper with white heightening
289 x 212
Adam vol. 57/80

The style of drawing and the use of chalk are not typical of the Adam drawings, though it is probably by someone in the Clérisseau circle, possibly Lallemand. The drawing itself may well be a study for the lower vaulting shown in several antique views.

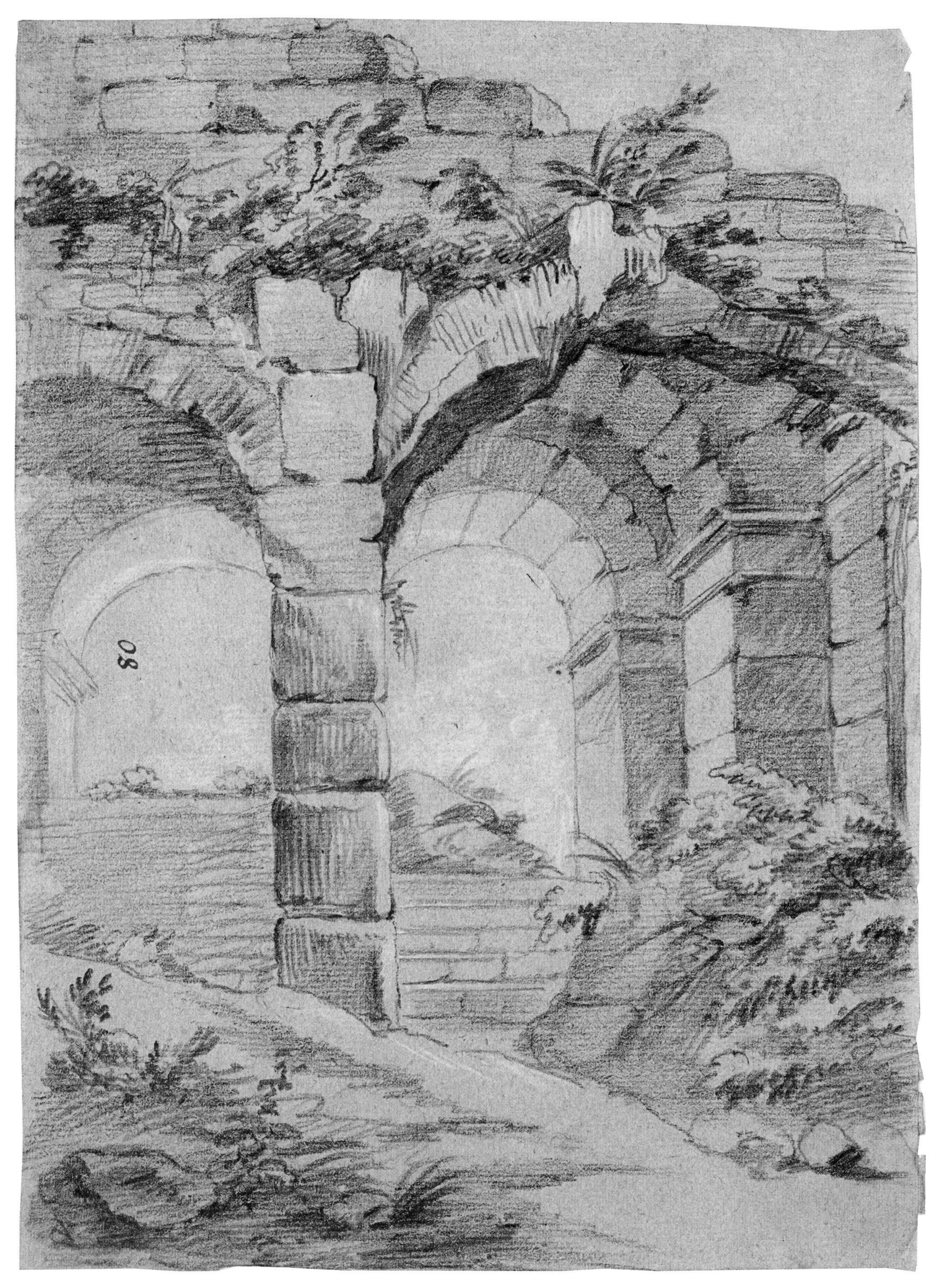

Robert Adam's

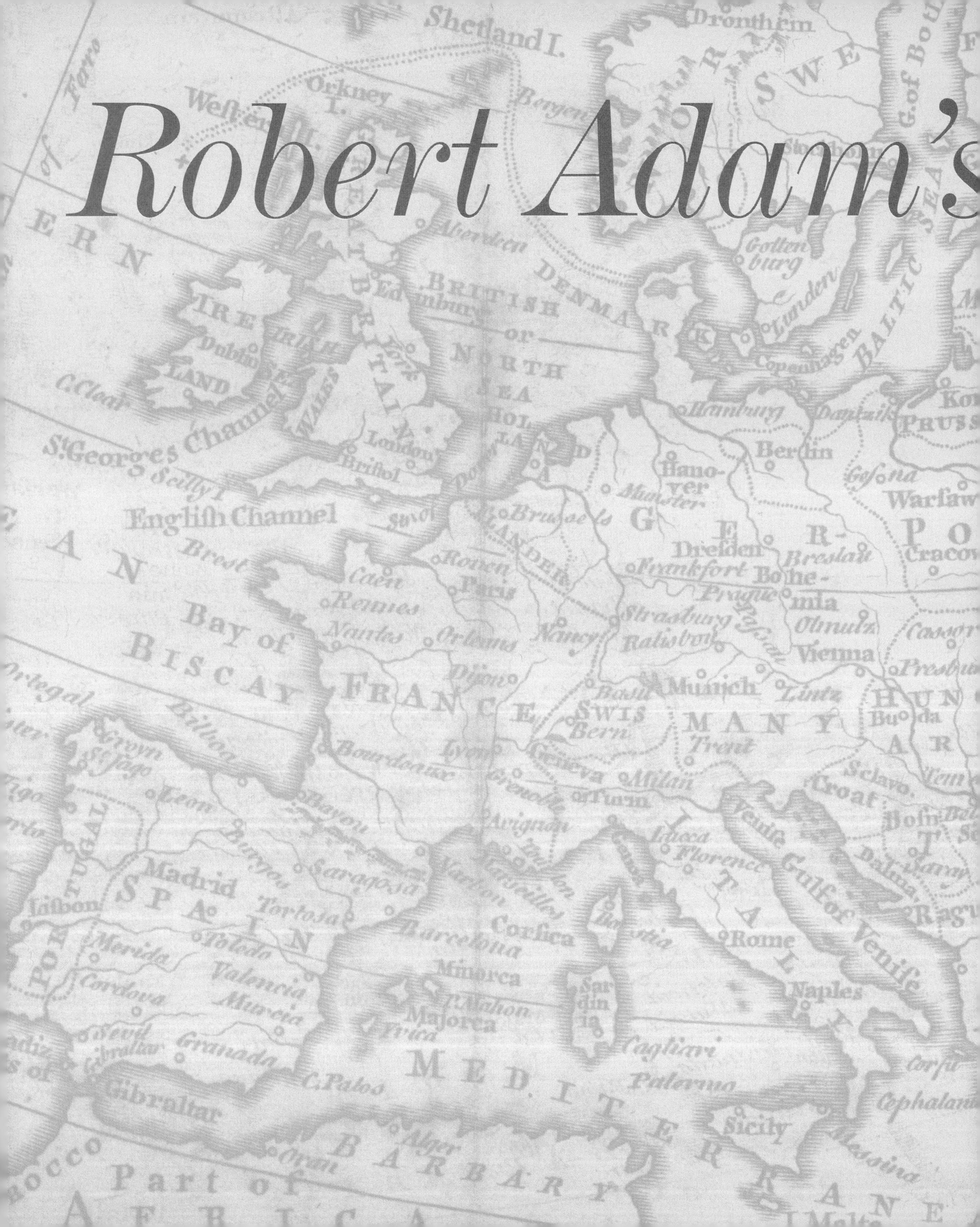

Grand Tour Rome

Robert Adam's Neapolitan tour, and the drawings he made under Clérisseau's tutelage, were a foretaste of what lay ahead in Rome, as had been intended. He returned in May 1755, when his academic drawing lessons in perspective and figure composition under Clérisseau and Laurent Pécheux, the young French painter, began in earnest. His lodgings at the Casa Guarnieri, near the Spanish Steps, were the centre for this activity and he described its organisation as 'a good bed-chamber for myself and a little one for my friend Clérisseau, a hall in which to have two or three tables for draughtsmen and other myrmidons of art whom we employ'. The atmosphere of the place was captured in an early pen drawing he made from his window over the tiled roofs of Rome [fig.37]. There, he wrote, 'we can sit and draw in one another's rooms or amuse ourselves as is most agreeable to us' and, in this way, 'the forenoon I devote to study and drawing; after dinner I ride out to see palaces and draw on the spot'. The routine was a comparatively relaxed one and details of the running of the Casa itself can be found on the backs of drawings and scraps of paper. There was a constant preoccupation with oil, the buying of pens and reusing paper, and even the purchase of a papier-mâché snuff box for everyday use. Robert was also taking language lessons, perfecting his Italian on his assistants while they in turn tried to come to terms with his English and with his Scottish accent. It was a regime followed later by James Adam, though on a grander and more extensive scale.

The drawings made in the Casa Guarnieri, after the return from Naples, were the bones of architectural composition, laborious lessons in perspective and the refinement of architectural detail. Robert was instructed to 'forbear inventing or composing either plans or elevations' and he found it hard to resist 'scrawling a plan of a temple or a bit of a front'. It was not until the end of that year that Clérisseau allowed him to escape from such a disciplined routine and Robert wrote to his brother saying that he found his 'ideas of architecture are a good deal enlarged and my principles of the grand more fixed than ever they were before [fig.39]. Clerisseau [sic] preaches to me every day to forbear invention or composing either plans or elevations till I have a greater fund, that is, till I have made more progress in seeing things and my head more filled with proper ornaments and my hand more able to draw to purpose what I would incline.' It is easy to feel his frustration when he wrote in January 1756 of the drudgery in 'labouring at perspective and doing cornices with modillions, viewed from an angle of a building, which has its own difficulties'. As an escape and an outlet for his burgeoning compositional powers, Clérisseau acquiesced in Robert's somewhat hare-brained scheme for rebuilding Lisbon after the earthquake of 1755. Robert noted that his grandiose project had 'the advantage of Clerisseau's [sic] assistance and council', but it never seems to have gone much beyond a small ink plan and bird's-eye perspective, annotated in French [fig.38]. There were, as he candidly admitted, 'a thousand chances to one it never will take place'. He was correct.

At this point, too, Robert was taking lessons in landscape composition, very likely from Jean-Baptiste Lallemand, another member of Clérisseau's wide Roman circle. He was determined that 'before I leave Rome I shall draw landscape tolerably, having a good master for that branch too', and Lallemand was not easy to satisfy. Both his and Clérisseau's inventions of landscaped ruins were well represented in Robert's collection, frequently with sets of watercolour views [fig.40]. To these names must be added Robert's two architectural mentors, of whom Giovanni Battista Piranesi was the most important. It was he, with his idiosyncratic archaeological enthusiasms, who was undoubtedly the driving force behind Robert's plan to make a complete survey of the Roman Baths and Hadrian's Villa, the project being underway in July 1755 when Robert described going with 'Signor Piranesi and Monsieur Clerisseau [sic] to see the ancient thermae or baths of Caracalla, the ruins of which are most magnificent'. It was part of his ambitious scheme to undertake a complete revision of Antoine Desgodetz's *Les Edifices Antiques de Rome*, an idea doing the architectural rounds in Rome in the 1750s. For more humdrum affairs, he relied on the minor architect, Laurent-Benoît Dewez, and after him nameless 'drudges' at a shilling a day 'who could absolutely do nothing, but work like a slave to little purpose'. Even Dewez and the decorative draughtsman, Agostino Brunias, were both condescendingly described by Robert in the following terms: 'I have got a young Lad from Liege that is become my great Draughtsman, is active, exact Expeditious & attentive. The lad I intend to bring to England & make him overseer of my Fineliners and Line Drawers. Then I have one for ornaments for Landscape figures & other things of that nature which will prove very useful & who I shall like wise plant in London.' But whatever their standing in his eyes, it was essential that he learn from them until he could match them technically 'in figures, in bas-reliefs and in ornaments, which, with any tolerable degree of taste so as to apply them properly, make a building appear as different as night from day' [fig.41].

For Clérisseau, Lallemand and Dewez, teaching was, for the most part, a lesson in emulation, once the basic principles had been absorbed. This is illustrated in a small, red chalk drawing by Lallemand that Robert enlarged into a capriccio of a circular and domed temple beside a small bridge, also borrowed from a Lallemand composition [figs 42, 44]. Evidence of a similar relationship can be found in several of Clérisseau's and Robert's watercolours of 1756, where, in a few examples, the hand is more or less indistinguishable. This is also true of the Dewez plans and elevations, where architectural stylisation and convention make it difficult to separate the two draughtsmen. However, several of Robert's plans have been clearly revised and corrected, often in red chalk, and this type of intervention was probably Dewez's form of instruction [fig.45]. They also show Robert advancing from the basic ink plan to scale – almost diagrammatic in character and in keeping with the style of the Edinburgh office – to grander compositions, some of which are in the form of a free, sketch plan with a bold use of ink and grey washes [fig.46]. This is best illustrated in a group of small-scale plans, obviously variants of each other and often growing in complexity, that also show what are perhaps Dewez's quick and sketchy initial contributions. In carrying out such exercises and making such variations and copies, Robert may have had in mind a notion of an architectural compendium, a paper museum, in the style of the Albani collection of prints and drawings that James was to acquire in 1763. Robert had gained access to the 200 folio volumes in 1755 and later reported that the 'Cardinal Albani and I are turned very thick as he has discovered my hidden talents for the hidden treasures of antiquity'. In studying these sheets and the variations on certain forms they revealed, he may have found a pattern for his studies with Dewez and, in this fashion, could bypass the sterility of endless copying. Stretched further, he could imagine himself and Dewez continuing in their drawings where the great Renaissance architects present in the collection had left off. This sympathy, however, did not extend to Renaissance architecture in general, and he and James affected surprise that Bramante 'could produce nothing more tolerable, nothing more correct, nothing more ingenious' than the tempietto at San Pietro in Montorio, and dismissed in the same manner the Palazzo Cancellaria as 'lacking genius, taste and elegance'.

After the Naples tour, Robert remained at the Casa Guarnieri for the next two years, apart from short excursions to Rimini, Sora and Viterbo, leaving Florence and Venice for his return journey to London in 1757. It was time well spent – on the surface, perhaps, an ideal existence. His biographer, John Clerk, described how 'he lived in a proper degree of splendour & kept in the first society at the same time that he applied with passion in the study of his profession which became more charming to him every day'. Architecture – ancient and modern – classicism, architectural drawing and capriccio invention, all were studied under the direction of Clérisseau and his associates. His pace was unrelenting, and he wrote of having 'so many projects in my head, of things to be drawn, plans and measures to be taken and perspective views to be made' that 'I am now determined to sally forth every morning by seven o'clock with paper and pen and draw till dinner time'. His drawing office in the Casa was so well known that, according to him, 'the students of the best Italian architects want to leave their masters in order to study in my House'.

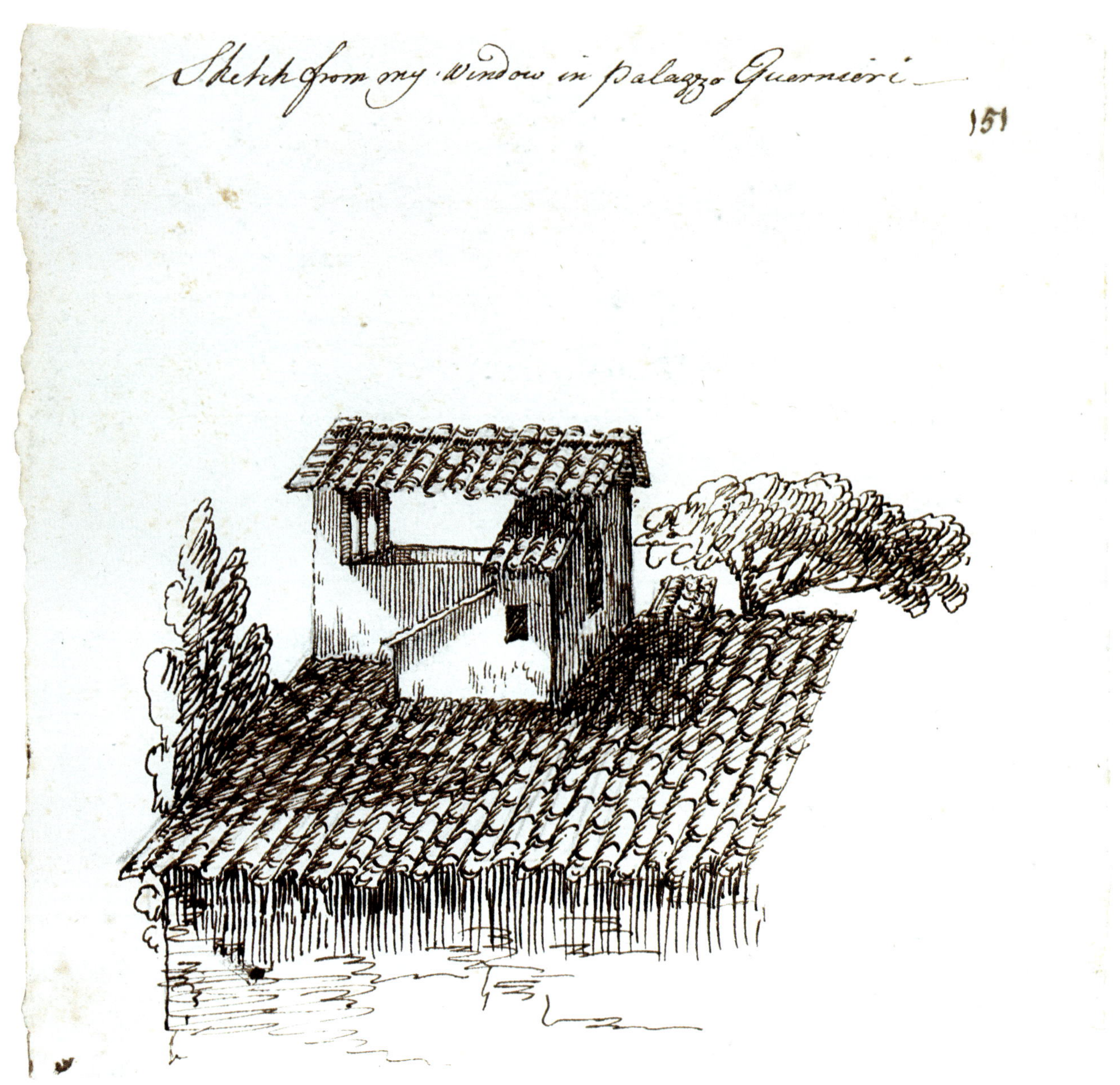

37. Robert Adam
View from the window of the Casa Guarnieri in Rome

*c.*1755
Pen
198 x 213 mm
Adam vol. 57/151

Robert Adam had lodgings at the palazzo (casa) Guarnieri from February 1755 until May 1757. This sketch is probably a view over the gardens towards the various buildings of the adjoining monastery and church of San Isidoro, a college of the Irish Franciscans.

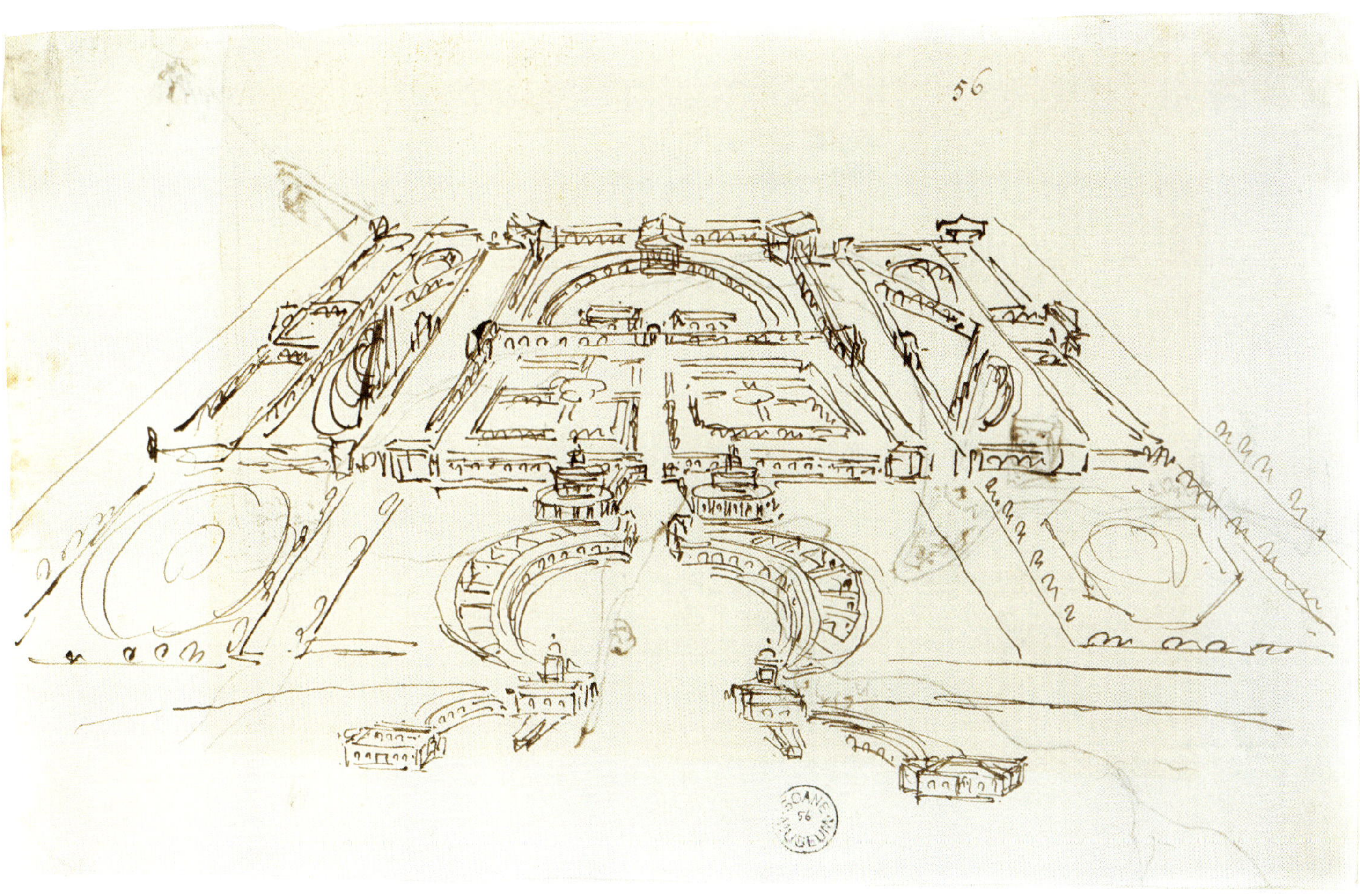

38. Robert Adam
Bird's-eye view of port city

1755
Pen
170 x 278 mm
Adam vol. 9/56

This aerial perspective shows Robert Adam's ideas for rebuilding the centre of Lisbon, which had been destroyed in the fire and earthquake of 1755. He toyed with the idea of gaining the commission for rebuilding the city but the scheme is in every sense an academic exercise and does not even fit the topography of Lisbon.

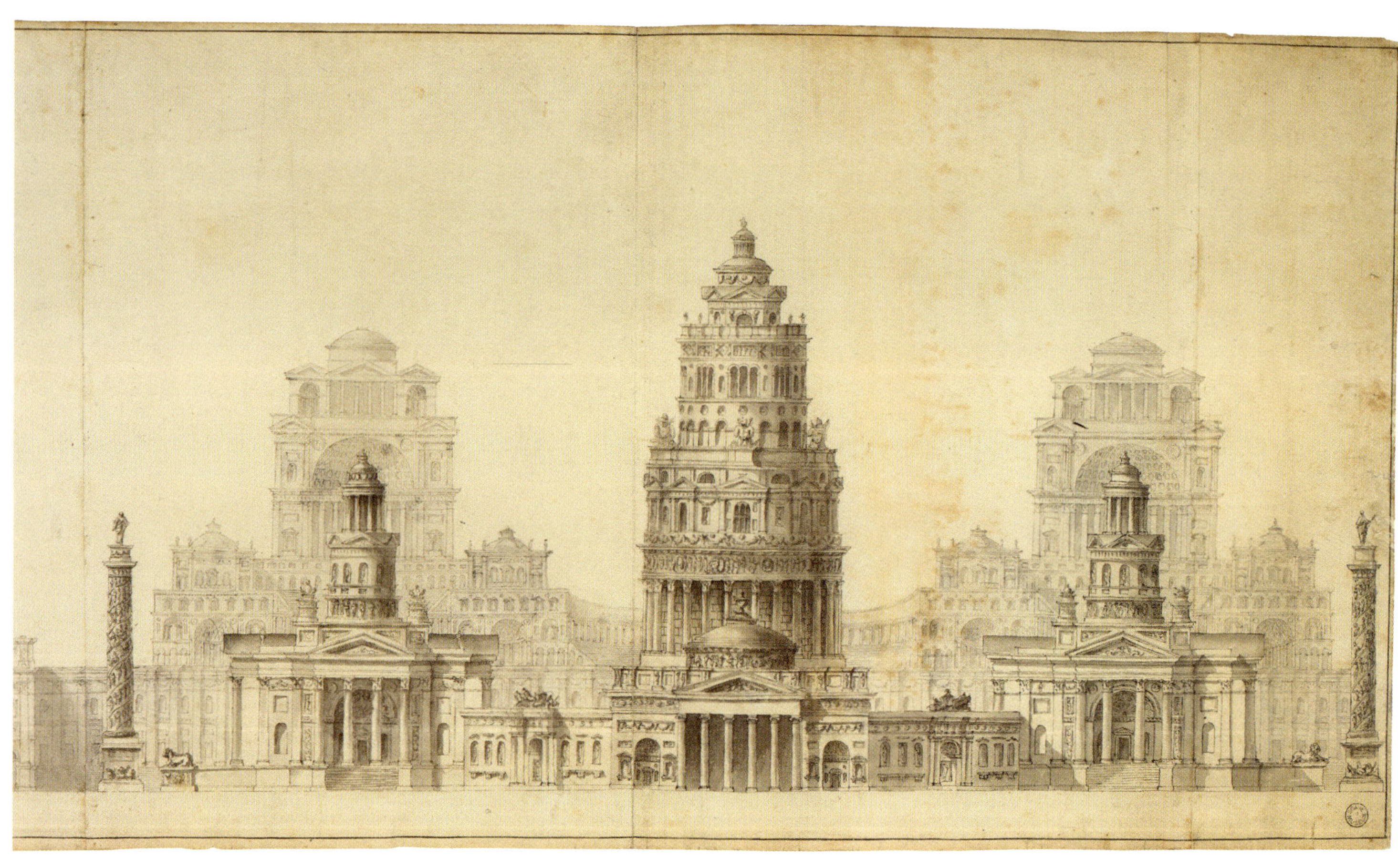

39. Robert Adam
Capriccio of a vast building

1757
Pen and grey wash
462 x 2764 mm
Adam vol. 28/1 (detail)

The grandest of Robert Adam's surviving Roman drawings, this composition recalls the scale of the Roman Baths whilst incorporating the outstanding monuments of imperial Rome, from Trajan's Column to Trajan's markets. He wrote in November 1756 that the baths had '...shown mankind that true Grandeur was only to be produced from simplicity and largeness of parts and that conveniency was not inconsistent with decoration'.

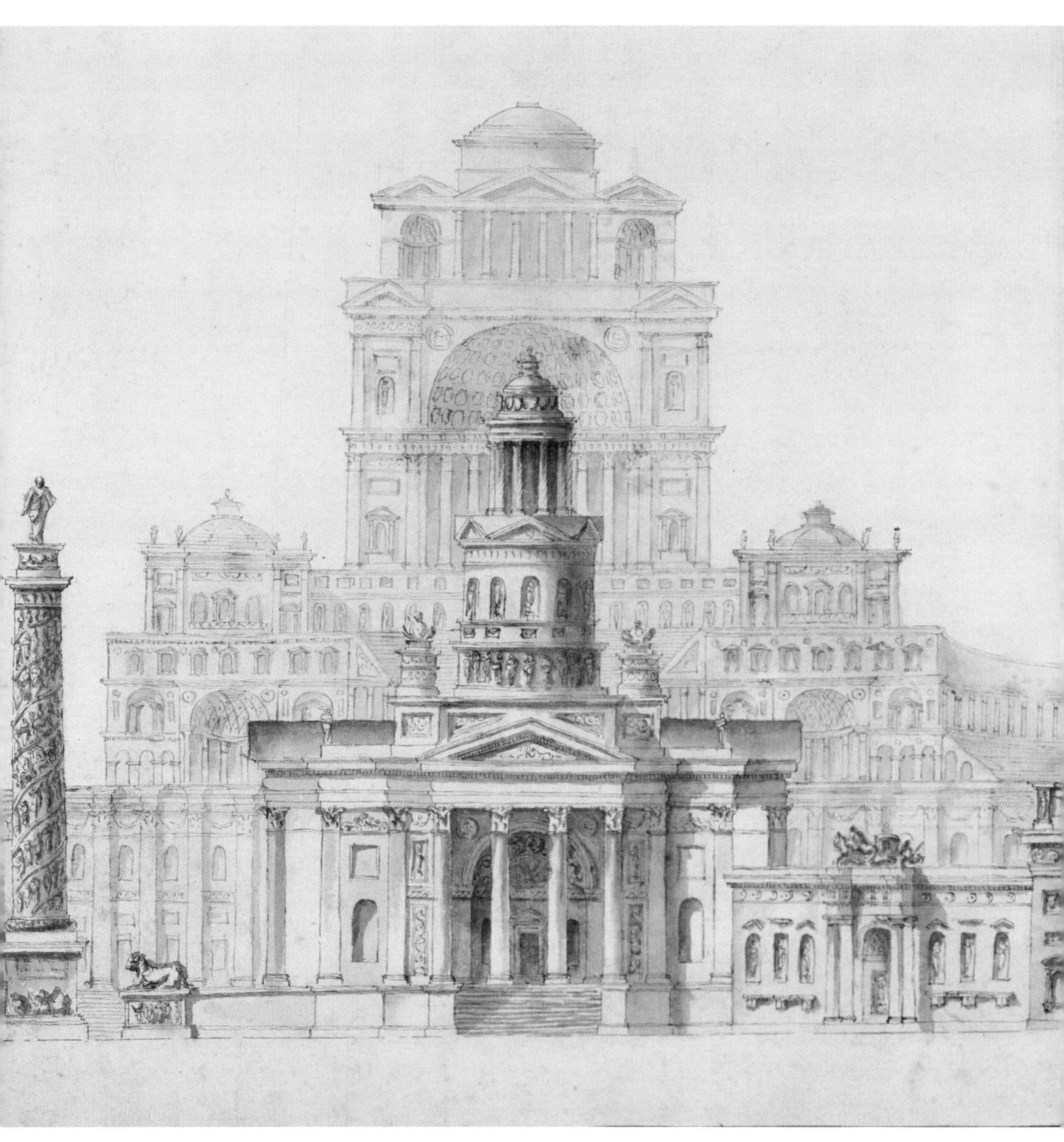

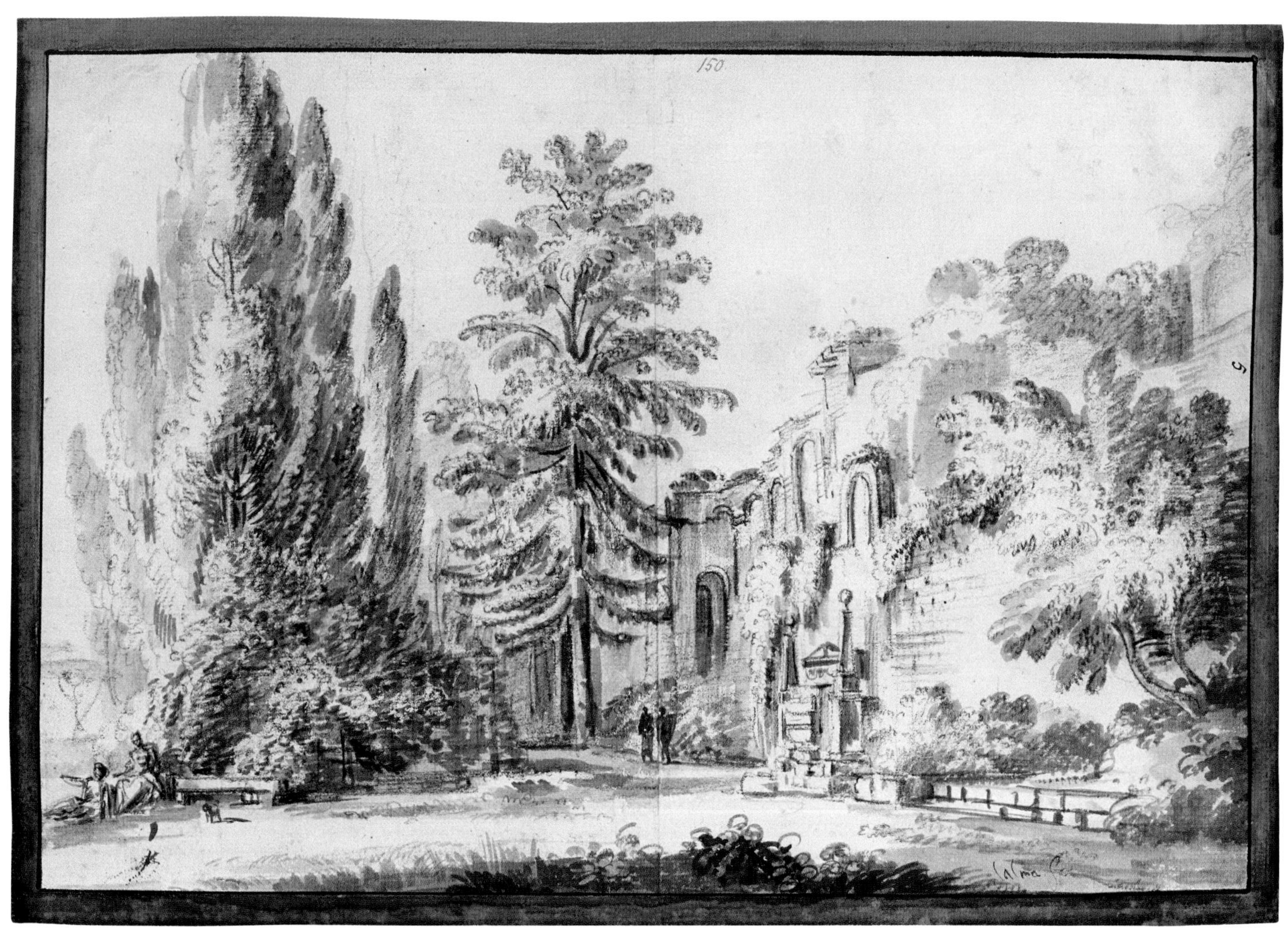

40. Jean-Baptiste Lallemand
View of garden of the Villa Ludovisi, Rome

*c.*1755
Pencil and grey wash, with a deep blue border
254 x 369 mm
Adam vol. 57/150

This is one of a set of six garden views by Lallemand, all of which have the contemporary blue borders. Lallemand taught landscape drawing to Robert Adam in Rome.

41. Robert Adam
Section through a design, possibly for a mausoleum

*c.*1755
Pen
204 x 202 mm
Adam vol. 55/38

This is a version of the section through the proposed mausoleum planned for the Adam family in Edinburgh. The plaques between the column capitals and sculpture are inscribed: *Lista delle anime di Purgatorio / Pater Noster de Ave Maria / Plen et[?] Indulgenzia*, all of which would have made strange reading in a Protestant churchyard.

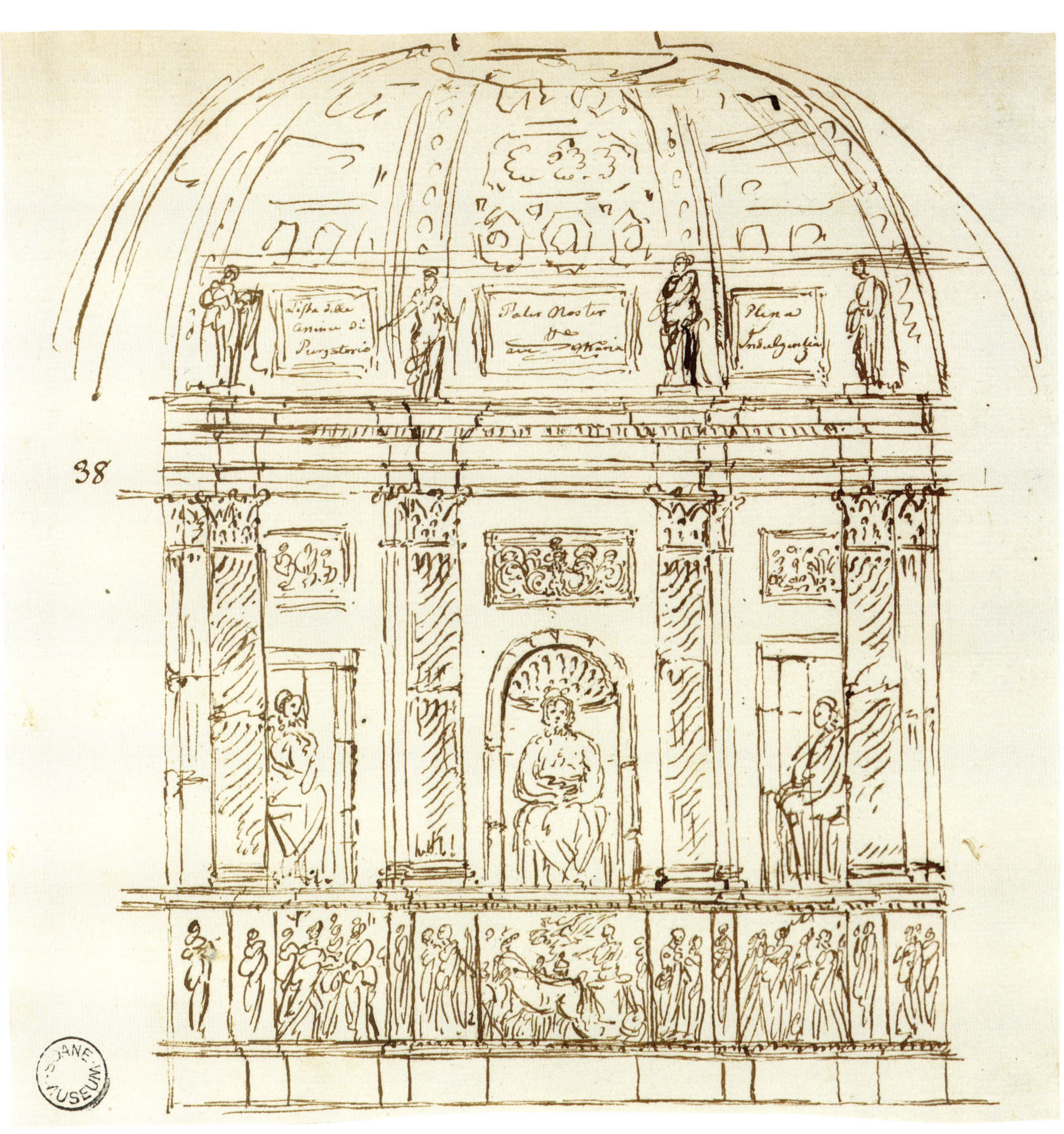
38

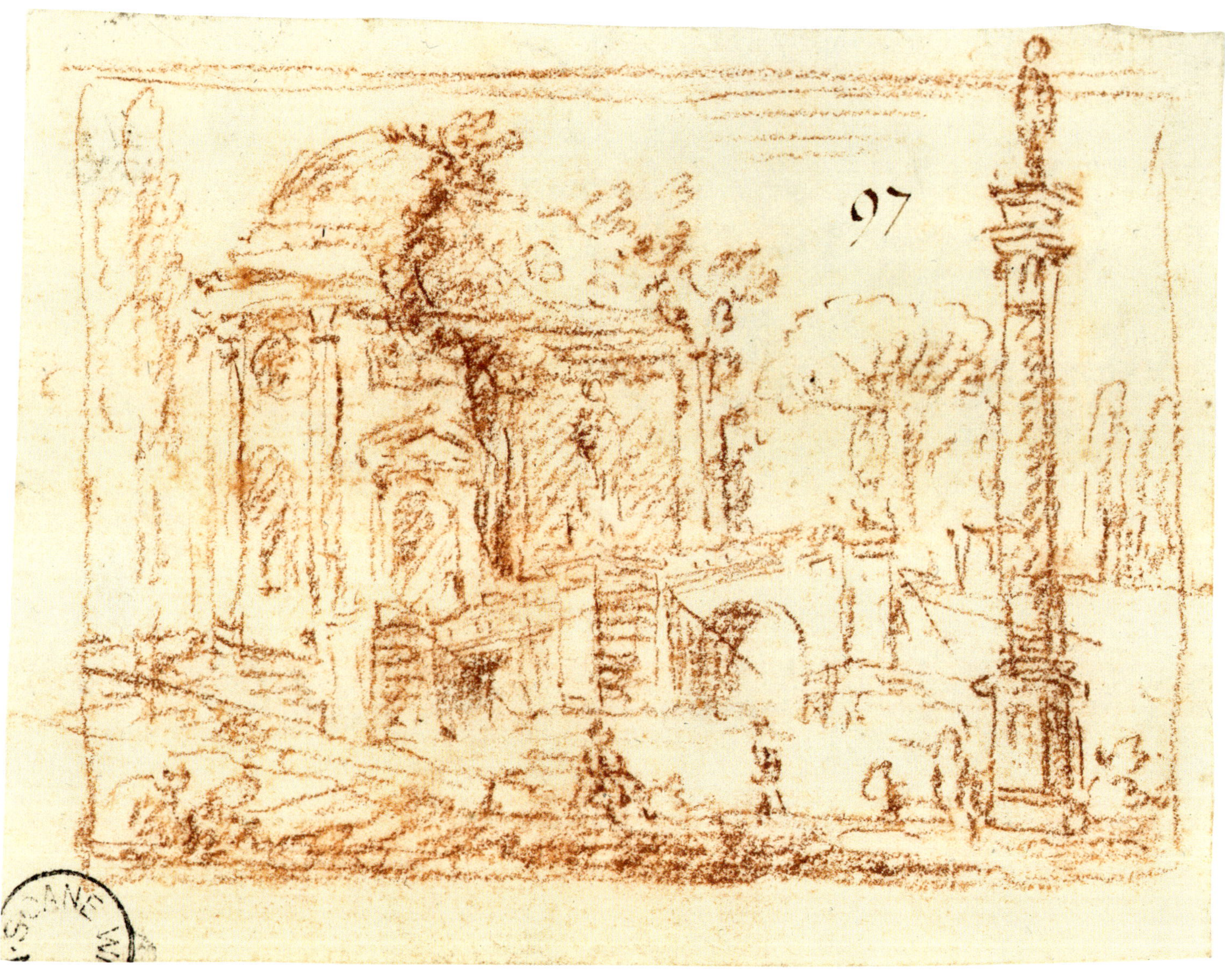

42. Jean-Baptiste Lallemand
Capriccio showing a ruined circular temple and a column in a landscape setting

*c.*1757
Red chalk
88 x 115 mm
Adam vol. 55/97

This small chalk drawing served as the basis for the larger pen and wash drawing by Robert Adam (fig.44). Part of his programme of architectural education, the drawing makes clear the connection between such small, very sketchy drawings and the grander essays in composition by Lallemand and Clérisseau, or the more architectural ones by Dewez.

43. Robert Adam *Attributed to*
Capriccio showing a three-bay portico of columns and pilasters with rectangular relief panels on either side

*c.*1756
Pen, and grey and brown washes over pencil
343 x 230 mm
Adam vol. 55/89

The composition of a deep perspective to one side, without any balancing interest, is typical of Clérisseau's influence. There are also similar but tamer compositions by both Clérisseau and Robert Adam and there is a view of this sort amongst the Adam drawings in the Victoria and Albert Museum, which may once have been part of Sir John Soane's collection.

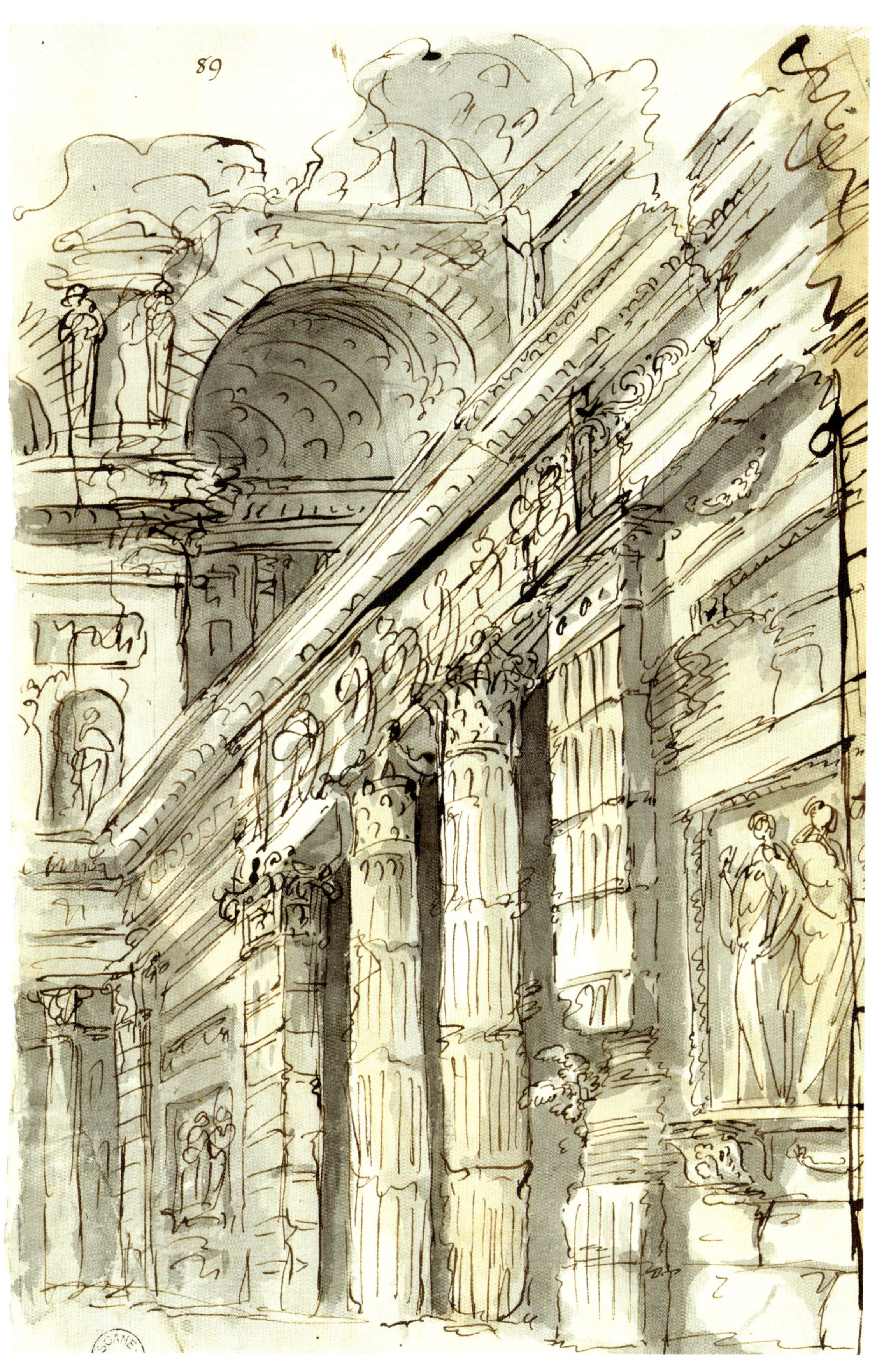

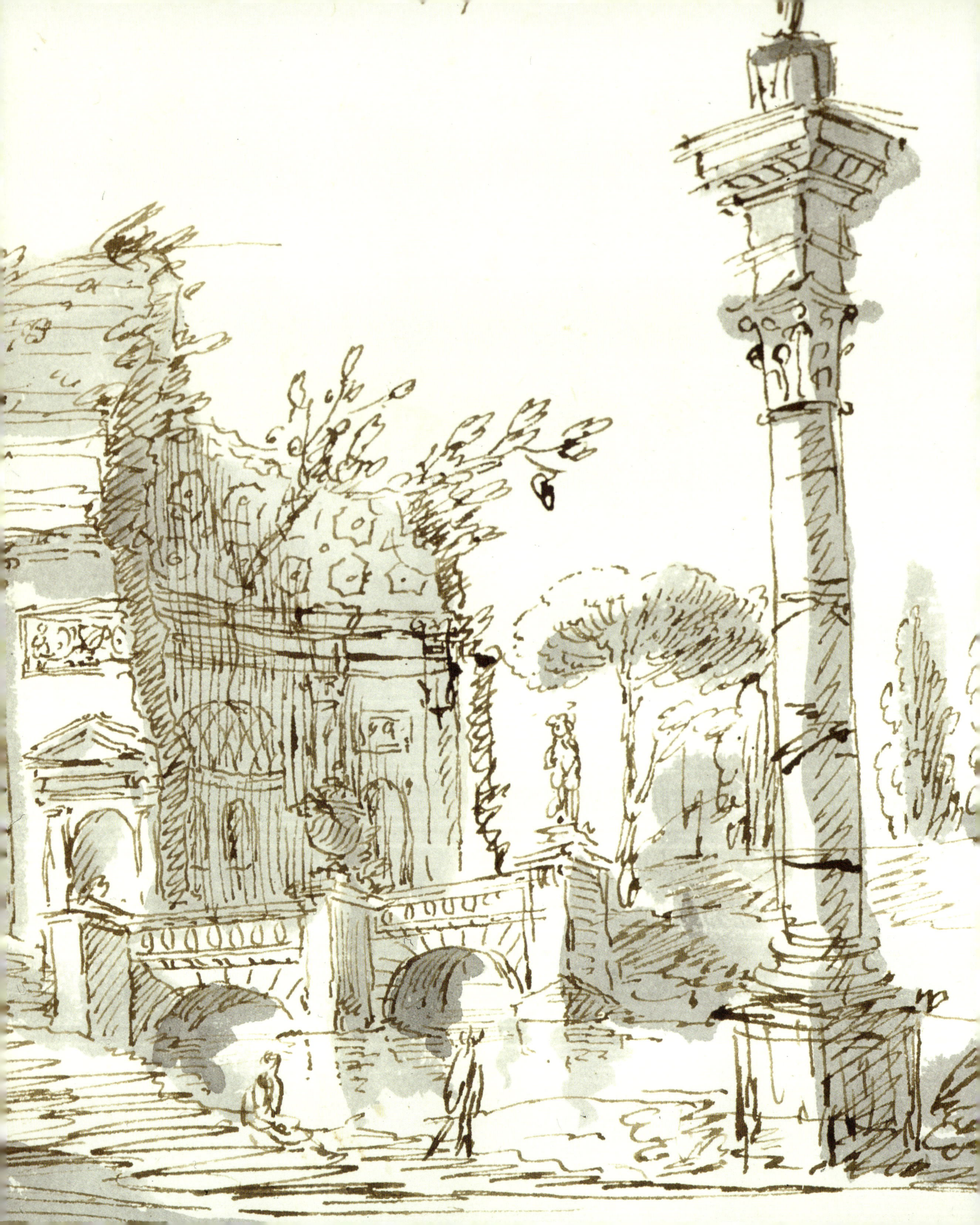

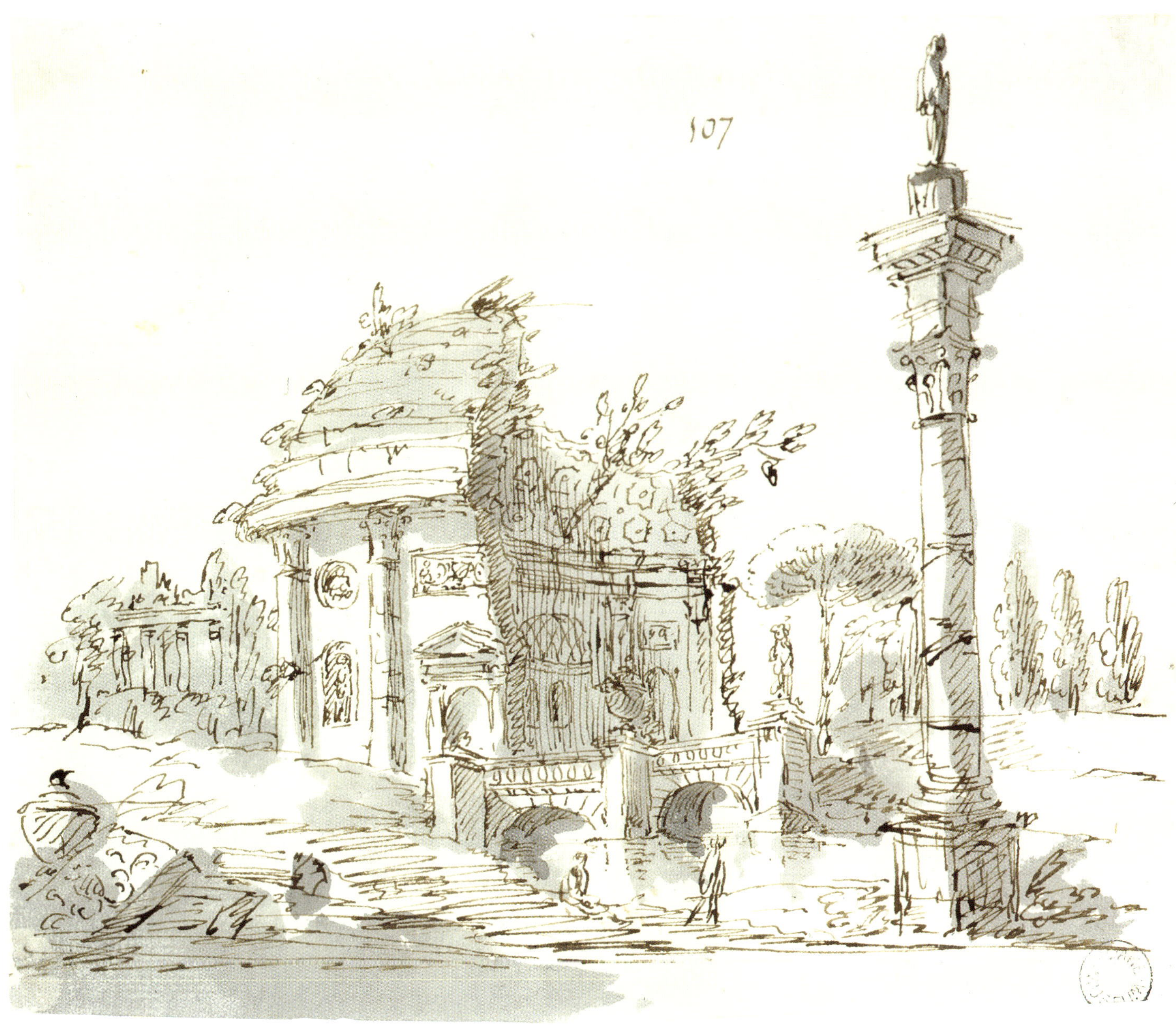

44. Robert Adam
Capriccio showing a ruined circular temple and a column in a landscape setting

c.1757
Pen and grey wash
179 x 215 mm
Adam vol. 55/107

This composition is an enlarged version of Lallemand's red chalk drawing (fig.42). The small bridge is also borrowed from Lallemand, as is the wash style of the drawing.

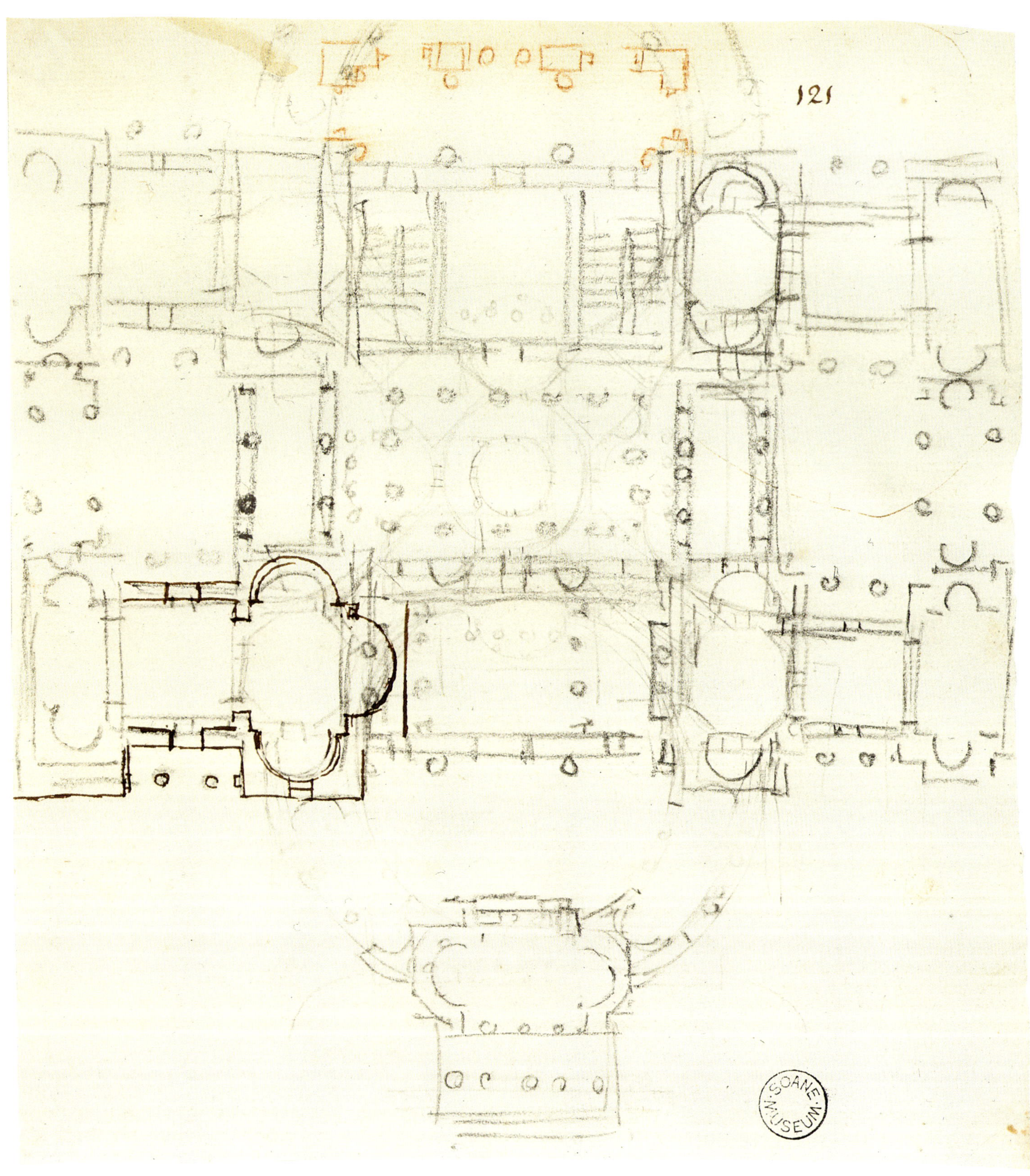
121
SOANE MUSEUM

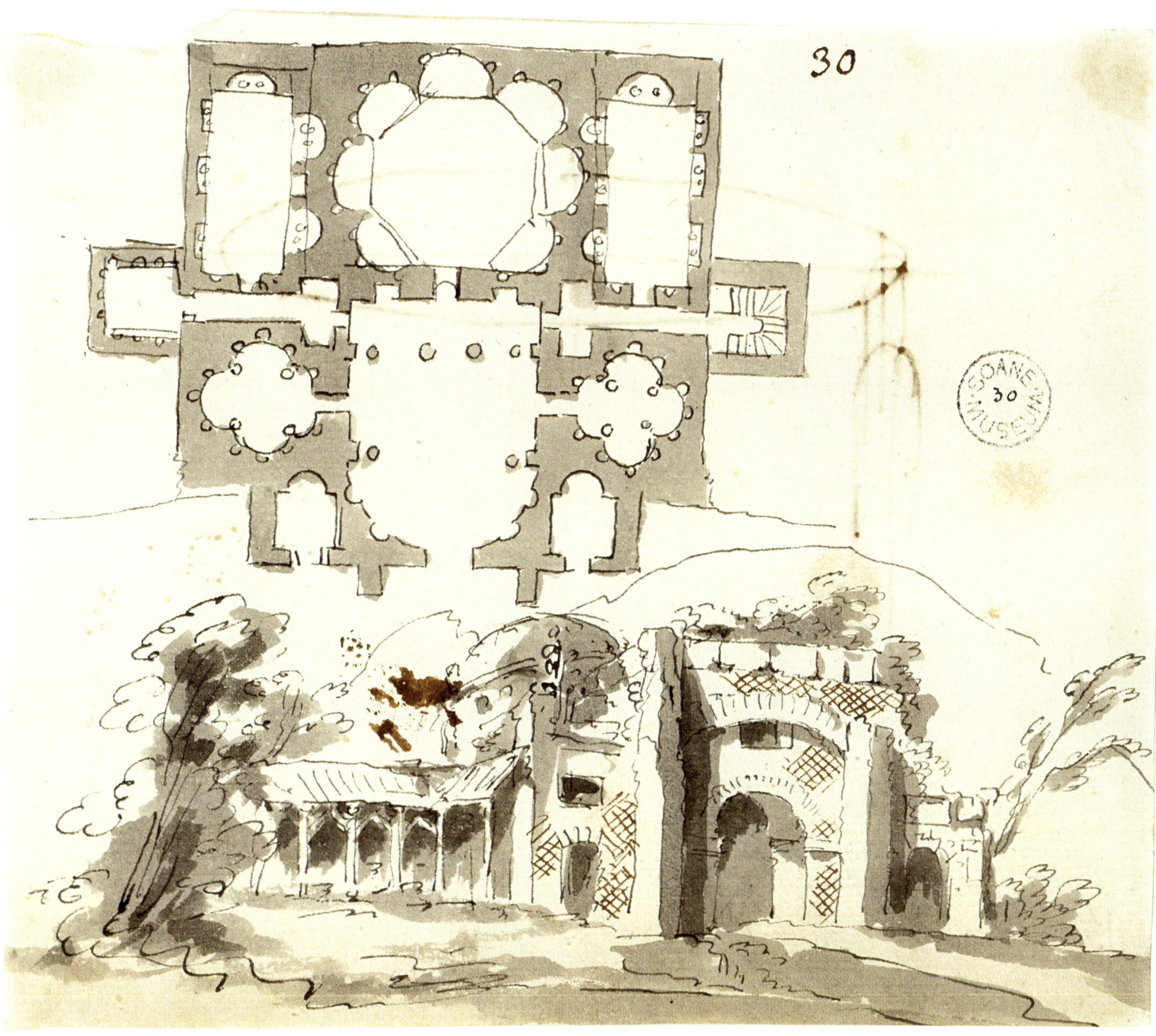

45. Robert Adam & Laurent-Benoît Dewez (1731–1812)
Academic exercise in planning a large building

*c.*1756
Pencil, pen, and black and red chalk
223 x 204 mm
Adam vol. 55/121

The plan on this sheet is typical of Robert Adam's studies in architectural composition. The drawing has overdrawing, or correction, in ink and red chalk, the latter possibly by his instructor, L-B. Dewez.

46. Robert Adam
Landscape capriccio and plan of a pavilion

1756
Pen, and brown and grey washes
144 x 169 mm
Adam vol. 9/30

The plan and perspective do not seem to be related, so this is possibly an example of Robert Adam reusing paper. The two drawings would seem to have been made at about the same time and possibly underscore Robert's simultaneous lessons in architectural and landscape composition.

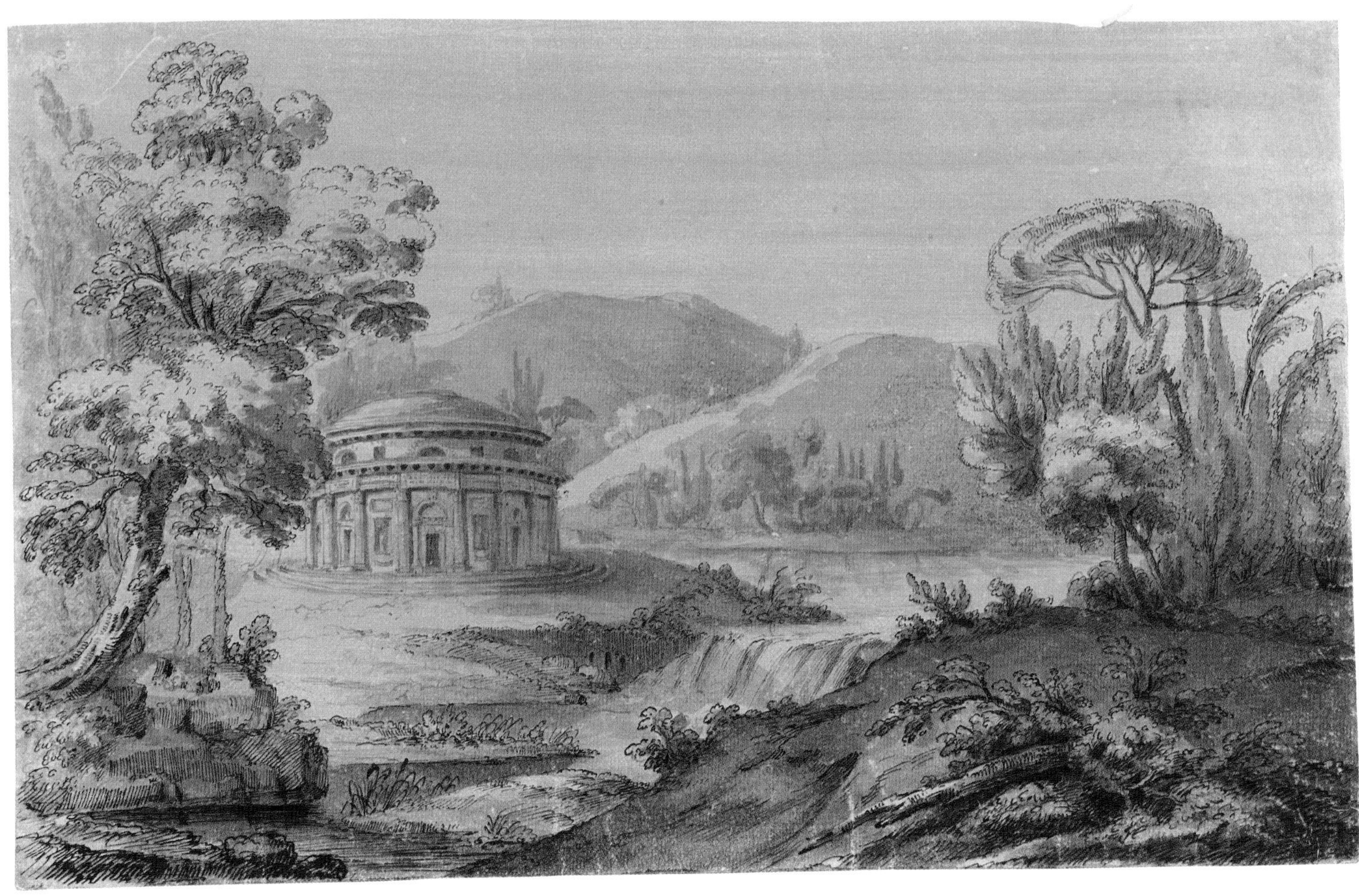

47. Robert Adam
Landscape capriccio showing, above steps, a large circular and columned building with a Pantheon-style dome

1755
Pen, and brown and grey washes
on grey washed paper
265 x 423 mm
Adam vol. 56/53

This drawing is part of a set of landscape compositions, probably after Lallemand. The circular building can be compared with that found in several small landscape sketches of this period.

48. Robert Adam
Capriccio showing the interior of a large barrel-vaulted and coffered hall with three-bay screens

*c.*1756
Pen, and brown and grey washes,
with black margins
290 x 325 mm
Adam vol. 56/132

This, and a similar composition with steps descending to a basin, can be compared with an interior amongst the Clérisseau drawings in the Hermitage.

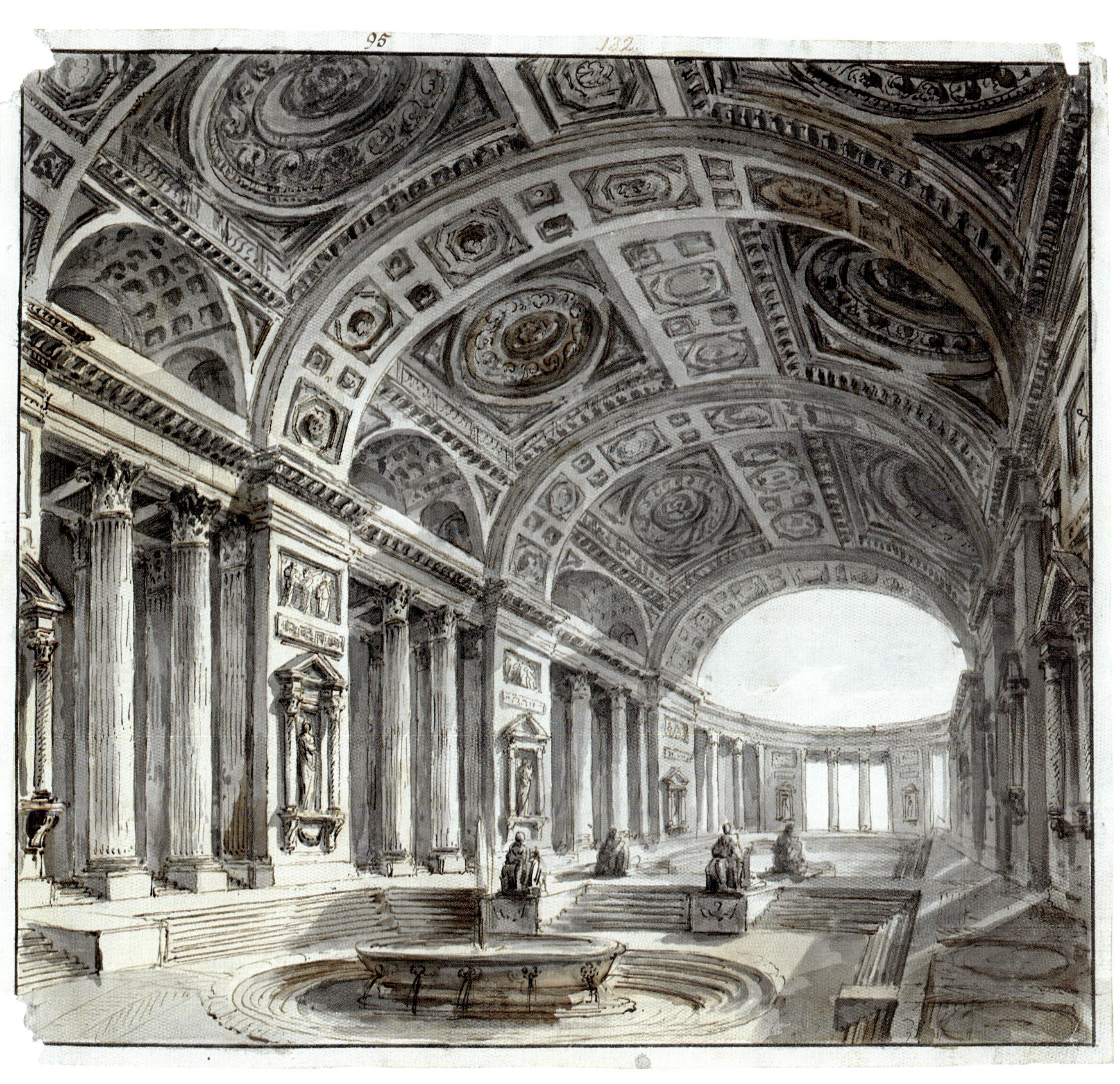
95
122

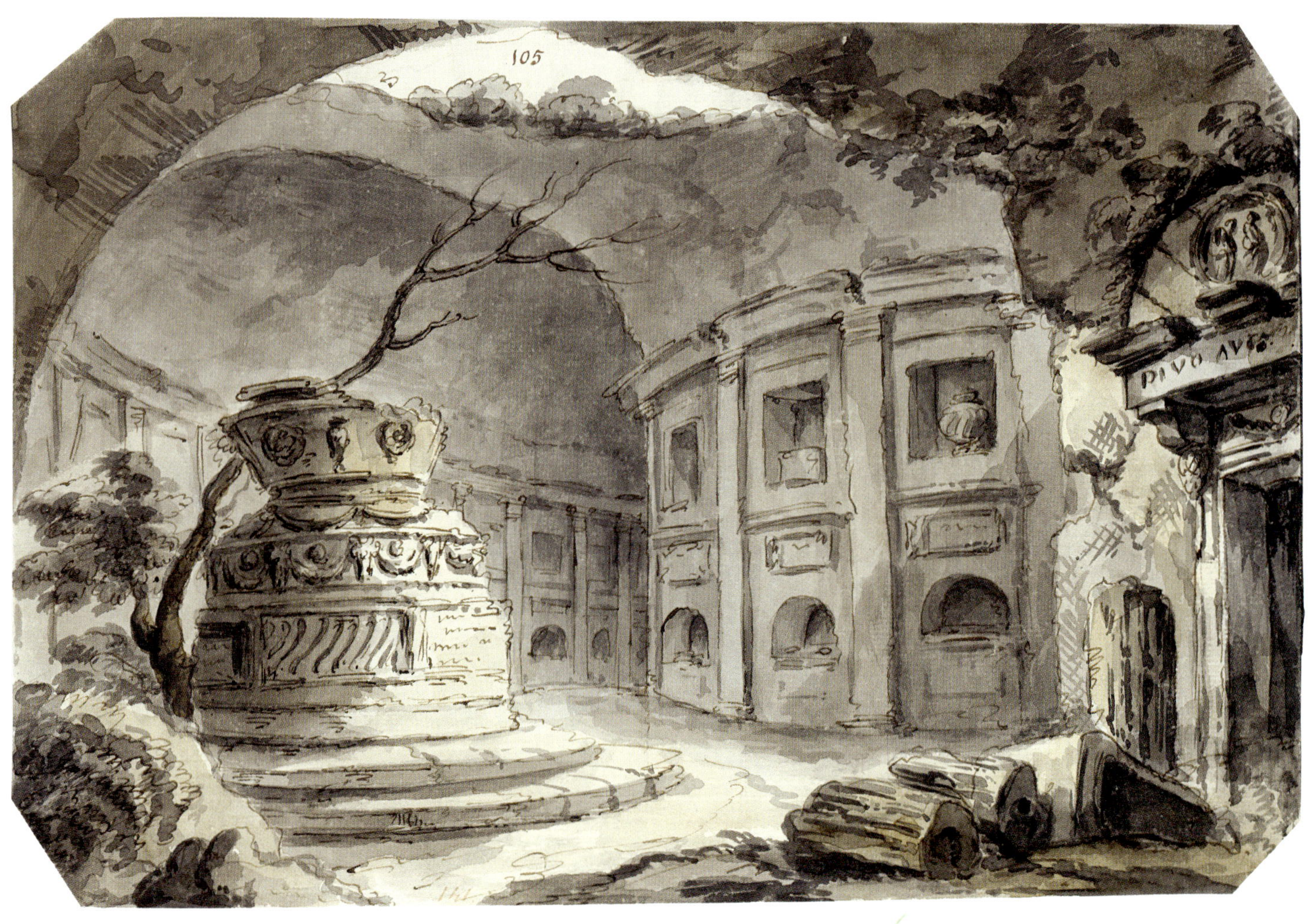

49. Robert Adam
Capriccio of a ruined interior or catacombs

1756
Pen, and brown and grey washes, with ink margins
230 x 346 mm
Adam vol. 56/141

The elaborate, free-standing sarcophagus on its tiered and decorated base is unlike others found in this set. The underground room, often under water, with a curving central pier, is a familiar theme in several of Robert Adam's classical capricci. The inscription *Divo Av-* is in Robert's hand.

50. Charles-Louis Clérisseau
Capriccio showing part of the interior of a curved and domed building, with parts of the ceiling coffering remaining

1756
Pencil, brown wash and watercolour
279 x 221 mm
Adam vol. 56/126

This composition can be compared with the grander *gouache* drawing by Clérisseau in the Hermitage, and there is another smaller version in the Adam collection.

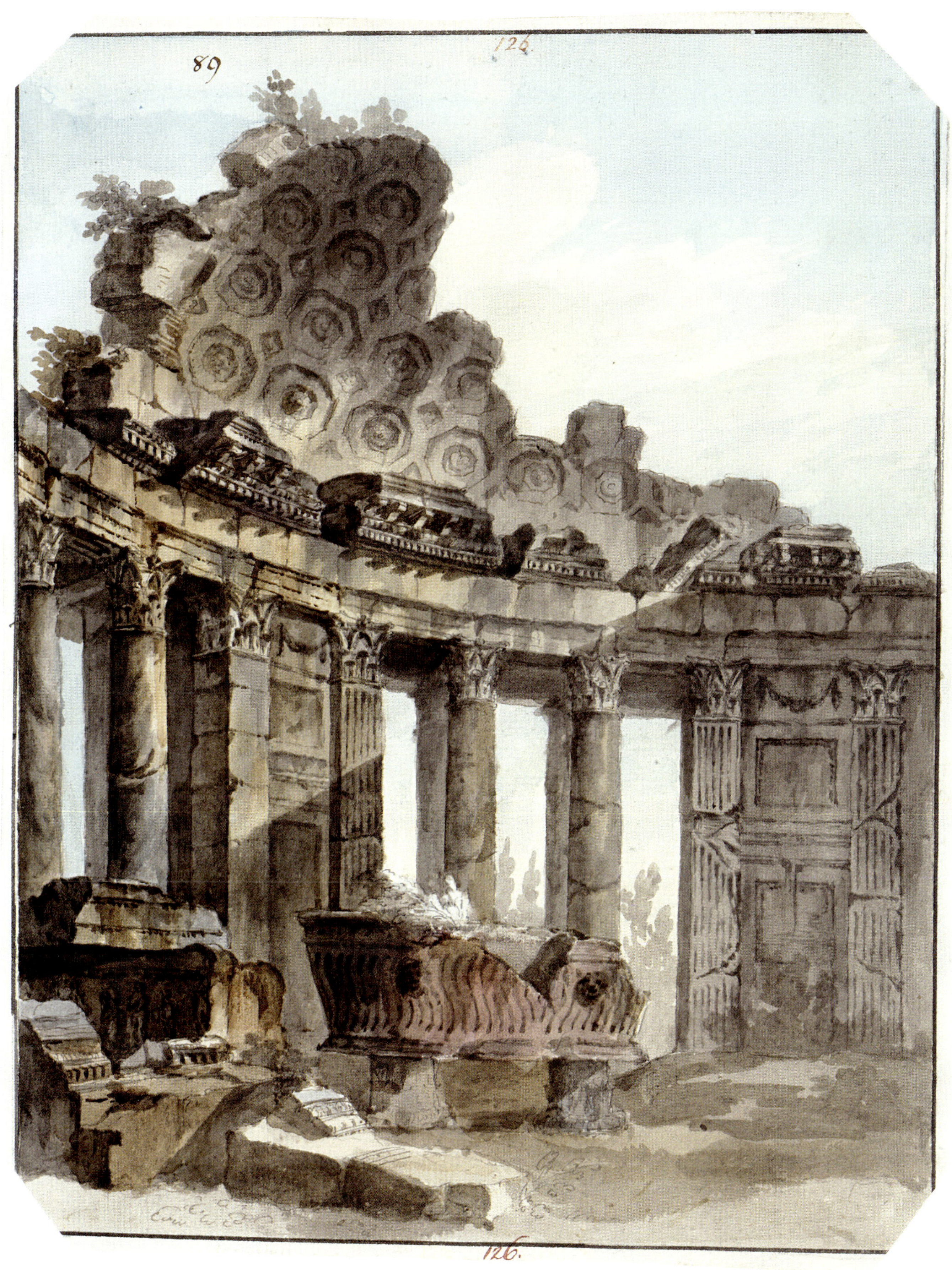
89
126
126.

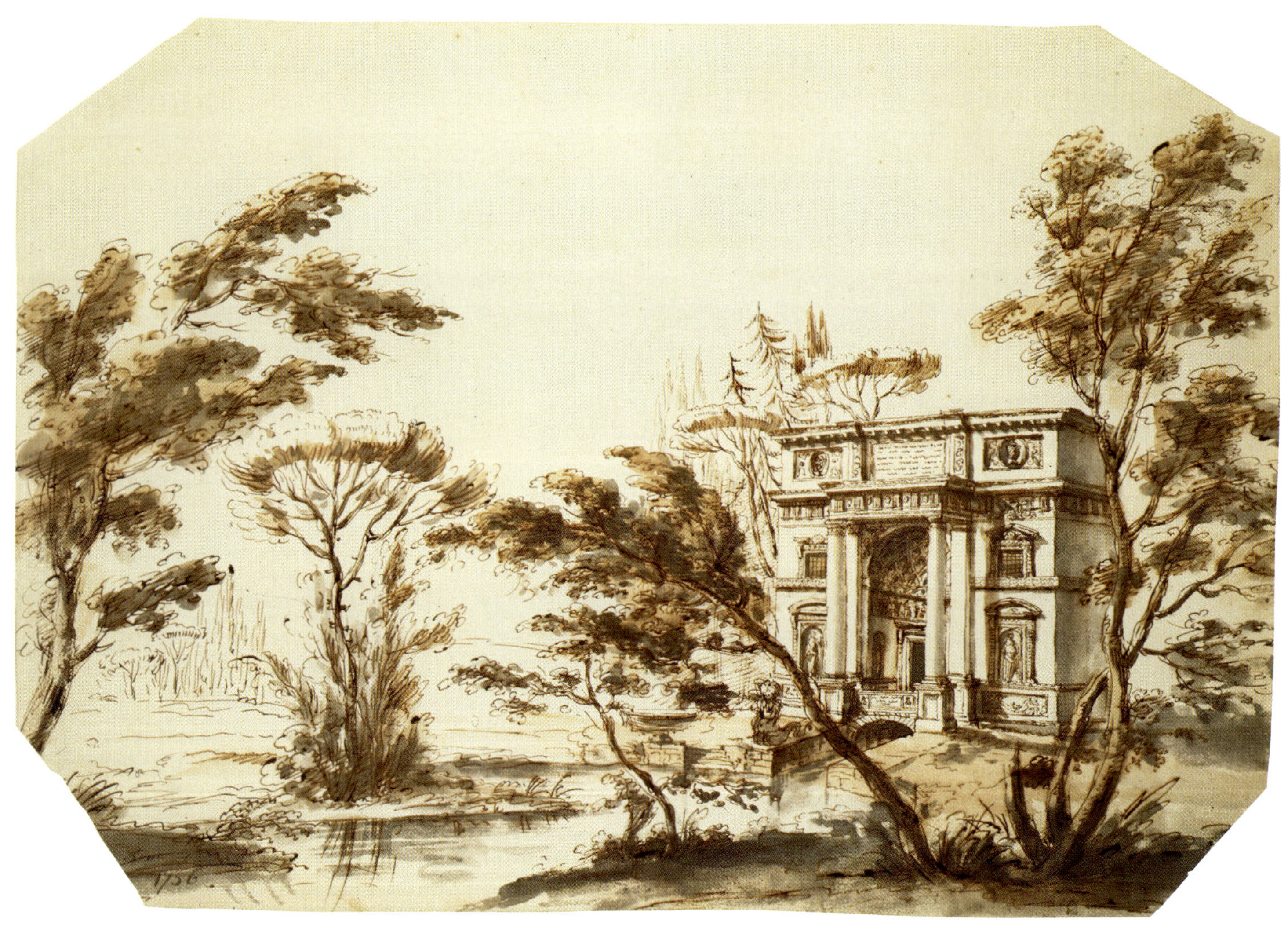

51. Robert Adam
Capriccio showing a three-bay triumphal arch richly decorated with a sculpture and relief panels framing a projecting Doric portico

1756
Pencil, pen, and grey and brown washes
384 x 560 mm
Adam vol. 56/41

The architectural composition is close to a larger scheme by Robert Adam, and the source for both may lie in the various projects of the early eighteenth century for the Trevi fountain, especially that of Nicola Salvi, which would provide both the central niche and watery setting. Robert was certainly impressed by that fountain and owned drawings of it (figs 69, 70).

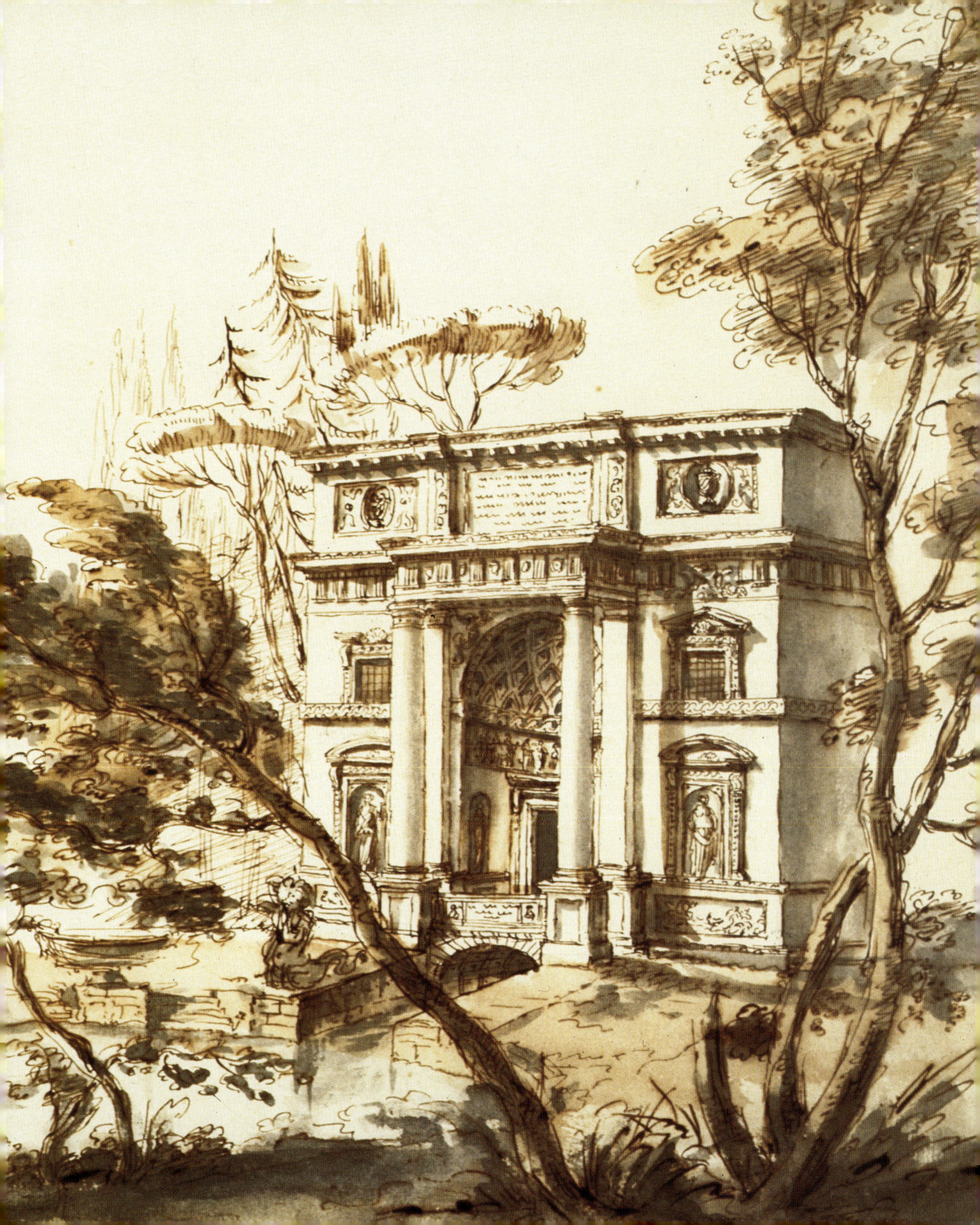

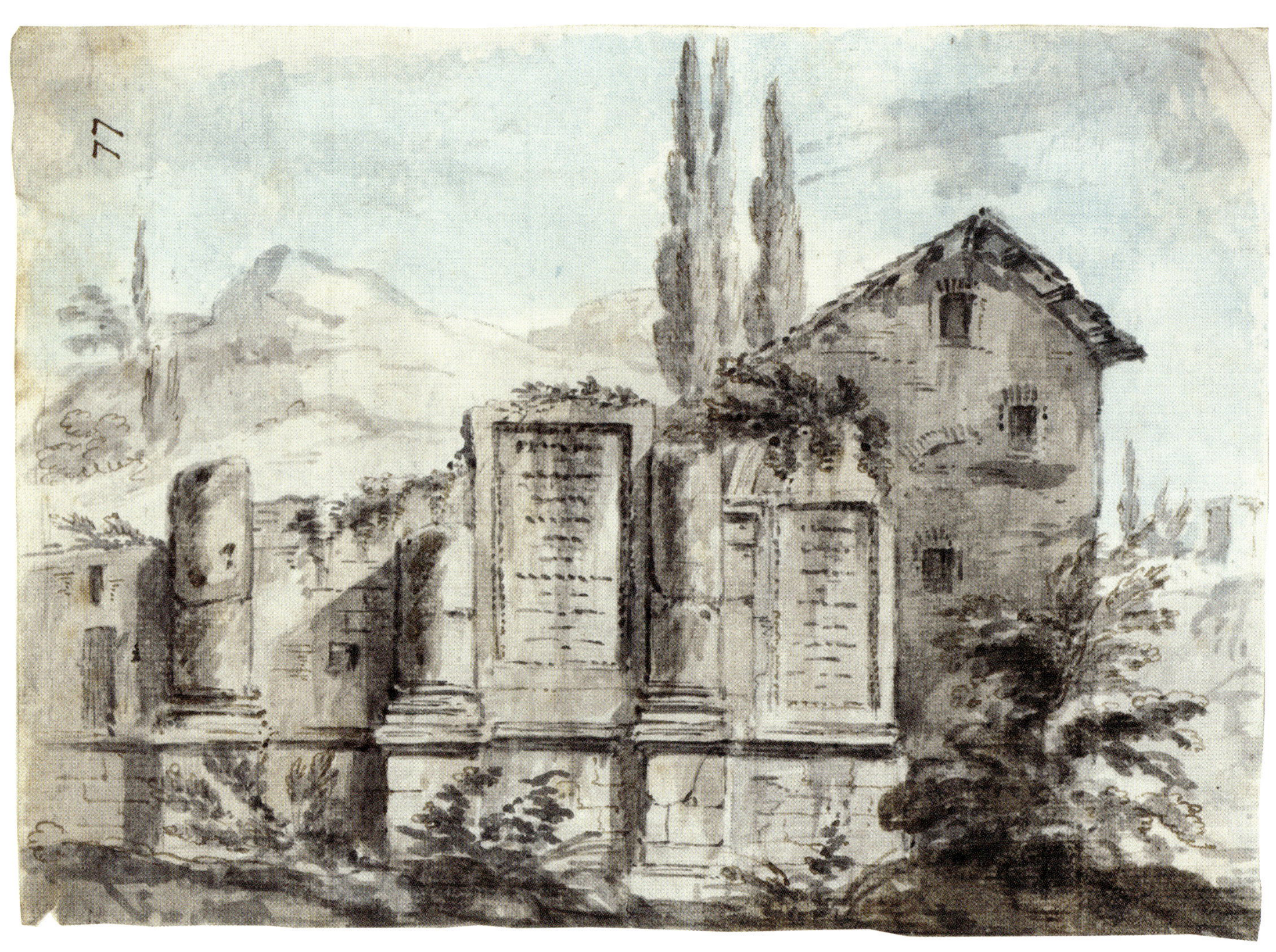

52. Charles-Louis Clérisseau
View of two inscription panels between three broken columns, with a tall house adjoining

1755
Pencil, and grey, brown and blue washes
129 x 183 mm
Adam vol. 57/77

This drawing would seem to show the scene at the Tomb of the Plautii, except it lacks the circular mausoleum shown just behind the inscription panels and opposite the house with a pitched roof. It may be compared with a similar view Robert Adam made on his Neapolitan trip of 1755.

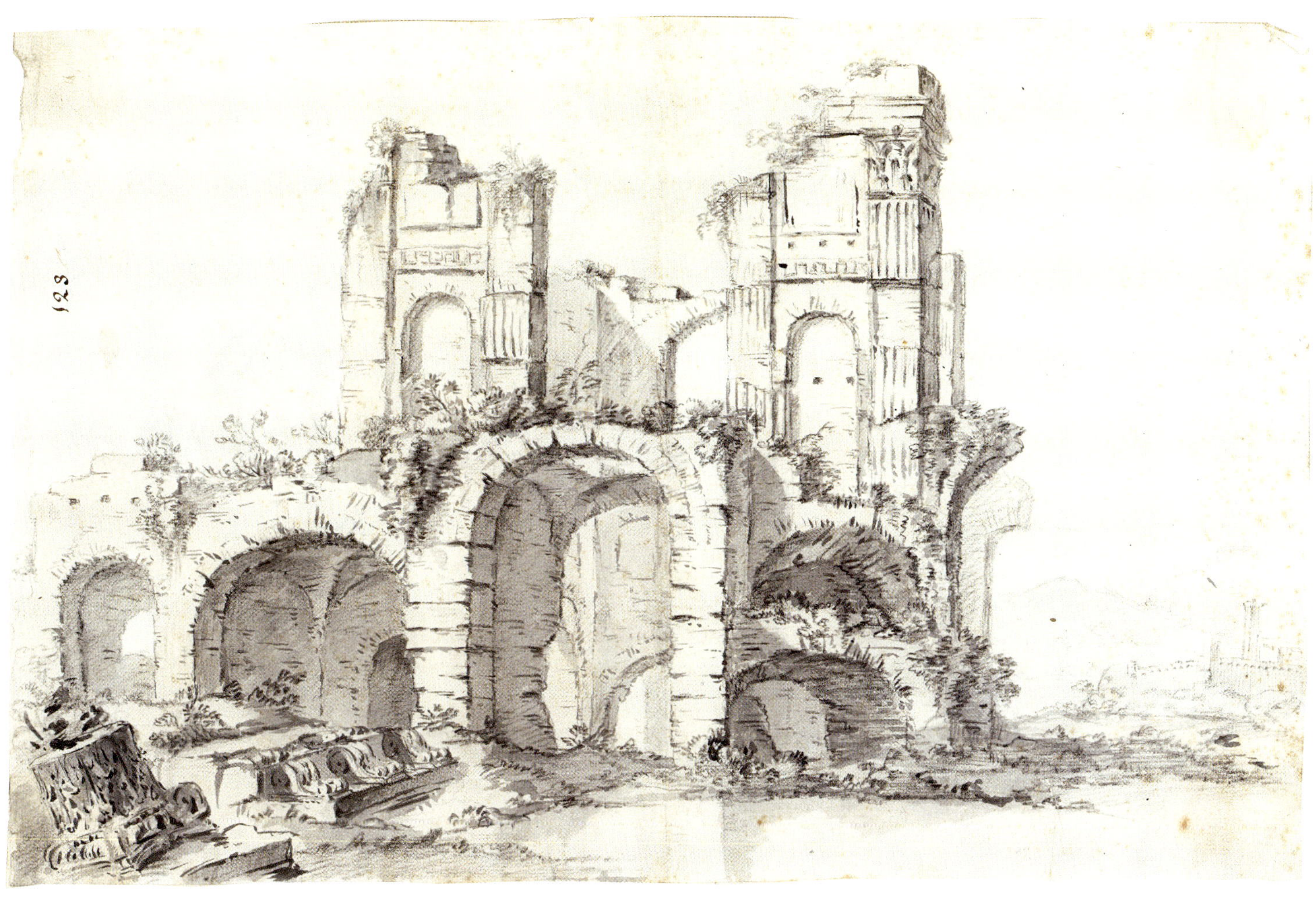

53. Charles-Louis Clérisseau
Capriccio of a ruined tower of three bays, with a niche with square panel above, between giant pilasters

c.1755
Chalk and grey wash
230 x 256 mm
Adam vol. 57/123

There is a highly competent version of this view by Robert Adam (fig.54), which shows more exactly the decorative detail of this ruin. The viewpoint for both sketches is precisely the same, though the source is possibly a capriccio based on several antique ruins. The niches with square panels above and raised on vaulting, seen at the Domus Praeconum of the Domus Augustiana, may be a formative source.

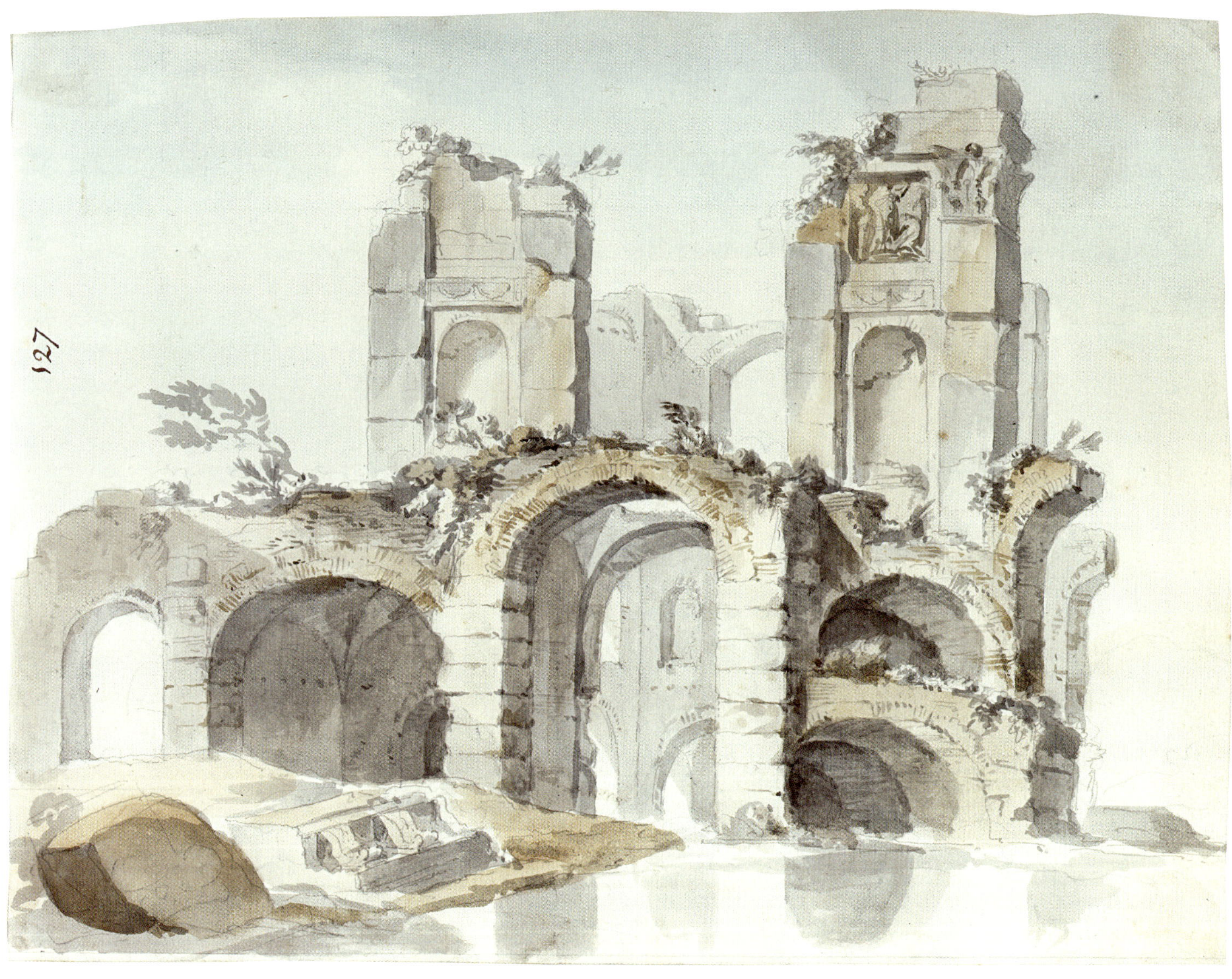

54. Robert Adam
Capriccio of a towered structure of three bays, with giant pilasters and niches with relief panels above on the shorter end bays

*c.*1755
Pencil, pen, and grey and brown washes
233 x 305 mm
Adam vol. 57/127

This is the same view as that by Clérisseau (fig.53), though it lacks the fortified background scene. Like the Clérisseau work, it is probably drawn from several antique sources and may be related to the tour Robert Adam and Clérisseau took to Albano in September 1755.

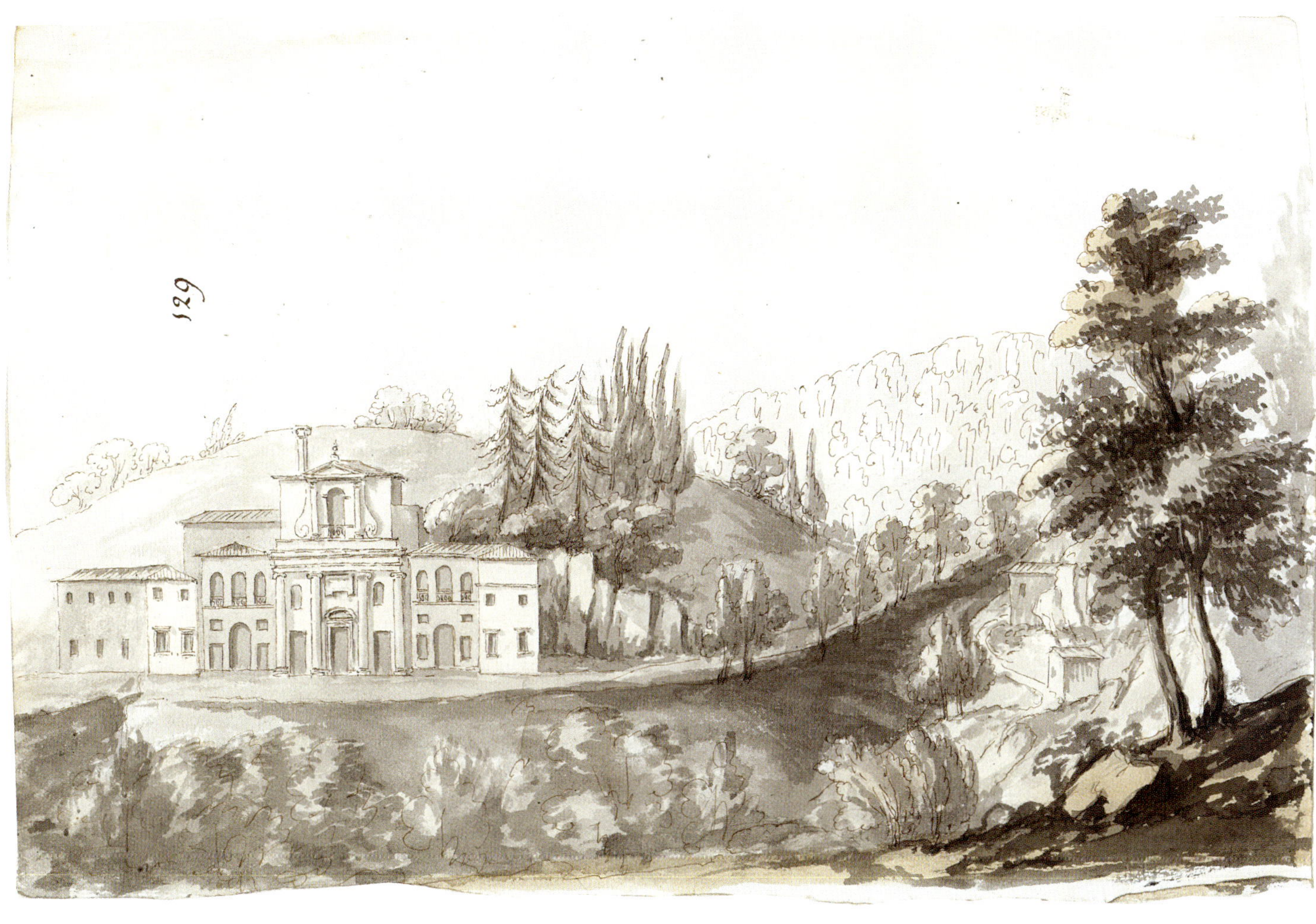

55. Robert Adam
Topographic view of a wooded landscape with road leading to an asymmetrical villa of sixteen bays and three storeys

1755
Pen, and grey and brown washes
230 x 341 mm
Adam vol. 57/129

This is an unidentified view of what is probably an early seventeenth-century villa in hilly and wooded countryside, presumably near Rome, or possibly seen in the journeys Robert Adam and Clérisseau made to Fano and Rimini in September 1755.

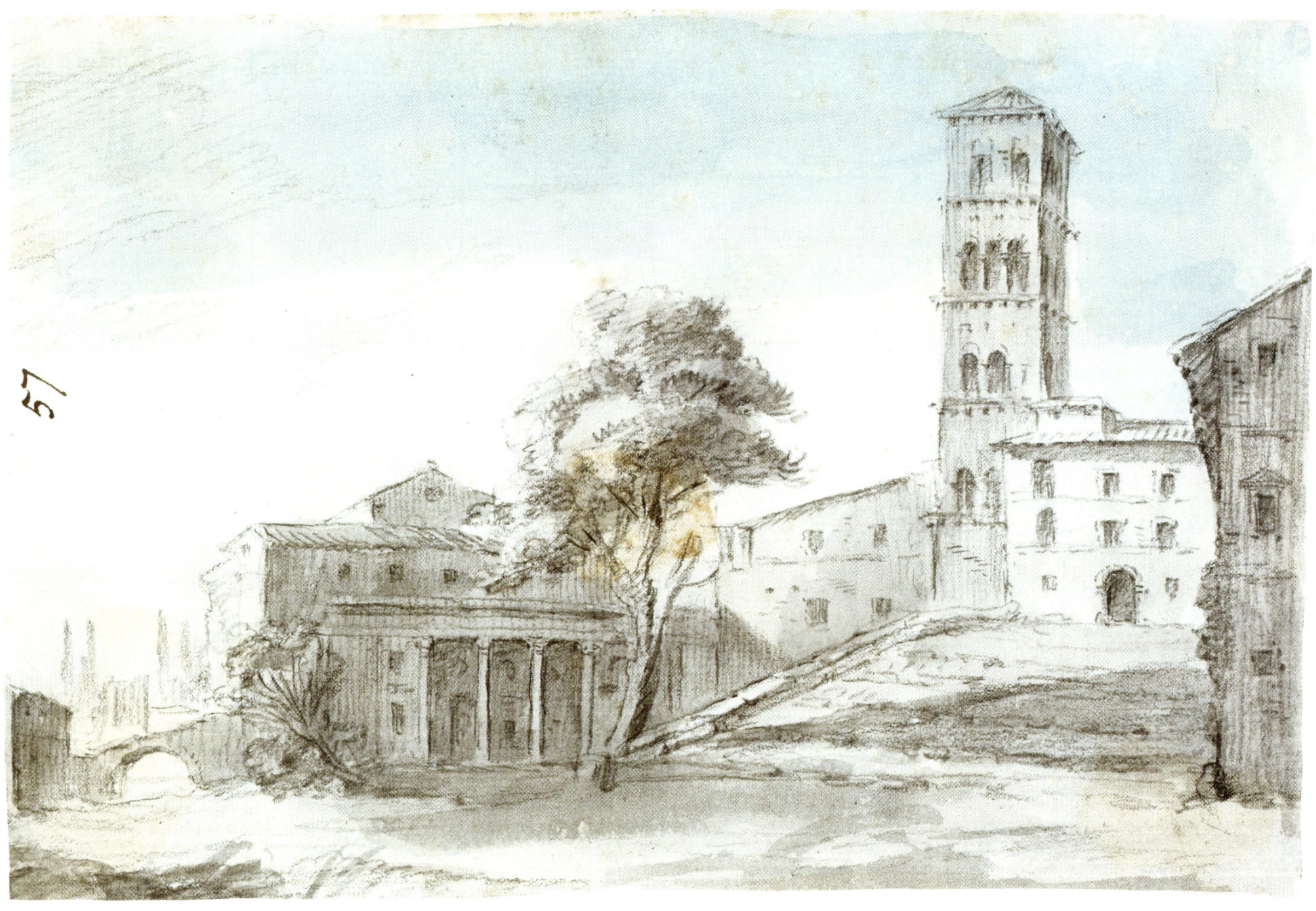

56. Jean-Baptiste Lallemand
View probably showing the entrance façade of the church of Santi Giovanni e Paolo and the adjoining campanile and monastic buildings

1756
Pencil, and grey, brown and blue washes
115 x 175 mm
Adam vol. 57/57

Santi Giovanni e Paolo was a short distance down the Monte Celio and below the Villa Celiomontana. Lallemand may have made this drawing when he was working here with Robert Adam. There is a further view by Lallemand, of the rear of the church from the alley of the Livus Scauri, that may have been made at the same time, and a similar one by Clérisseau.

57. Robert Adam
Capriccio showing the façade of a church with a central rose window and composed with three spires above heavily decorated towers

1757
Pen
156 x 133 mm
Adam vol. 54 / Series 4/2

This drawing is Robert Adam's only reference to the German Gothic he saw in his passage up the Rhine, though the arcaded entrance is Romanesque rather than Gothic and may have been inspired by the sight of St Gereon in Cologne. The inscription at the top of the composition is in Robert's hand.

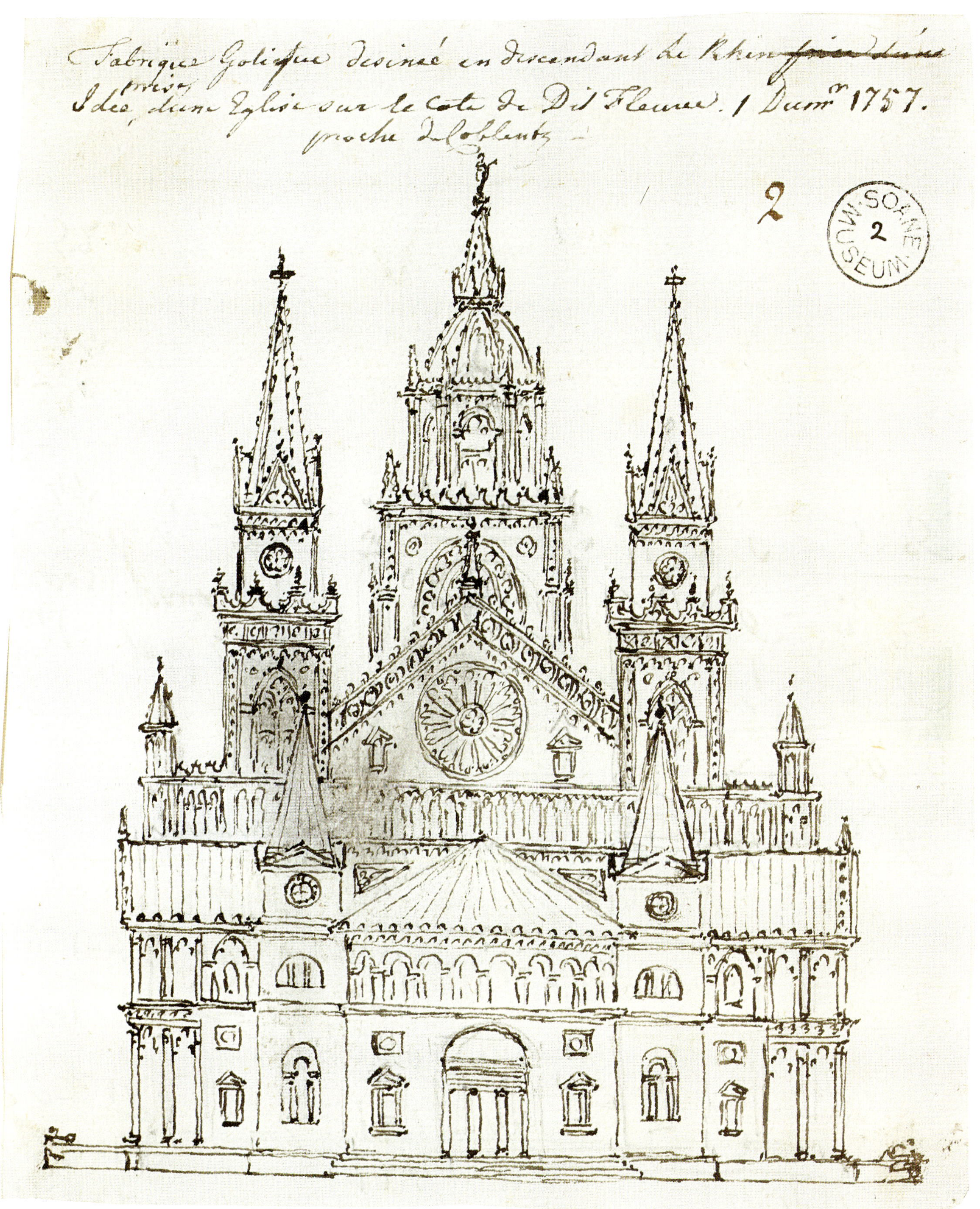
Fabrique Gotique desinée en descendant le Rhin
Idée d'une Eglise sur le Cote de dit Fleuve. 1 Decmr 1757.
proche de Coblentz
2
SOANE MUSEUM 2

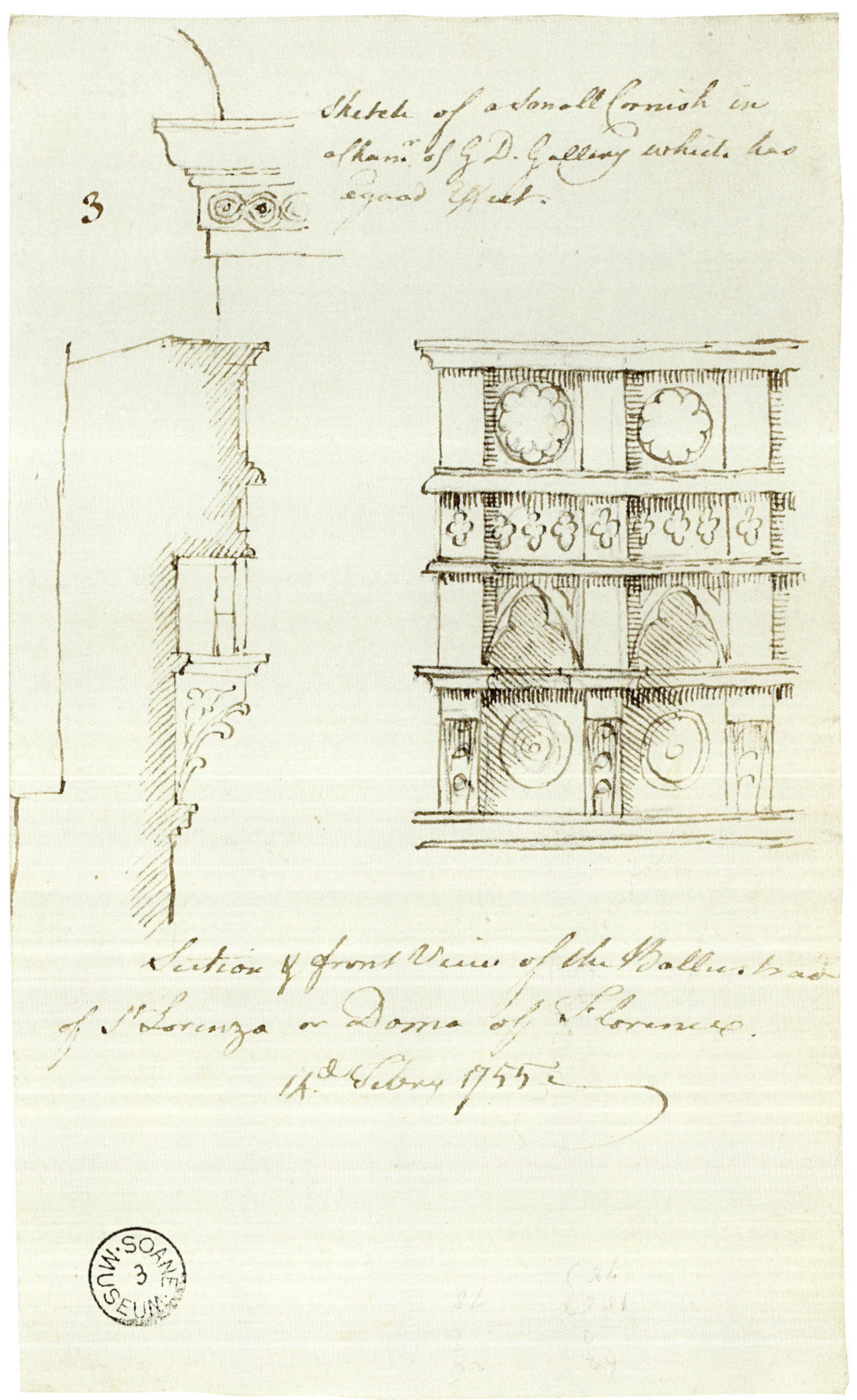

58. Robert Adam
Detail of an elevation and section of the balustrading in four tiers, from Florence cathedral, and a cornice detail from the Uffizi, Florence

1755
Pen
184 x 114 mm
Adam vol. 54 / Series 4/3

Robert Adam was in Florence from 30 January until 20 February 1755. The fruit of this visual experience led him to conclude in a letter of February that Florentine and Tuscan architecture '...though a little heavy is composed of parts far from disagreeable, with doors and windows no less ingenious than agreeable'.

59. Robert Adam
Capriccio showing a gorge, or pass, cut through mountains beside a sarcophagus with a large Gothic cathedral-like structure above

1757
Pen
210 x 184 mm
Adam vol. 54 / Series 5/18

The cathedral-like building in this composition is similar in style to that of the Gothic buildings Robert Adam admired for their picturesque architecture while on his return journey to London.

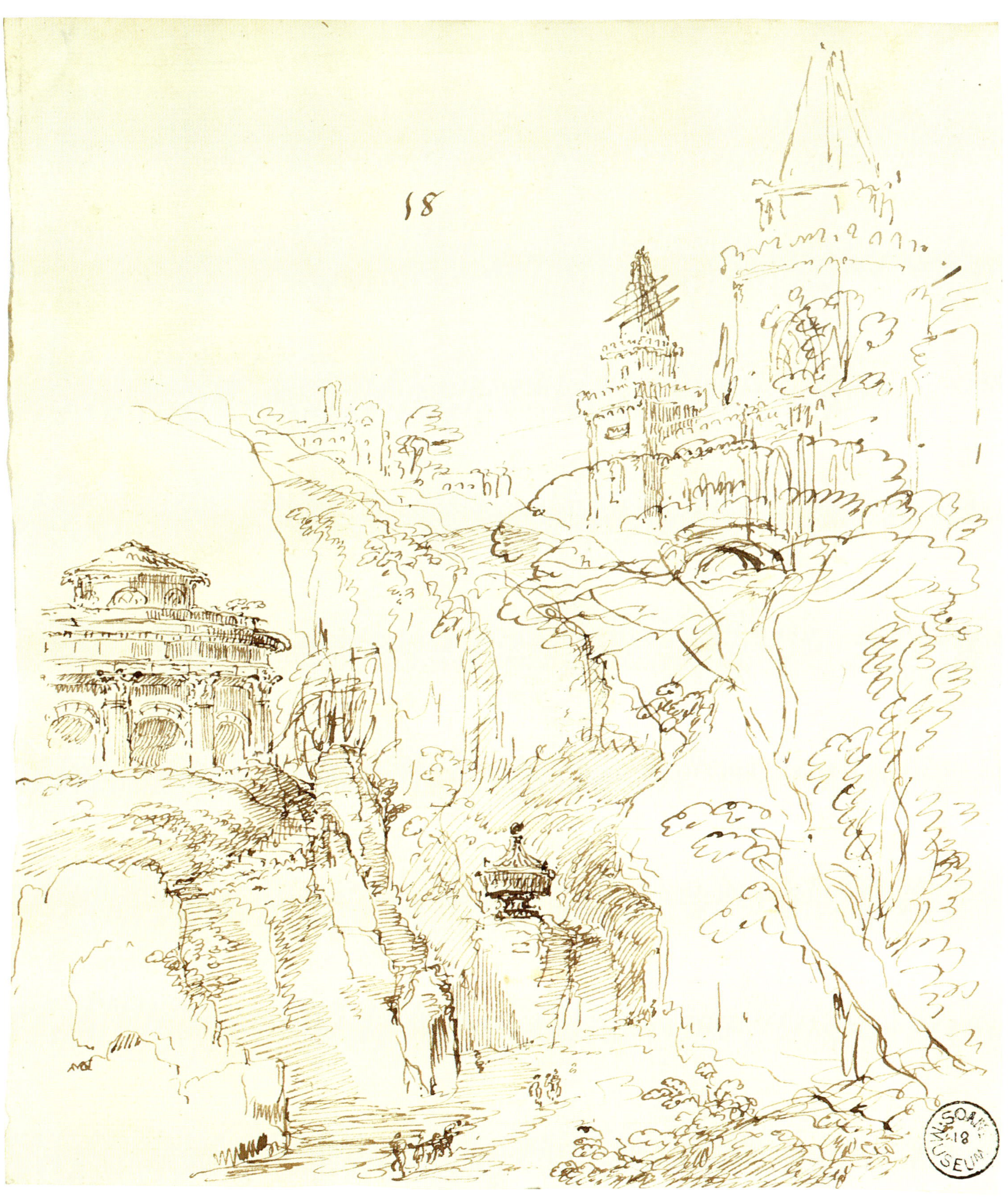
18

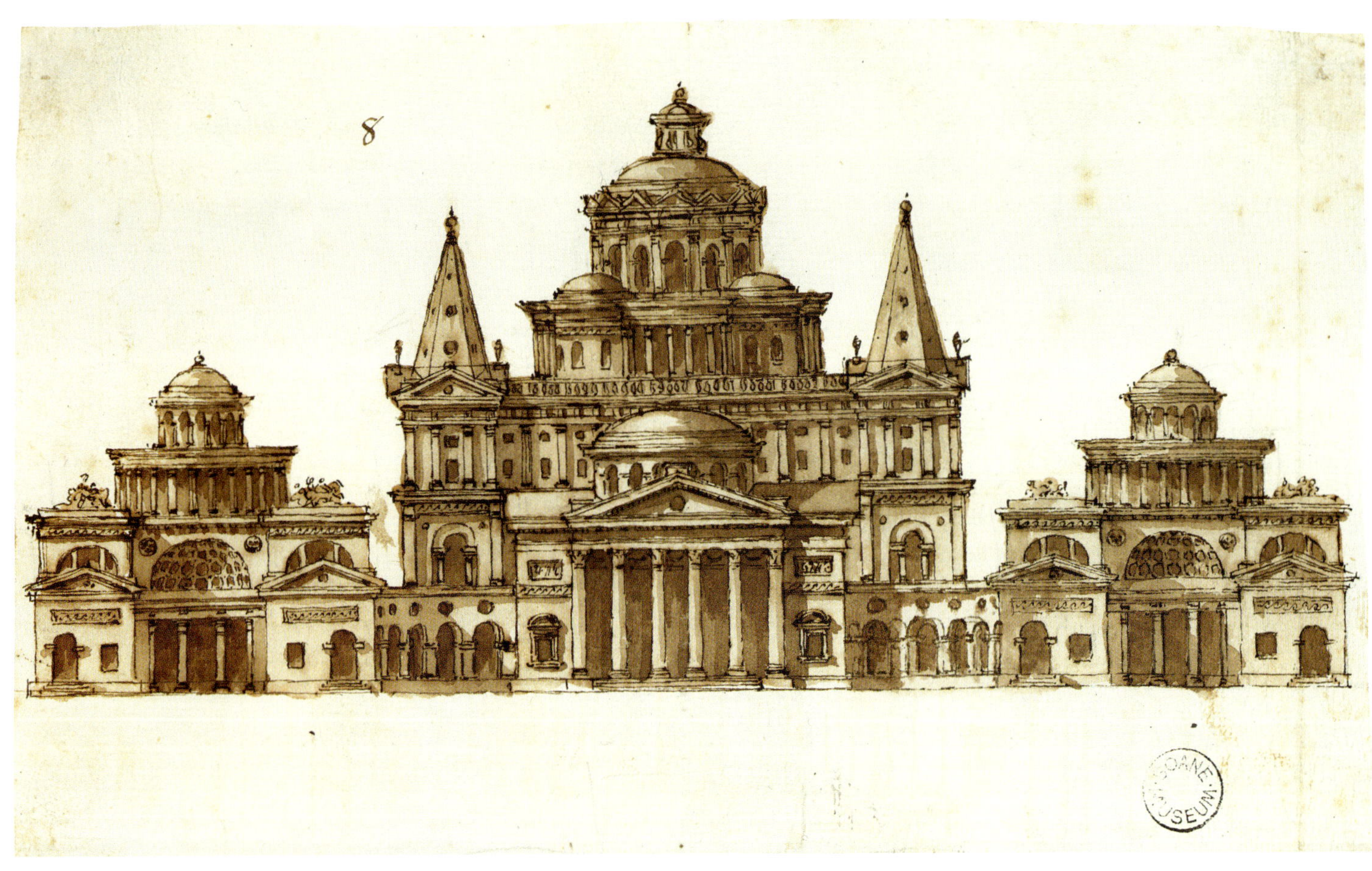

60. Robert Adam
Capriccio showing in elevation a main block with a dome on two drums flanked by spires

*c.*1756
Pencil, pen and brown wash over pencil
271 x 230 mm
Adam vol. 55/8

This composition may be compared with the perspective views that Robert Adam made. They were all probably part of the architectural exercises he undertook with Dewez and Clérisseau.

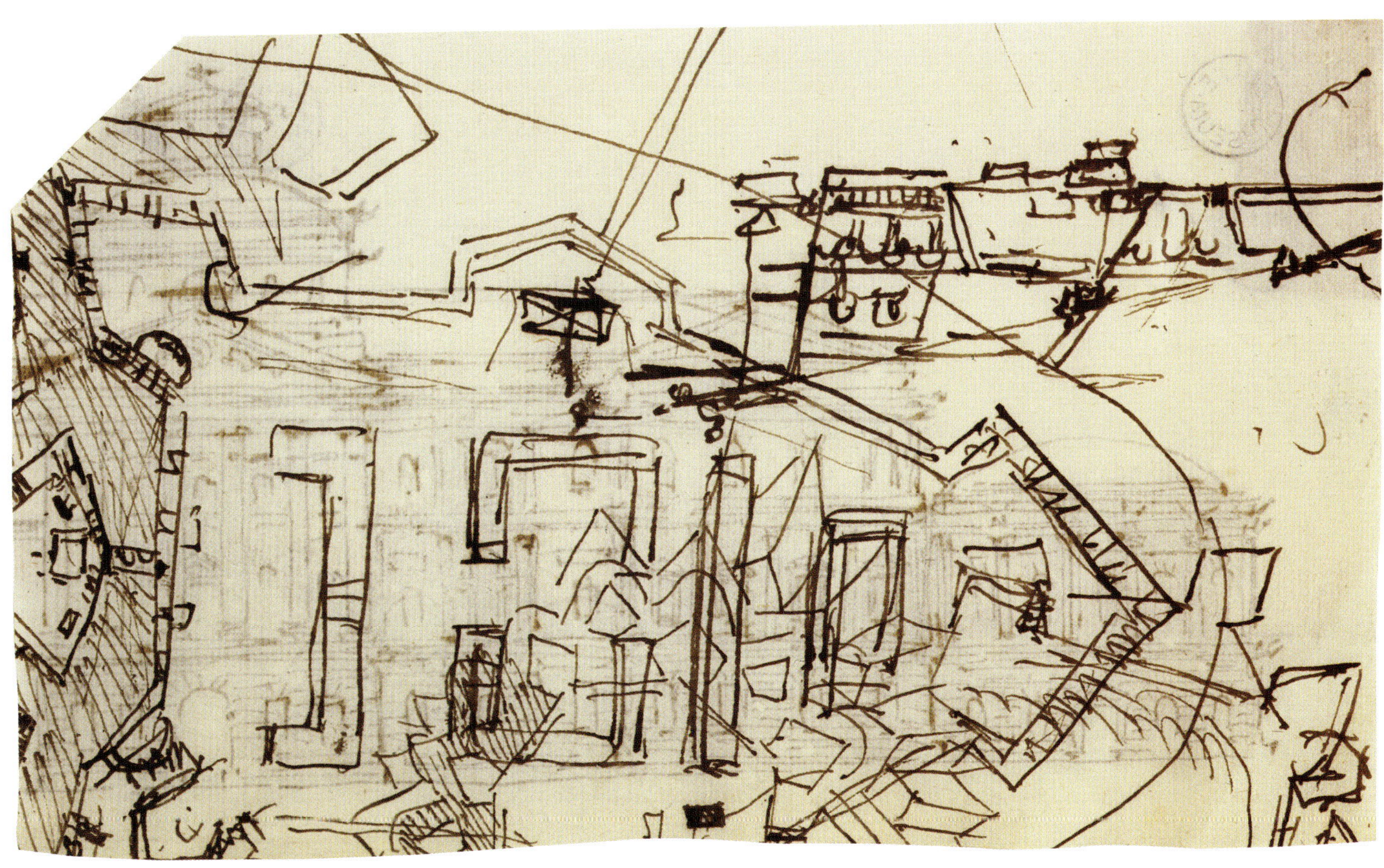

61. Robert Adam
Outline of diagrams, in plan and elevation, of a group of military fortifications and buildings, possibly Fort George, Inverness

*c.*1753
Pen
109 x 187 mm
Adam vol. 55/5 verso

The plan of the fortifications may well be associated with Robert Adam's work at Fort George, Inverness, after 1748 and before he left for Italy. There is a version of this plan in the Blair Adam collection. Apart from this drawing and another similar one at Blair Adam, there is nothing in the collection concerned with Fort George – a building that was clearly the past for Robert and James Adam.

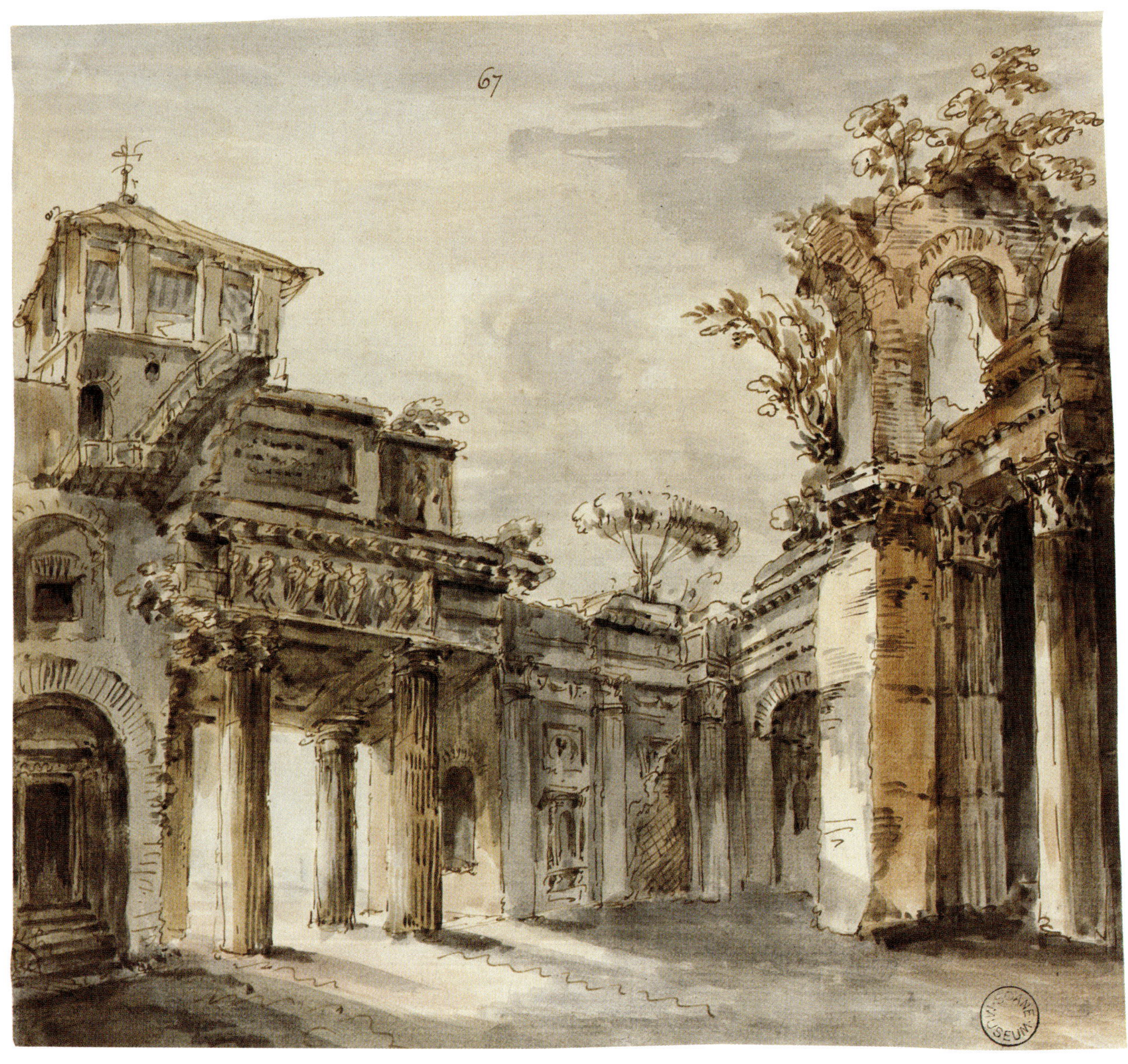

62. Charles-Louis Clérisseau
Capriccio of overgrown classical ruins showing two walls of a courtyard with two porticoes

1755
Pen, pencil and watercolour
237 x 265 mm
Adam vol. 55/67

The subtle handling of watercolour and the sophisticated use of light are more typical of Clérisseau than Adam, Robert reluctantly accepting the other's superiority. He wrote in February 1755 that Clérisseau had '...the utmost knowledge of architecture, of perspective, and of designing and colouring I ever saw or had any conception of. He raised my ideas. He created emulation and fire in my breast.'

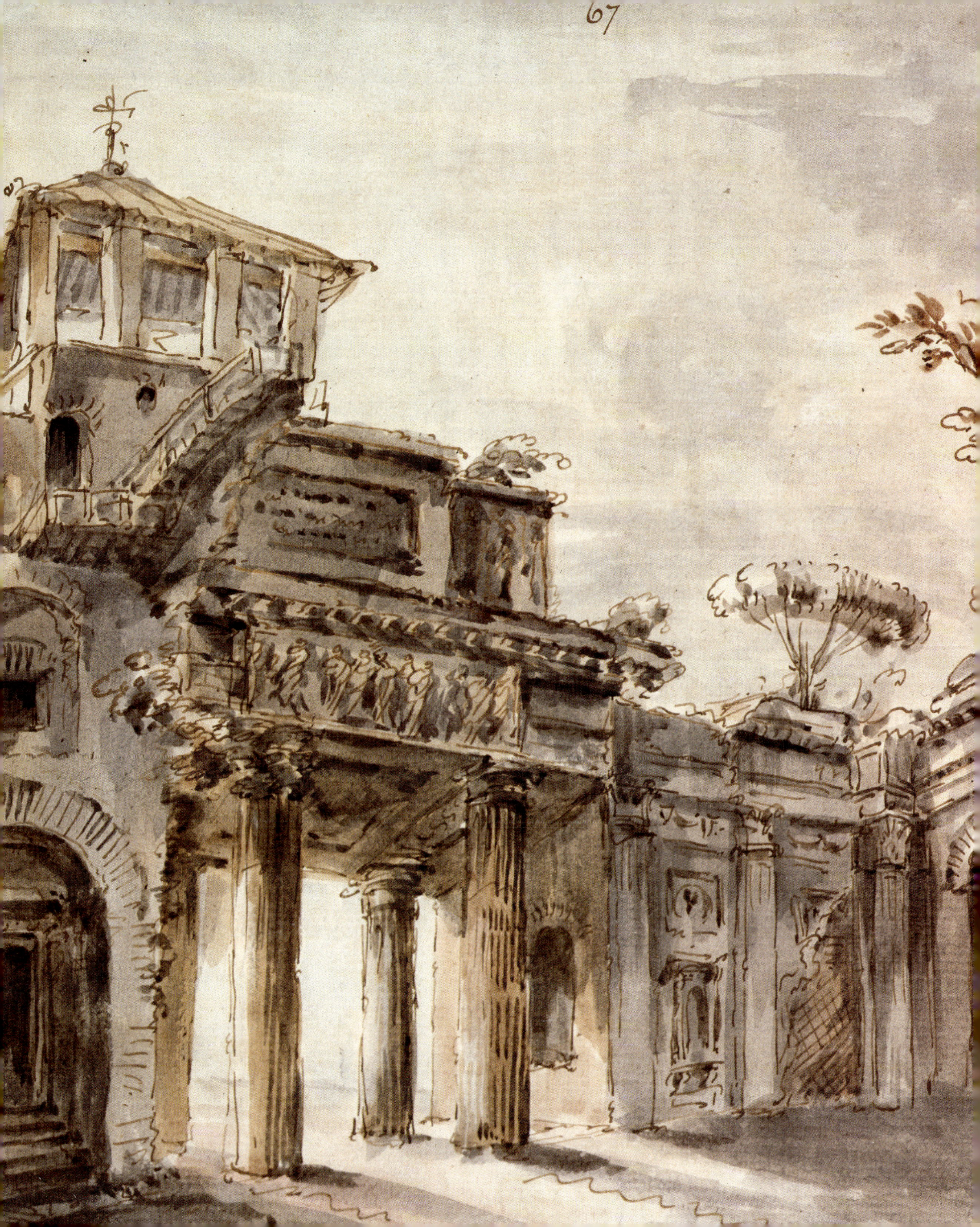
67

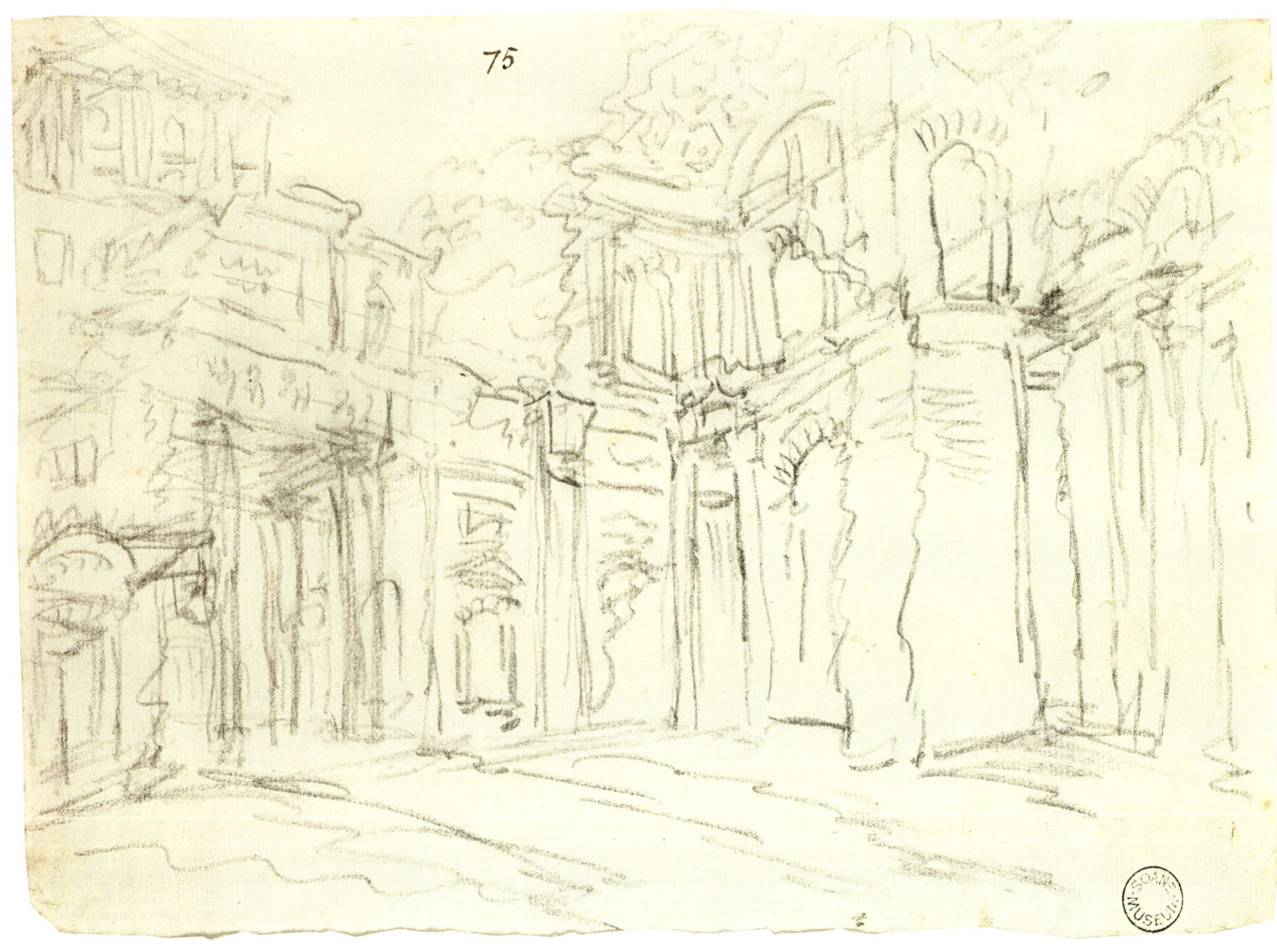

63. Charles-Louis Clérisseau *Attributed to*
Capriccio showing a group of classical ruins around a courtyard with two walls and the remains of a coffered ceiling

1755
Black chalk
190 x 270 mm
Adam vol. 55/75

There is a larger version of this composition in watercolour by Clérisseau (fig.62), which shows perspective lines, indicating that it was taken from a sketch such as this one and worked up either by Robert Adam or by Clérisseau.

64. Robert Adam
Studies of a centralised building showing elevation, plan and section with Italian notes

*c.*1756
Pen
180 x 158 mm
Adam vol. 55/37

This sheet of academic exercises shows Robert Adam at work also on his Italian lessons, a language he mastered sufficiently to be able to sing well.

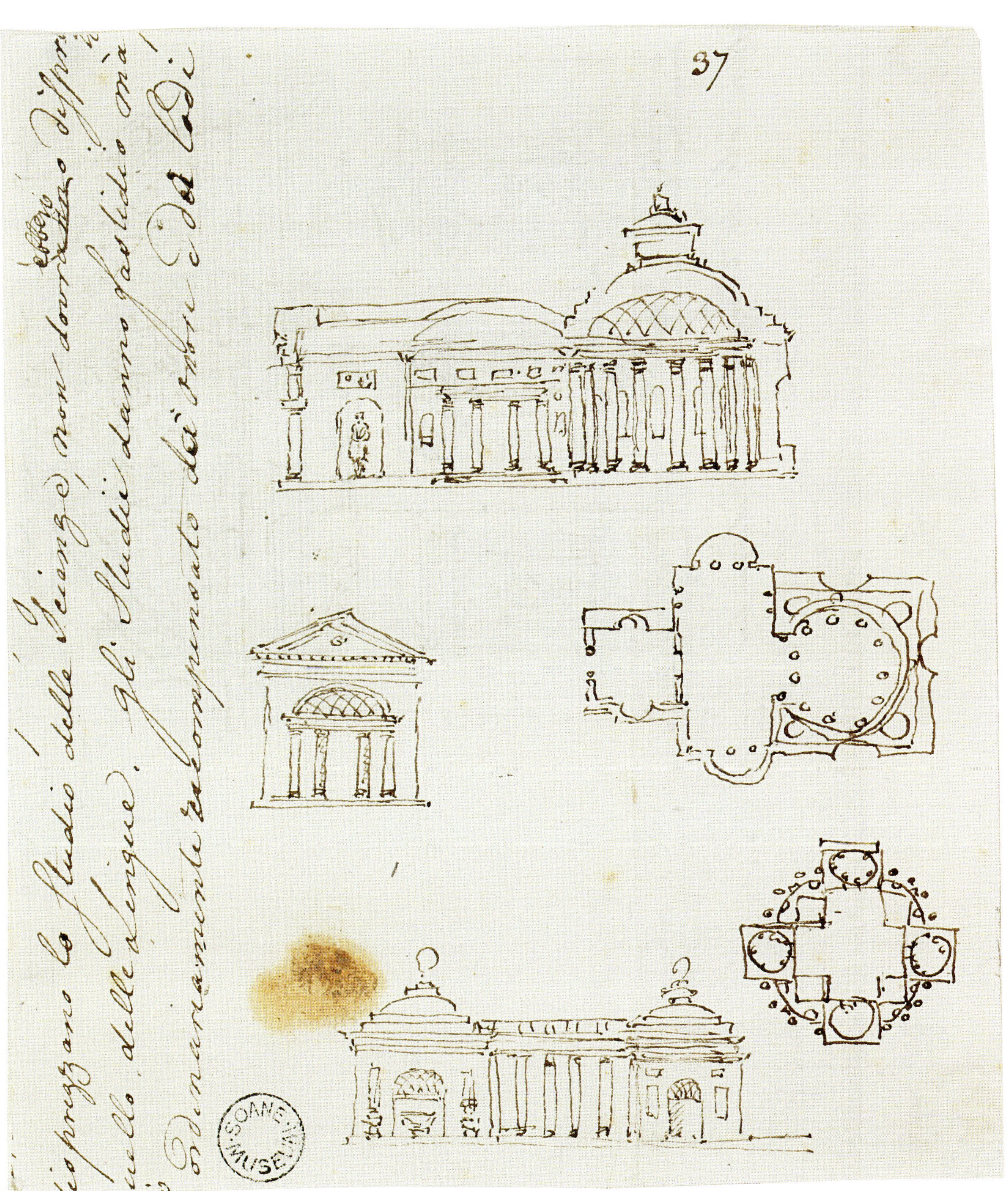

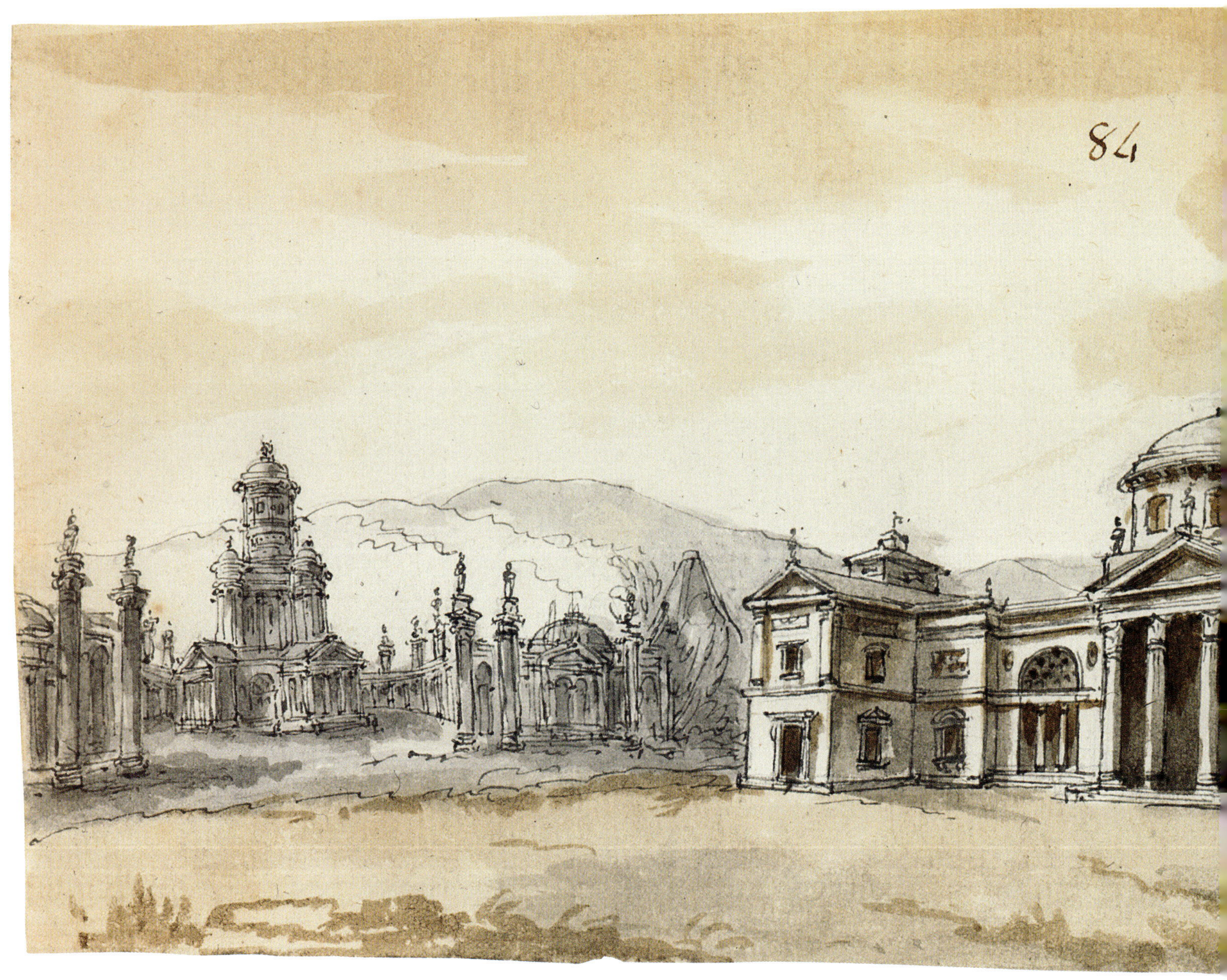

65. Robert Adam
Capriccio showing a large group of buildings with statues on columns in a park-like setting

*c.*1757
Pen, and grey and brown washes
106 x 273 mm
Adam vol. 55/84

There are several versions of this sort of scheme amongst the Adam volumes, where the composition is enlarged or reduced. Composed in a variety of media, they can all be related to the vast palace elevation of 1757 (fig.39).

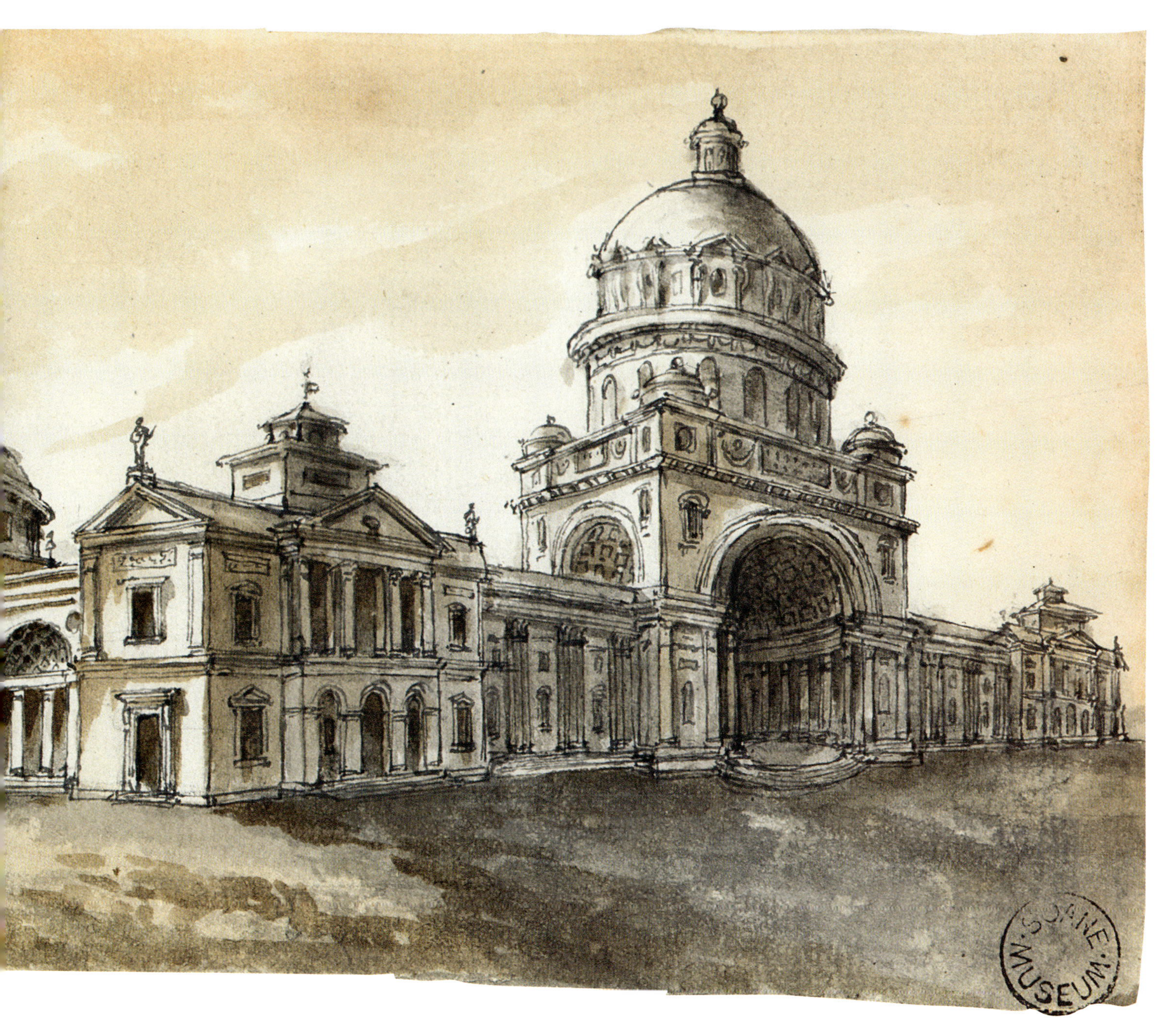
SOANE MUSEUM

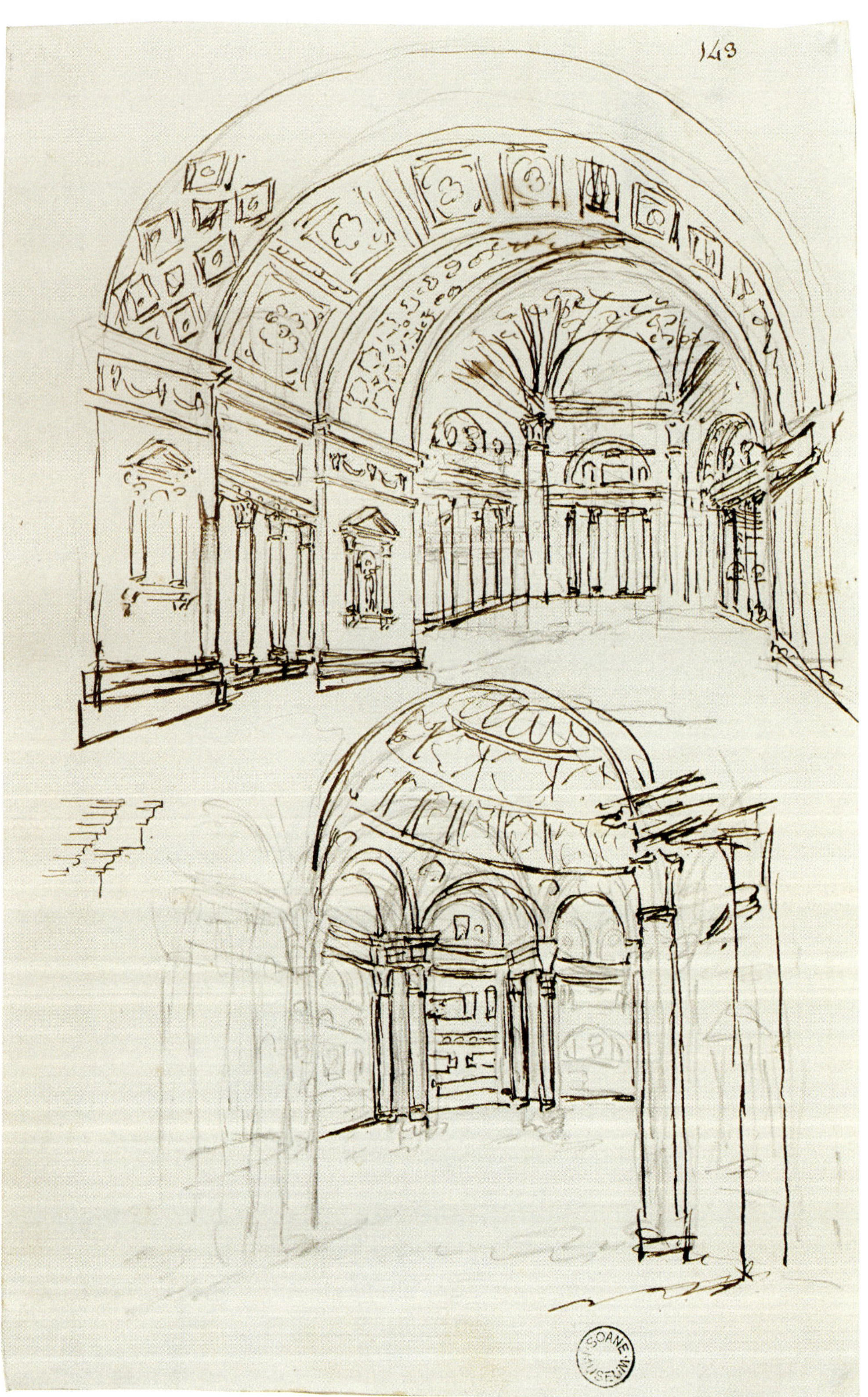

66. Robert Adam *Attributed to*
Architectural capricci of the interiors of two domed halls

1755
Pencil and pen
313 x 302 mm
Adam vol. 55/143

The inspiration for the upper capriccio may be the interior of Santa Maria degli Angeli, which Adam visited and studied in June 1755.

67. Robert Adam
Capriccio showing in plan the end elevation of a shallow domed pavilion of nine bays, with sculpture on the dome

*c.*1756
Pen and grey wash
285 x 215 mm
Adam vol. 55/109

This drawing has been compared with several of Dewez's schemes in the surviving albums of his Italian drawings in Brussels. The use of casual penwork and a grey wash is also typical of Dewez's teaching.

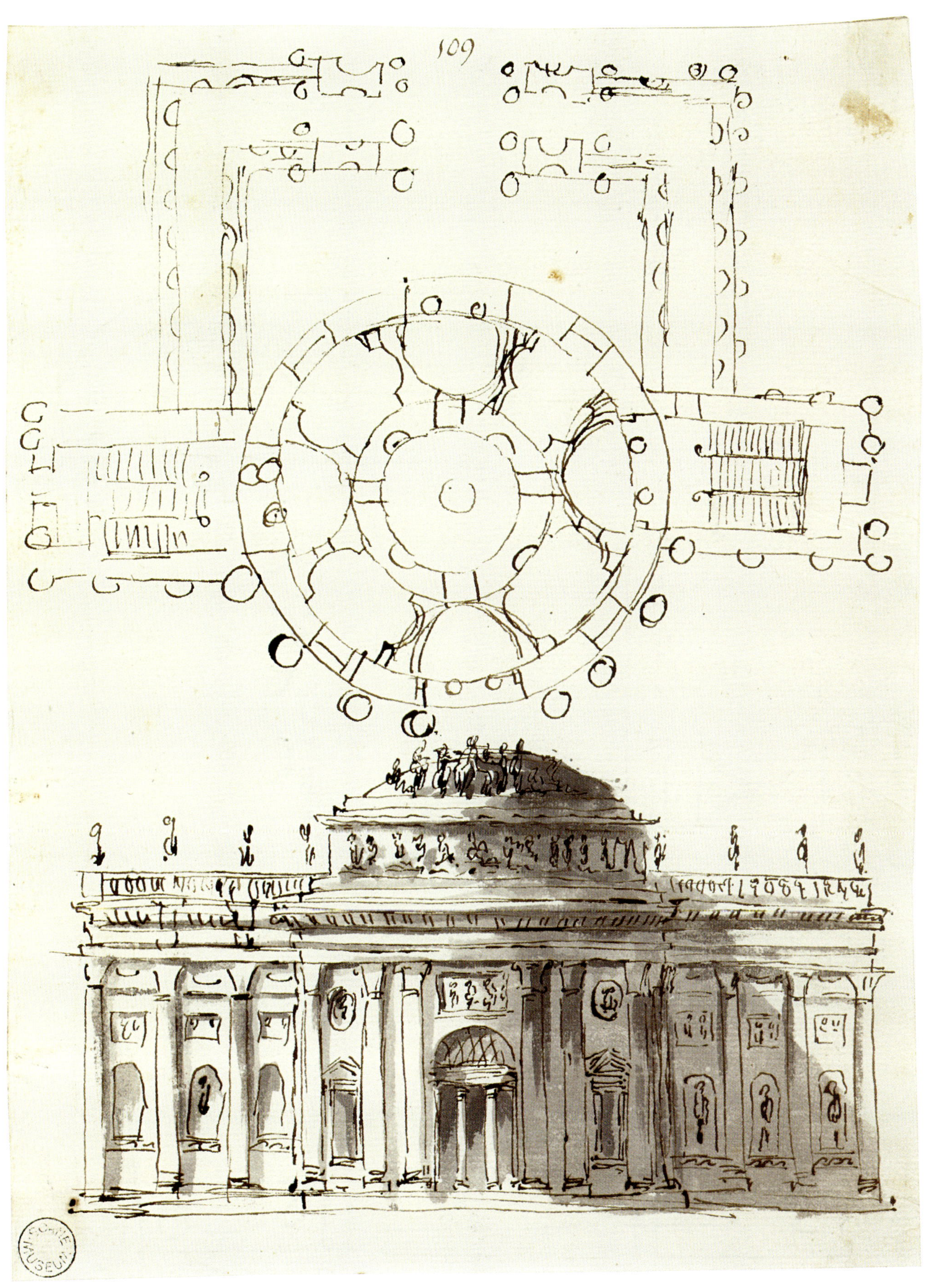

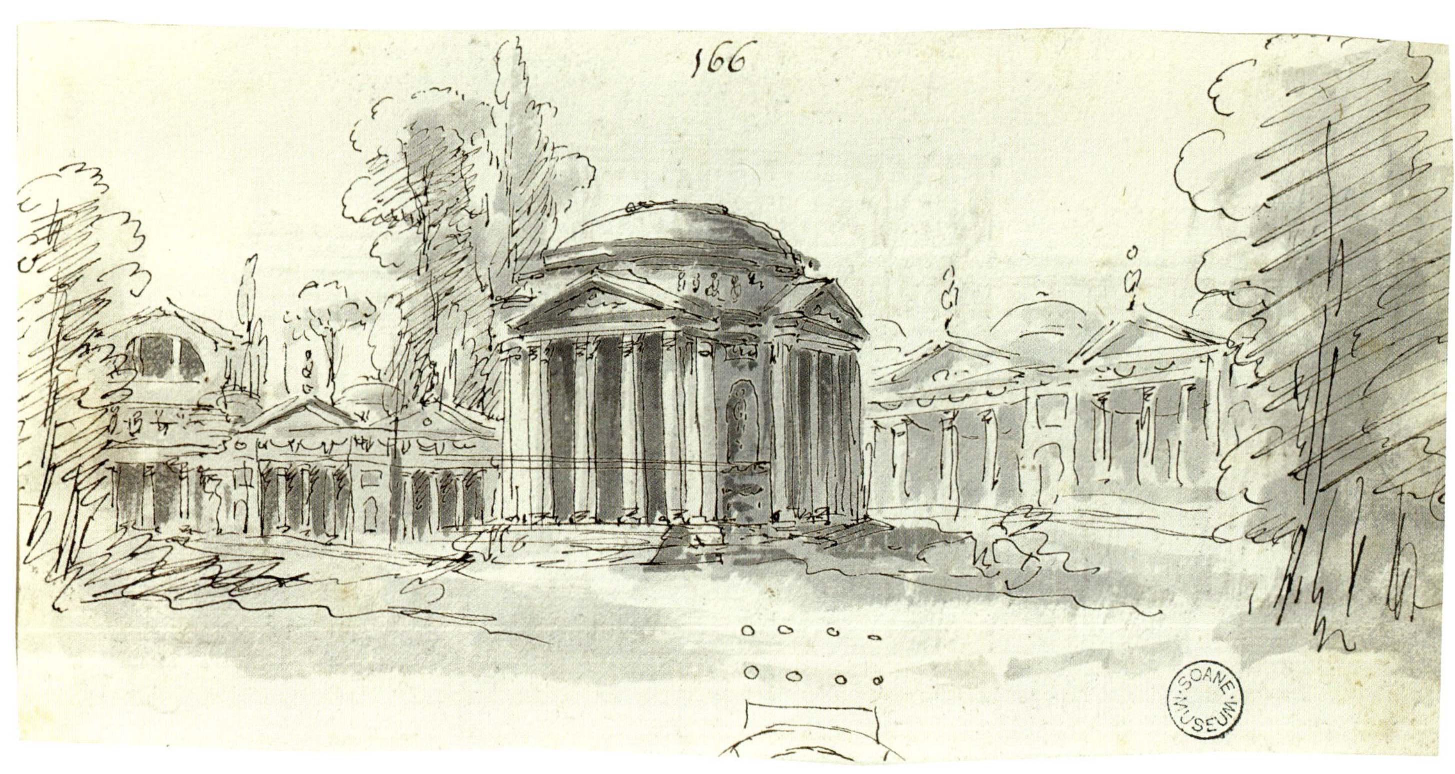

68. Robert Adam

Capriccio showing a symmetrical domed and pedimented pavilion with three-bay porticoes on steps in a woody landscape setting

*c.*1756
Pen and grey wash
126 x 256 mm
Adam vol. 55/166

The pavilion with a symmetrical plan is a frequent Adam–Dewez exercise. The inclusion of a landscape setting is a further development and it shows Lallemand's influence.

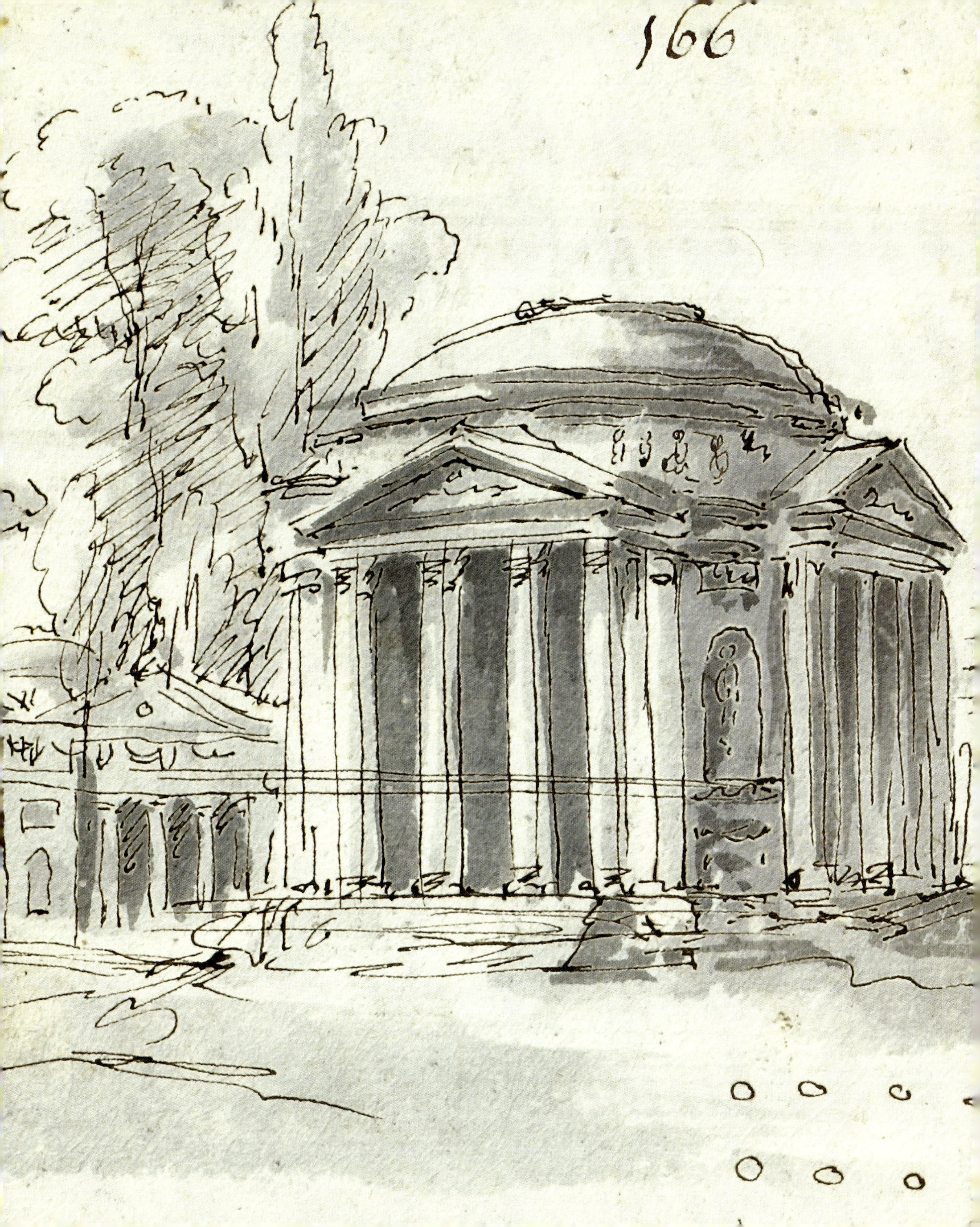
166

Robert Adam's

Col

Grand Tour

lecting

Robert Adam's other face was that of the indefatigable collector and connoisseur, the typical role played by the Grand Tourist, though rarely by the travelling artist or architect. In this, he had two aims: the first was to recover some of his capital through the sale, on his return to London, of his pictures and antique sculpture, the other to build a reference library of books, and especially drawings, for the use of his projected practice. His biographer, John Clerk, described the results of Robert's endeavours as a 'handsome Collection of Pictures, Bronzes and plaster casts of the most beautiful Mouldings of ancient Architecture, together with an infinite number of Sketches of Antique ceilings discovered on the roofs of the remains of the Palace of Nero, the Baths of Caracalla, Diocletian etc… Mr Adam bestowed as assiduous attention to that branch of his art eagerly diving with great labour & expence into all the crypts of Rome & its environs, he discovered there much hidden treasure. To this he added a large collection from the best modern masters: the works of Raphael, & of Michael Angelo, Pyrro Ligorio & Algardi all of which he picked out himself in the happiest manner (& it may with great truth be said, that his success in this branch of his art stands unrivalled in modern Europe.' Despite Clerk's remarks to the contrary, Robert did have a degree of professional help, principally from the Jacobite émigré, the Abbé Grant, who dabbled in picture dealing as well as acting as a cicerone to the more well-heeled tourists. Certainly both Robert and the Abbé Grant were known to Thomas Jenkins, the leading English picture dealer and broker on the Corso, and one who '[did] not enjoy the best reputation in the world'.

Though the Adam collection of Old Masters and drawings has disappeared, it has not done so without trace, and much of its character can be reconstructed from the various Adam sales of 1765, 1773, 1785 and the posthumous ones of 1818 and 1821. Nor, for that matter, did either of the Adam brothers intend from the outset that their collection should remain intact. In 1755, Robert wrote that he would soon be 'master of a very pretty collection well chosen & cheap, In so much that I am fully convinced on selling one half of my pictures in London, I shall have t'other for nothing at least.' However, the sale of the more pedagogic end of the collection was not one he anticipated and the loss of his antique casts, surveys of Roman monuments and topographical drawings by Pécheux was a professional loss. He had, after all, claimed in 1756 that 'there will not be one good thing in or near Rome that wont be included in my Collection either by way of Plan, or perspective view or Geometrical elevation according as the subject was interesting'.

Apart from the records of the various sale lots, little remains of this ambitious survey of ancient and modern Rome. Of what is left, the outstanding set of three large drawings, attributed to Pécheux, of Nicola Salvi's unfinished Trevi Fountain in the heart of Rome, is a painful reminder of what has been lost [figs 69, 70]. Robert may have had these drawings in mind when he wrote in May 1755 about 'a sett of Drawings in red chalk from the best antique statues, there is nobody can do them more exquisitely or with better taste, than he does', and they were no doubt included in his scheme 'to do the fountains... using my own and our myrmidons'. Something of the same topographic character was apparent in the bulk of the drawings by Clérisseau and Lallemand that have survived and which are listed in the various Adam sale catalogues. Some are studies by Robert in the style of these two, but more are groups of watercolours that Robert had clearly collected before he left Rome in 1757. Lallemand had a considerable reputation for decorative landscape drawings, especially in *gouache*, and a group of garden scenery views of a largely topographical sort was typical of his and of Robert's taste. Several appeared in the 1818 sale, helpfully catalogued as by 'L'Alma'. The relationship with Clérisseau was obviously a closer one and Robert came nearer to perfecting the Clérisseau copy than he did that of Lallemand, with its more difficult and subtle atmospheric moods. Certainly this was true of the run-of-the-mill compositions, like the small, circular and brightly coloured capricci of classical subjects, though even here Adam was defeated by Clérisseau's small and lively sketches [fig.72]. It was clearly not through want of trying. As early as December 1755, he wrote from Rome that 'I intend to enclose for you in this letter a little bitt of a view of a Ruinous Inside of a temple in the Antique Stile, done in Clerisseau's [sic] stile, but it is too small that you cannot judge of its effect so well as if it was sufficient size to express mouldings, ornaments, etc.' They came much closer in the larger *gouaches* and watercolours, though Clérisseau still excelled in compositional terms [fig.73].

These groups of drawings aside, there is little left to suggest the sweep of the rest of the collection, extolled by Clerk and ranging from Cortona to Rembrandt, with a sizable print collection strong on the seventeenth century in France and Italy. There were also Robert's two drawings by Piranesi which, apart from the dedicated plate in *Il Campo Marzio dell'Antica Roma* of 1762, showing 'my head and his own joined', is all that remains of the intense relationship Piranesi shared with Robert for three years and with James for four. The two chalk and ink compositions may be related to those mentioned by Robert in 1755 – '[Piranesi is] just now doing two drawings for me which will be both singular and clever' – though their unfinished character suggests there may have been others [figs 75, 76]. Apart from these, there were, of course, complete sets of Piranesi's engravings that included the dedicated volume of *Il Campo Marzio dell'Antica Roma*, bound, as the sale catalogue of 1818 had it, in 'red morocco, elegant', and a capital in the Egyptian taste that had probably been given by Piranesi to Robert [fig.74]. There were also the odds and ends of rather battered Old Master drawings, such as that for a tomb in the Venetian church of the Madonna dell'Orto and the architectural manuscripts by Vasari, Montano and Fontana, which may have been acquired from the Albani collection while it was in Adam hands [fig.77].

'I am sorry to think of leaving this place where I have lived so happily with many agreeable and good friends, unmolested by kirk or state, esteemed and respected by all good people and hated and envied by the wicked and villainous only; master of myself, with a proper mixture of application and amusement and a constant improvement in my own business in the most elegant and lordly way.' So wrote Robert, sadly, from the Casa Guarnieri in the spring of 1757, shortly afterwards succumbing to the familiar 'Very severe cold & Rhumatism' that so often afflicted him during times of stress and that now delayed his departure, cutting short his leisurely return journey to London.

His decision to leave was as much financial as anything else. His capital was exhausted, his family impatient and his Roman objectives mostly realised. He was equipped to take his place in the world, well above the measuring and surveying of the Edinburgh office and ready to devote himself 'entirely to giving designs and receiving my money'. His trunk – of 'a most enormous magnitude, made a-purpose to contain all my drawings, sketches and studies, the books necessary on the road, with all my habilments and utensils of war' – was packed. His collection of paintings and sculpture had already left by sea from Livorno and a further trunk was sent from Venice in August 1757. In October he was in Vicenza and Venice, where he made a large but lacklustre drawing of the Salute, and he arrived back in London in January 1758 [fig.78]. His two principal assistants, Brunias and Dewez, had boldly agreed to return with him to London and his new office. Dewez went overland and was in Augsburg with him in November, where Robert was still drawing on odds and ends of paper and sightseeing without end, enchanted by the picturesque and Gothic [fig.79]. Brunias, 'who never was without the walls of Rome till he came with me', was sent by sea from Venice.

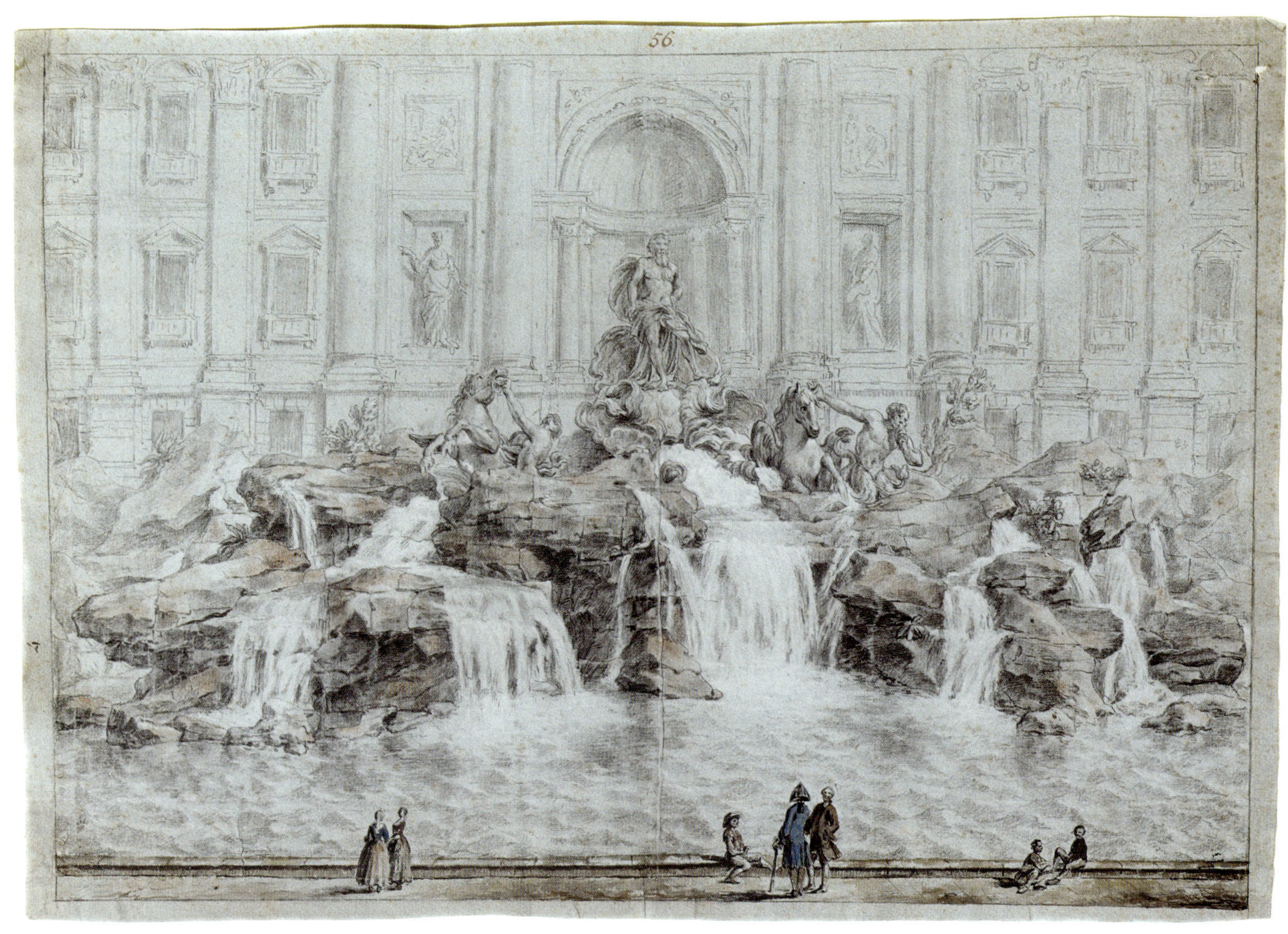

69. Circle of Laurent Pécheux (1729–1821)
View of the Trevi fountain in Rome

*c.*1755
Pencil, chalk and bodycolour on grey paper
418 x 606 mm
Adam vol. 56/56

This drawing is one of a set of three views of the Trevi fountain that Robert Adam owned, and was executed as part of his survey of Roman fountains. The drawings emphasise and exaggerate the sculpture of the fountain, at the expense of the architecture behind.

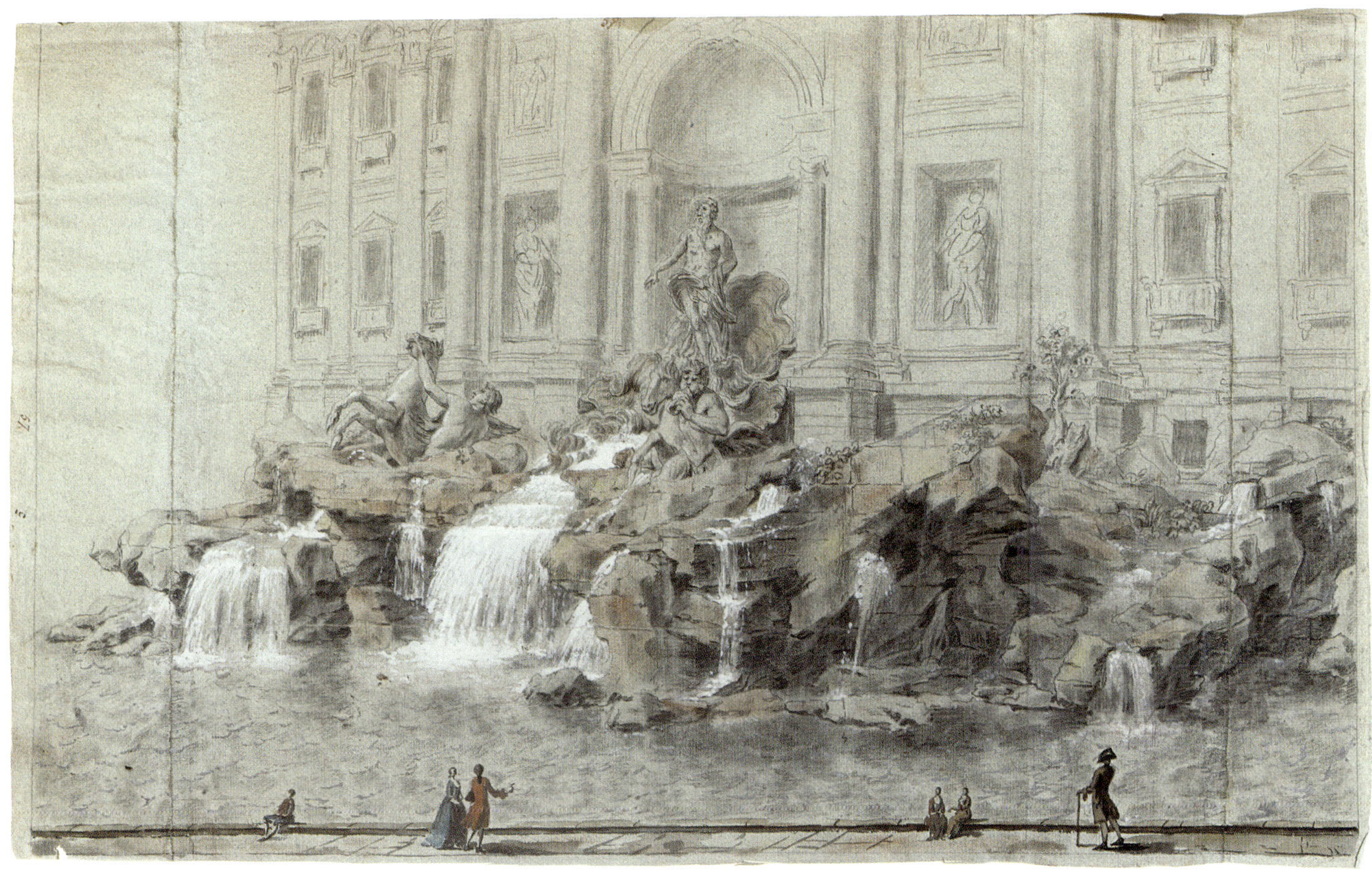

70. Circle of Laurent Pécheux
View of the Trevi fountain in Rome

*c.*1755
Pencil, chalk, water and white bodycolour on grey paper, with two pieces added
454 x 738 mm
Adam vol. 56/57

A companion view to fig.69, and, like it, given a sense of theatre by the audience in the foreground.

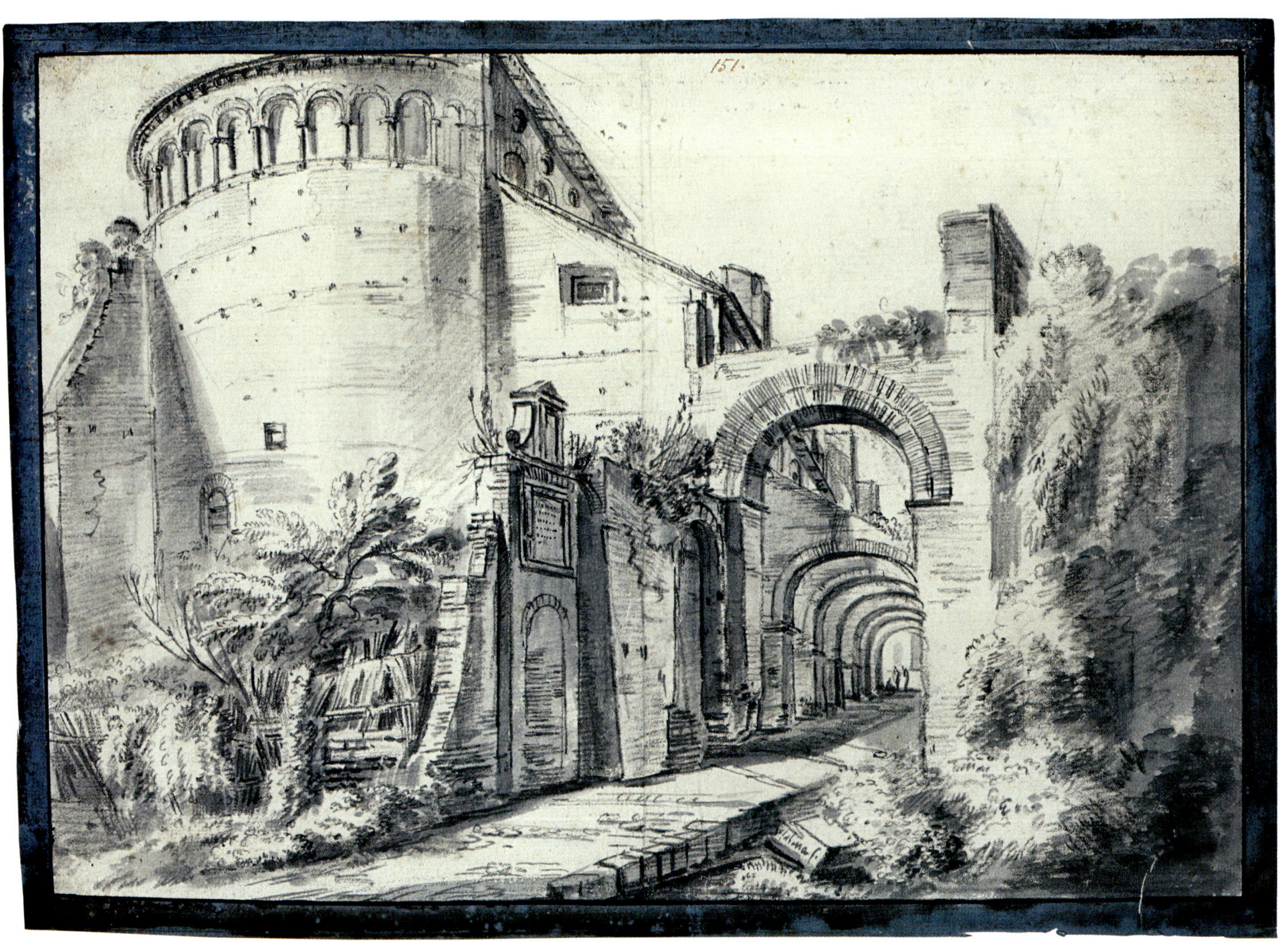

71. Jean-Baptiste Lallemand
View under the arches of the Via Clivio di Scauro

*c.*1756
Black chalk and bodycolour, with deep blue border
267 x 380 mm
Adam vol. 56/151

The church of Santi Giovanni e Paolo, seen on the left, was a popular subject for the Adam circle. It was drawn more than once by Lallemand and also by Clérisseau.

72. Robert Adam
Circular capriccio

1755
Pencil, watercolour and oxidised white heightening, with ink border
201 x 201 mm
Adam vol. 56/121

This capriccio is probably inspired by mausolea such as the Roman tomb of the Plautii or that of Cecilia Metella, both of which were well known to Robert Adam, as was the Arch of Titus, seen in the distance.

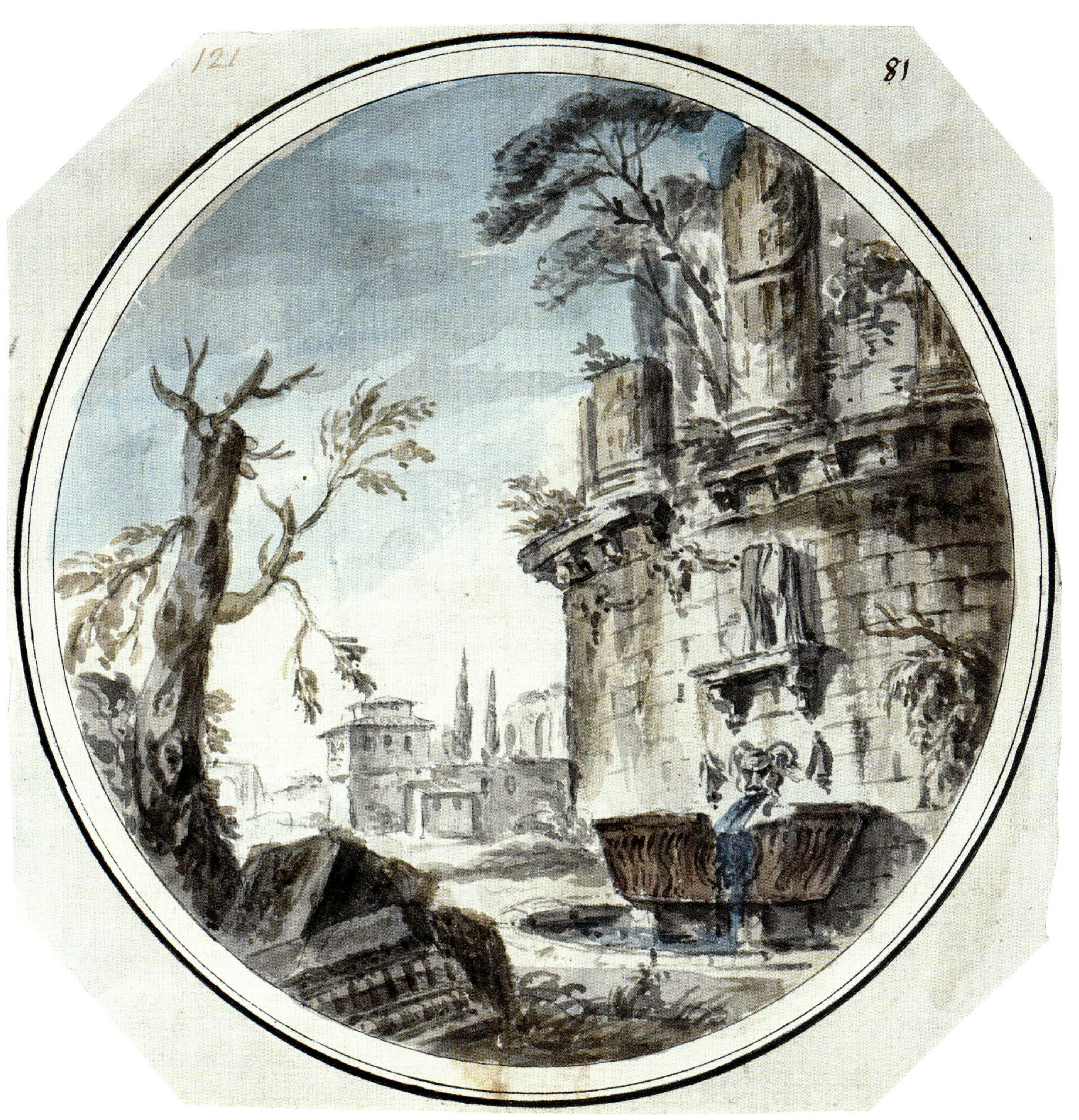
121
81

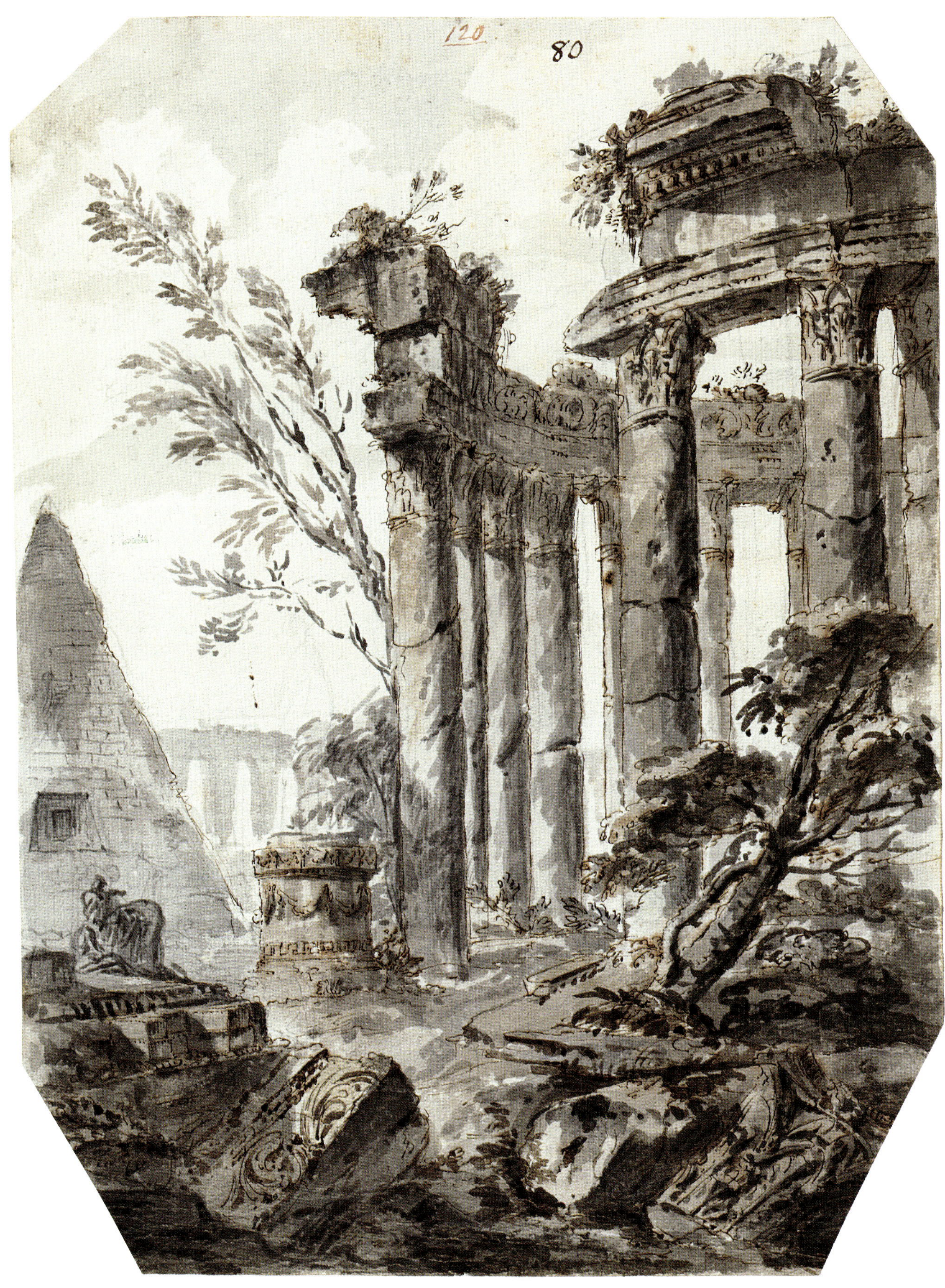
120
80

73. Charles-Louis Clérisseau *Attributed to*
Capriccio of ruined buildings

1755
Pencil, pen, and brown and grey washes
272 x 206 mm
Adam vol. 56/120

This is one of several such compositions based on the ancient ruins of Rome, executed by both Robert Adam and Clérisseau. Here the attribution to Clérisseau is based on the sophisticated handling of light and the liveliness of the brown and grey washes.

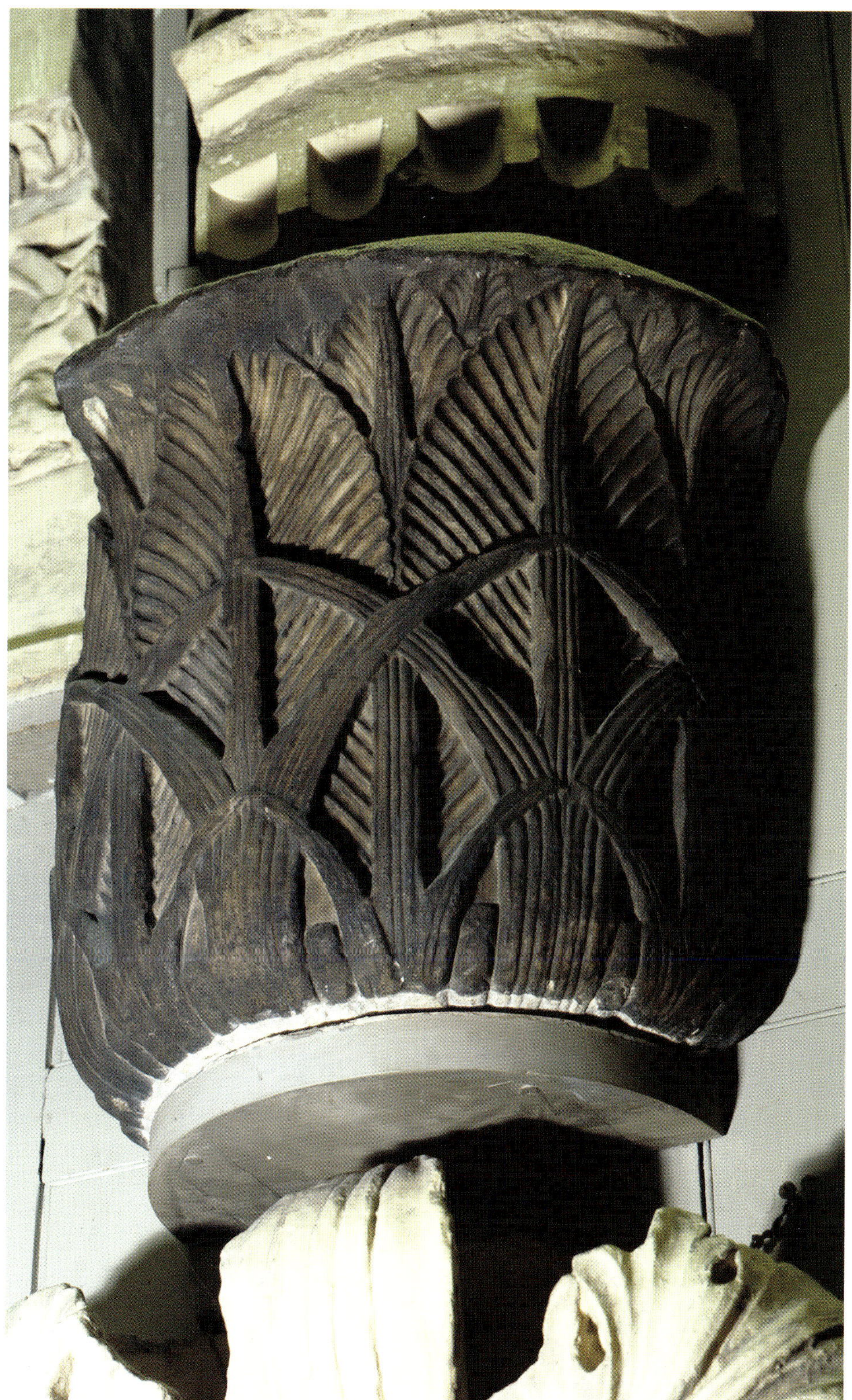

74.
Capital of an engaged column

Roman, *c*.150 BC
Limestone or marble
610 x 580 mm
Soane Museum M76

This capital is in the Egyptian style and possibly comes from one of the temples dedicated to Egyptian deities in the Campus Martius area of Rome. Sir John Soane bought it for £2.2s at the 1818 Adam sale.

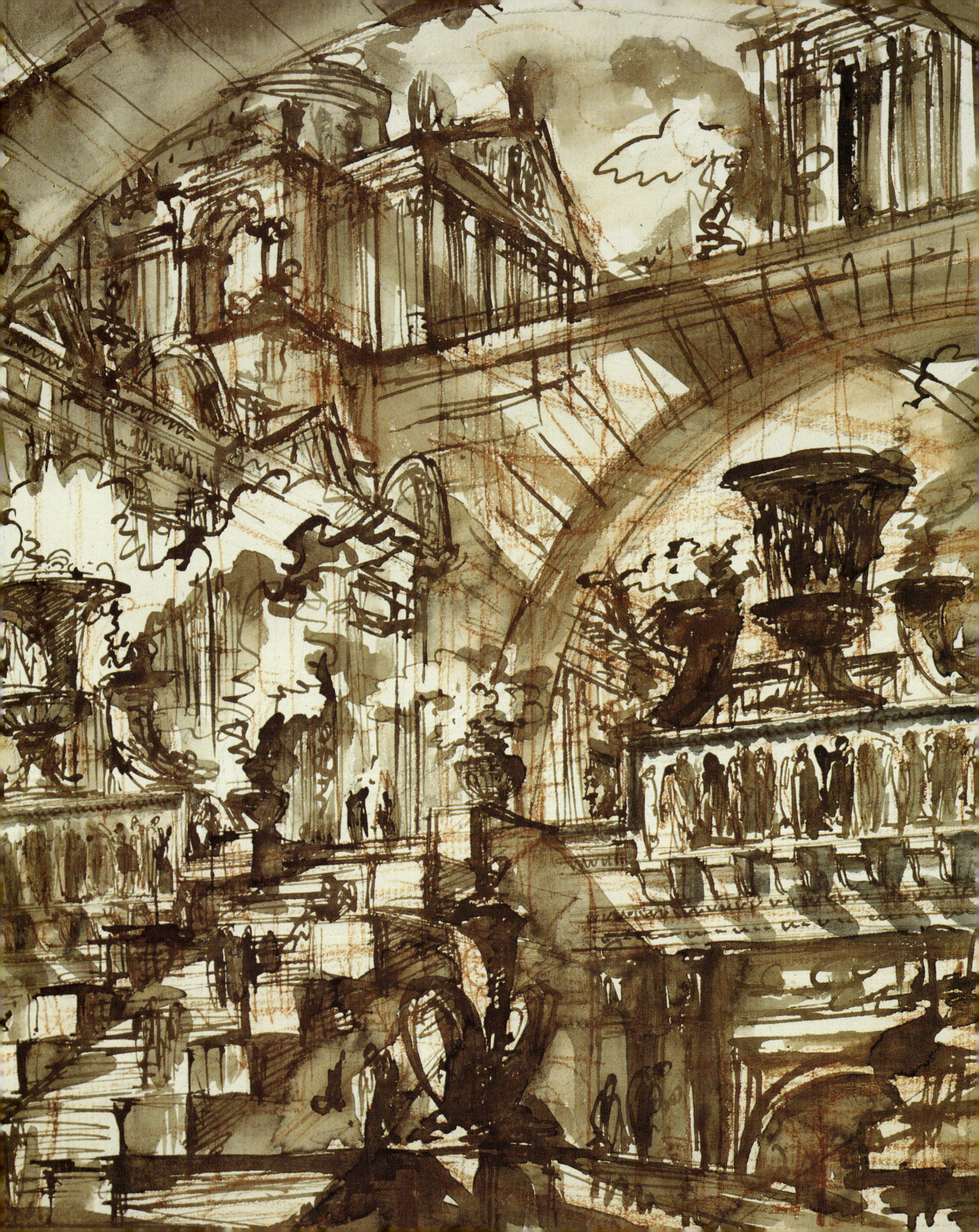

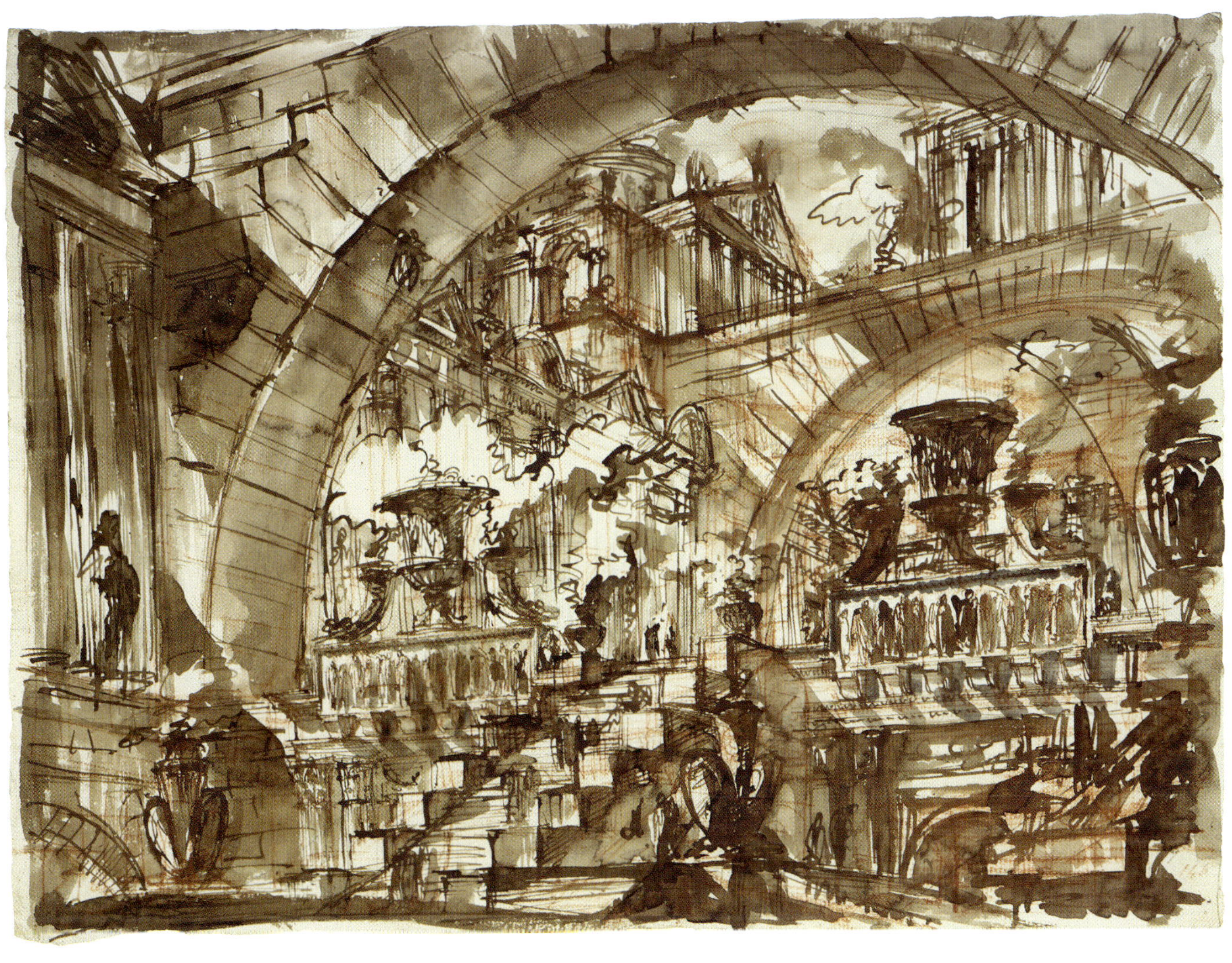

75. Giovanni Battista Piranesi (1728–80)
Capriccio

*c.*1755
Red and black chalk, ink and brown wash
385 x 530 mm
Adam vol. 56/146

The composition, building upwards from left to right via staircases, and the flamboyant use of wash, are typical of Piranesi's *Carceri* drawings of the mid-1740s. However, the watermark suggests the 1750s. Piranesi's imaginative use of the remains of antiquity was to have a profound effect on Robert Adam.

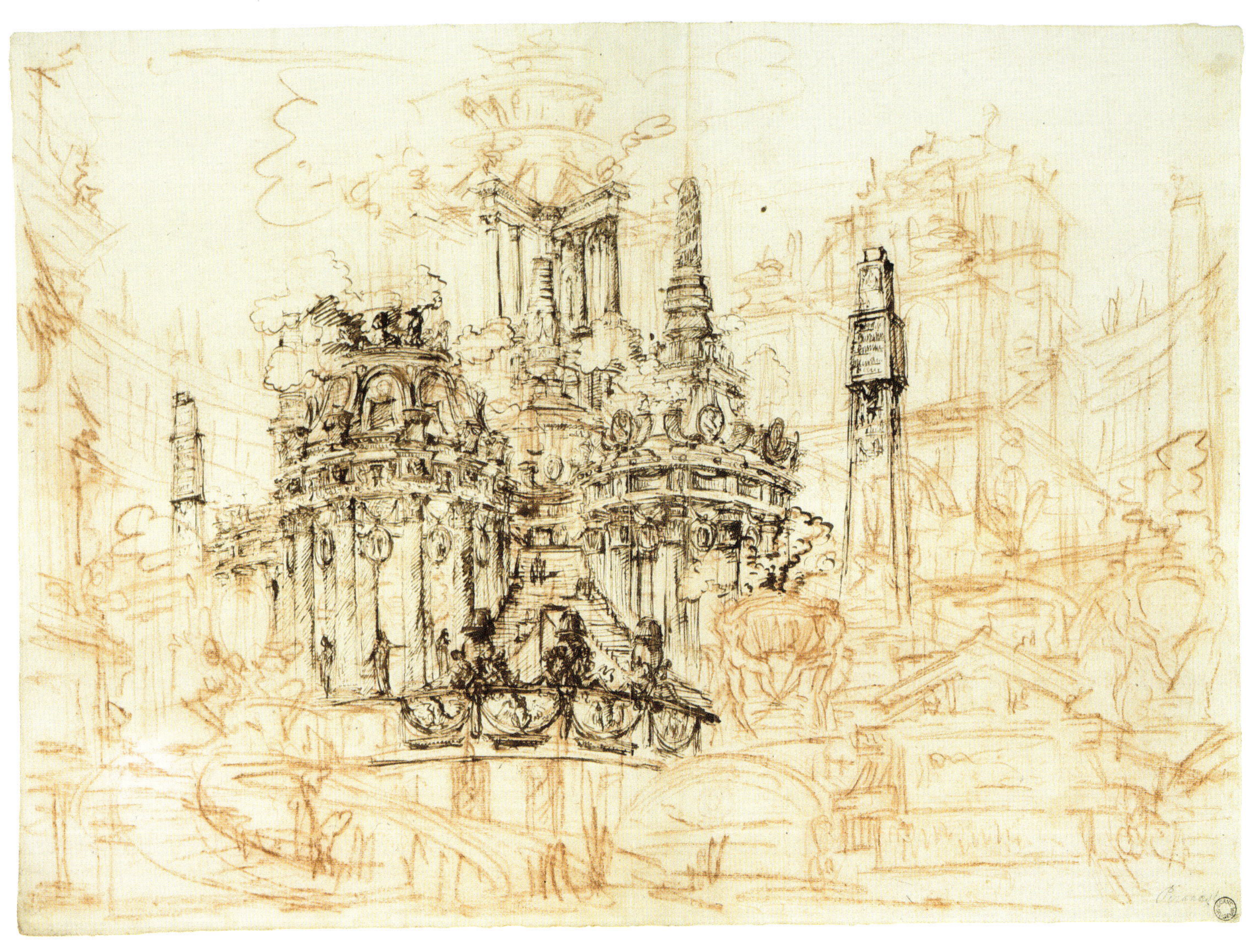

76. Giovanni Battista Piranesi
Unfinished capriccio including a group of tiered funerary monuments

*c.*1756
Red chalk and ink
535 x 750 mm
Adam vol. 26/163

The subject matter of funerary monuments can obviously be related to Piranesi's *Antichità Romane* (1756), where volume two dealt with *sepolchri antichi*, to which this drawing may be related. Robert Adam's name appeared in the dedicatory plate of volume two of the *Antichità Romane*, and the *Pianta di Roma e del Campo Marzio* of 1762 was dedicated to him. James Adam, to whom this drawing belonged, handled the negotiations about this and according to him, Piranesi '...hinted at a dedication to me...' in July 1761.

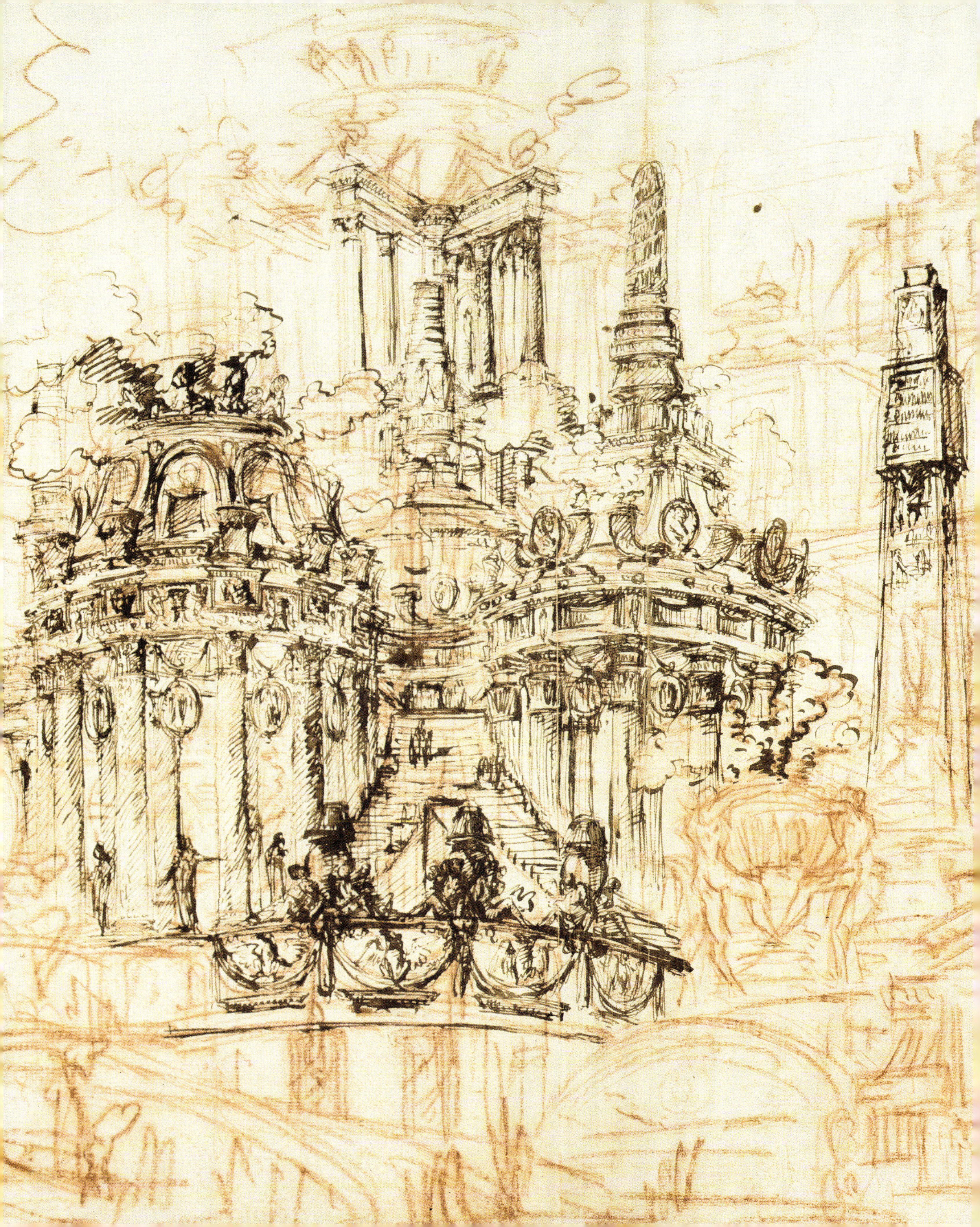

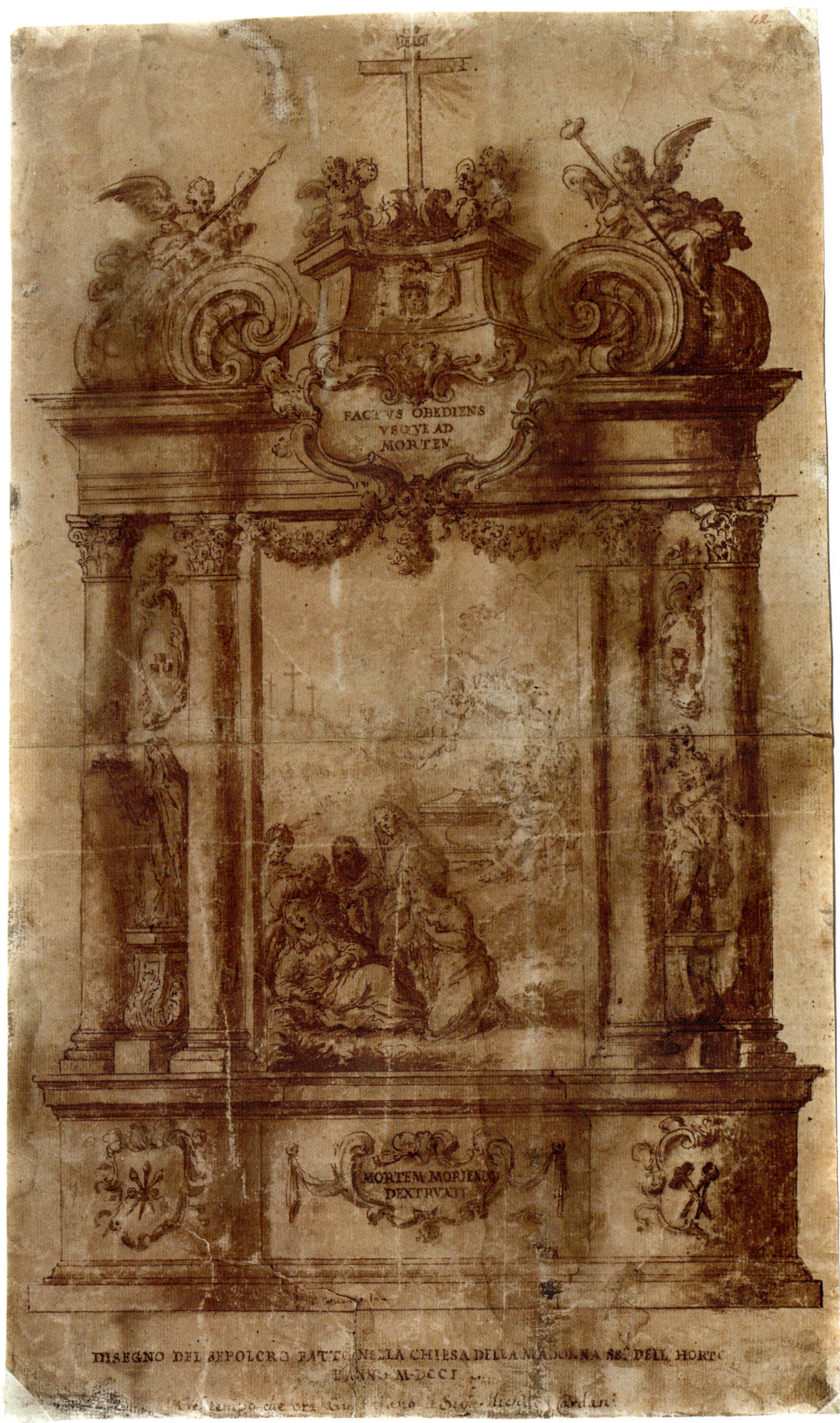

77. Unidentified 18th-century artist
Design for an altarpiece, including a painting, probably of the death and apotheosis of the Virgin

Dated 1701
Pen and brown wash on buff paper
515 x 315 mm
Adam vol. 56/42

The church of the Madonna dell'Orto in Rome is distinguished by paintings by Tintoretto and Bellini: this design is probably for a minor side-chapel. Although signed by L. Cardango – or Cardocco – there is no account of him as a painter or architect. This altarpiece may have disappeared during nineteenth- and twentieth-century restorations. The rather battered drawing, which is dated 1701, may have been acquired by accident (as part of a lot) rather than by design, possibly during Robert Adam's time in the city in 1757.

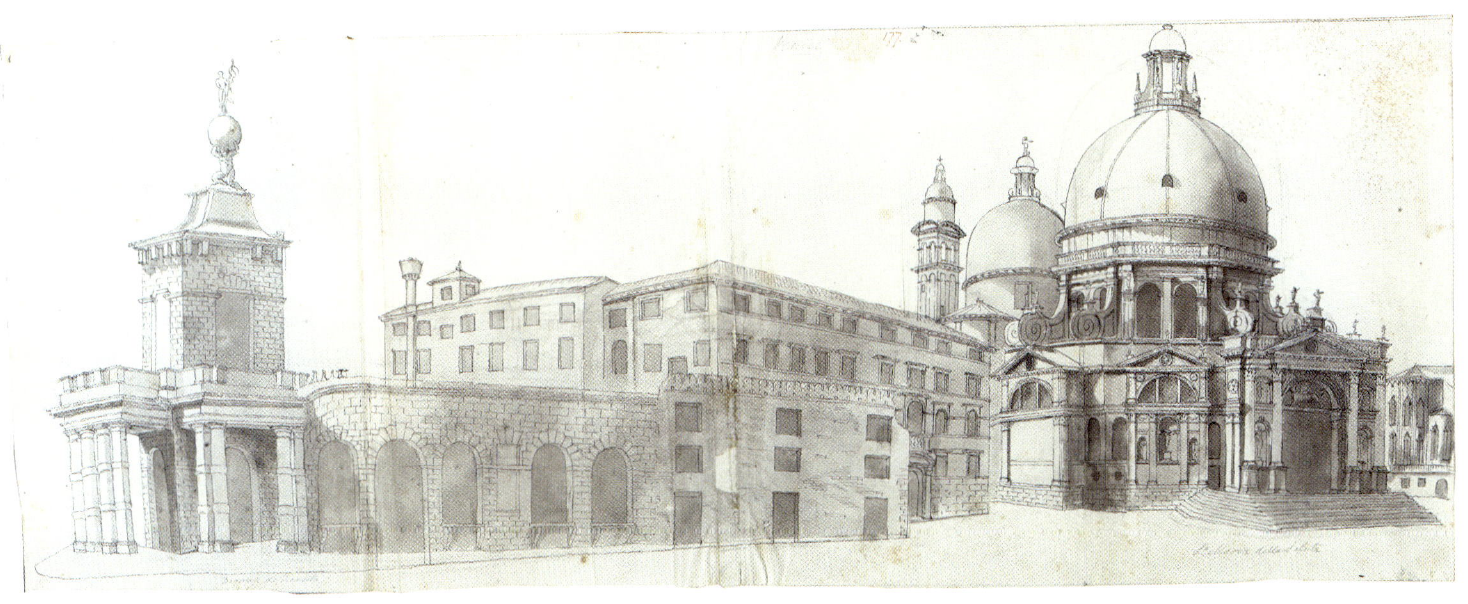

78. Robert Adam
View of the entrance façade of Santa Maria della Salute and the adjoining customs buildings in Venice

1757
Pencil, pen and grey wash
201 x 795 mm
Adam vol. 56/177

Robert Adam was in Venice from June until October 1757 and this drawing was almost certainly made during that time. It is one of the few Venetian views to have survived. He also used the city as a base for his expedition to Diocletian's palace at Spalatro in Dalmatia.

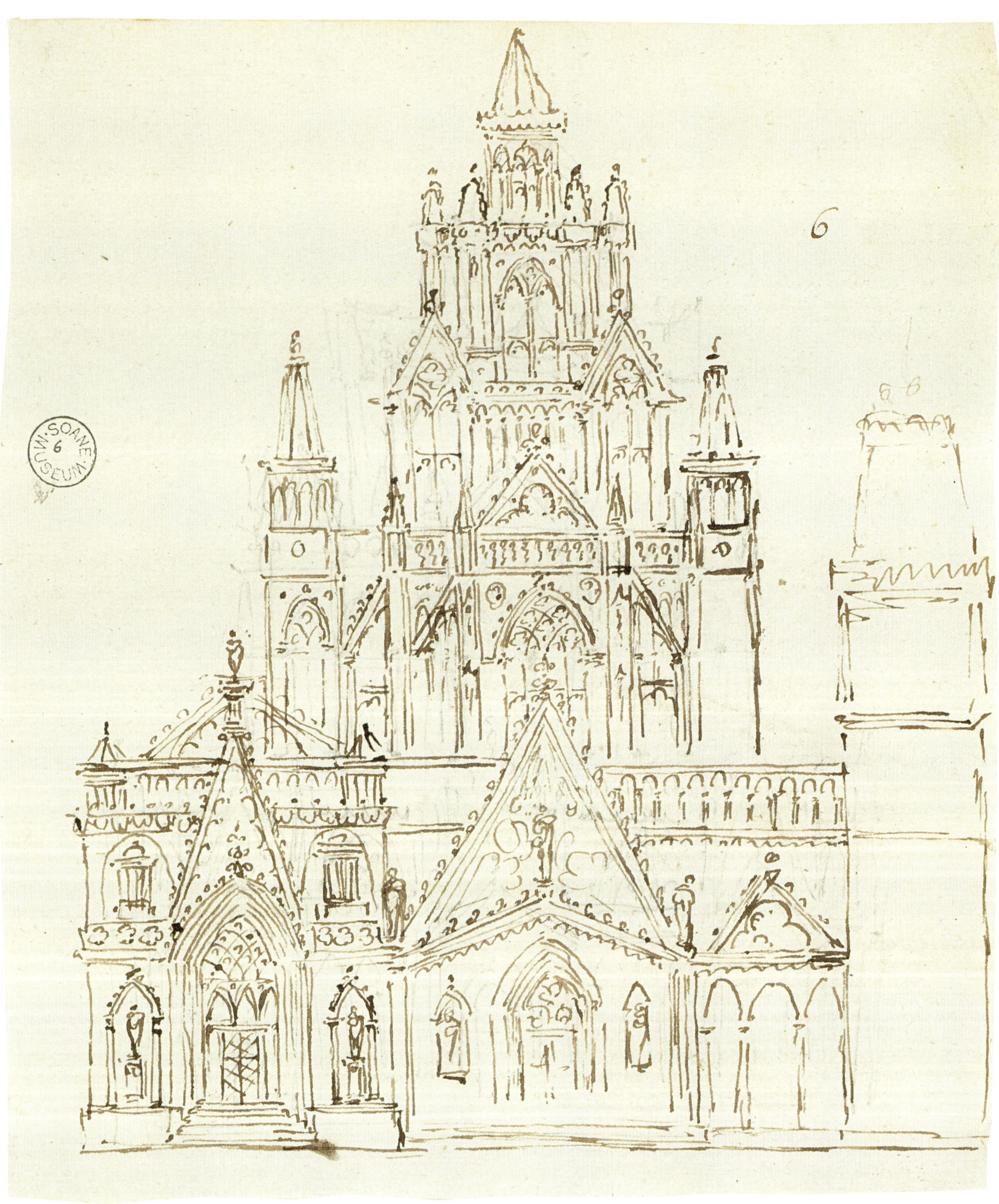

79. Robert Adam
Capriccio of a Gothic façade

1757
Pencil and pen
227 x 198 mm
Adam vol. 54 / Series 4/6

This drawing shows the sort of building that engaged Robert Adam's imagination, especially on his return from Italy through Germany in 1757. Although this is an invention, he made several topographical views at this time of similar subjects.

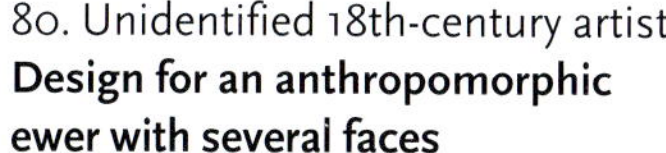

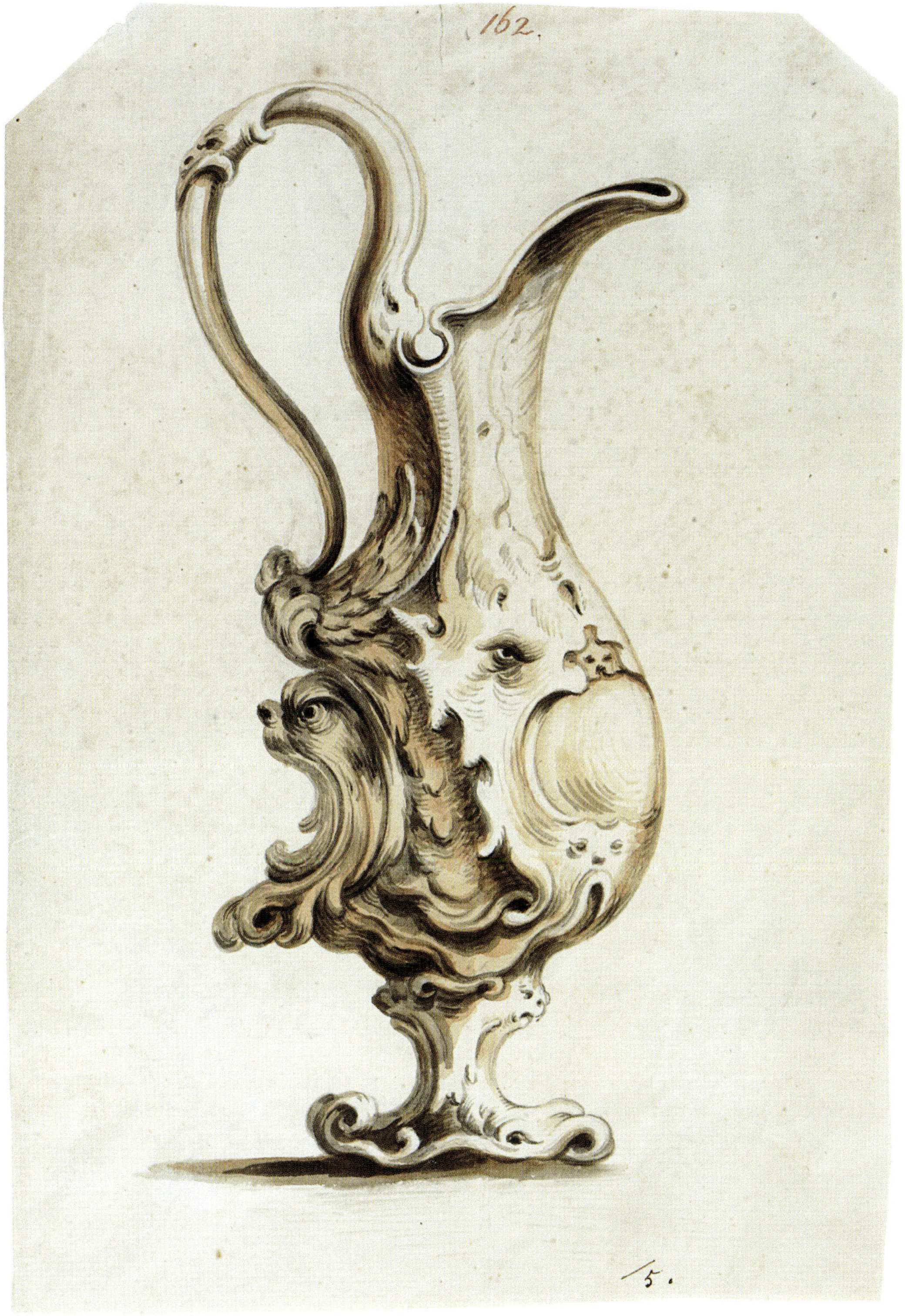

80. Unidentified 18th-century artist
Design for an anthropomorphic ewer with several faces

*c.*1740
Pen and brown wash
262 x 185 mm
Adam vol. 56/162

This drawing is a larger copy of a plate from Adam van Vianen, *Modelles Artificiels de divers Vaisdeaux d'argent*, of 1650, a copy of which was presumably held in the library at Blair Adam, the Adam family home.

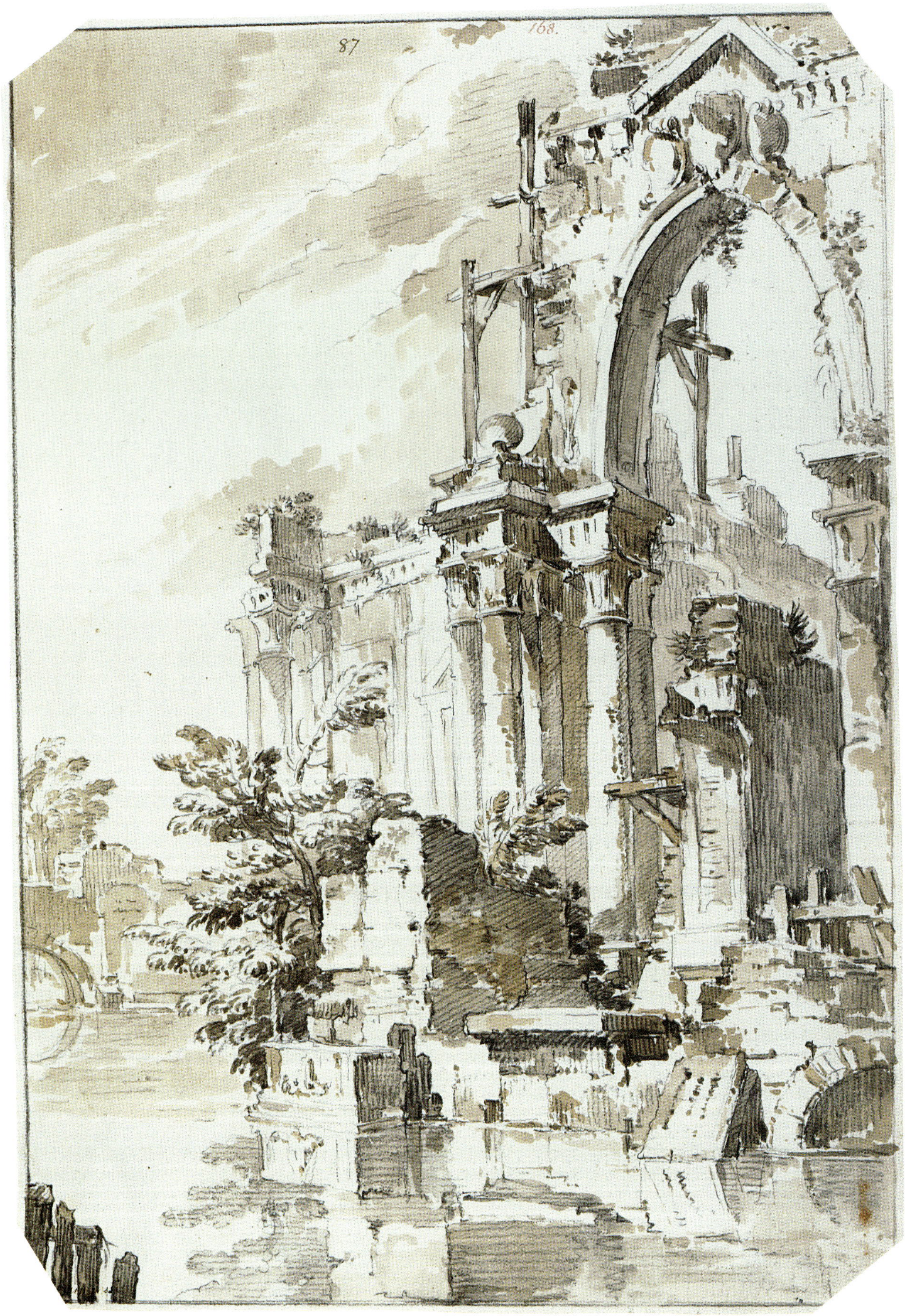
87
168.

81. Unidentified 18th-century artist
Capriccio showing large ruins around an arch

*c.*1755
Black chalk and brown wash, with chalk margins
413 x 295 mm
Adam vol. 56/168

This sheet and its companion show similar compositions of classical ruins beside water. It was possibly collected by Robert Adam as an example of this kind of draughtsmanship.

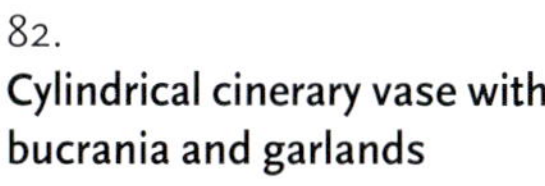

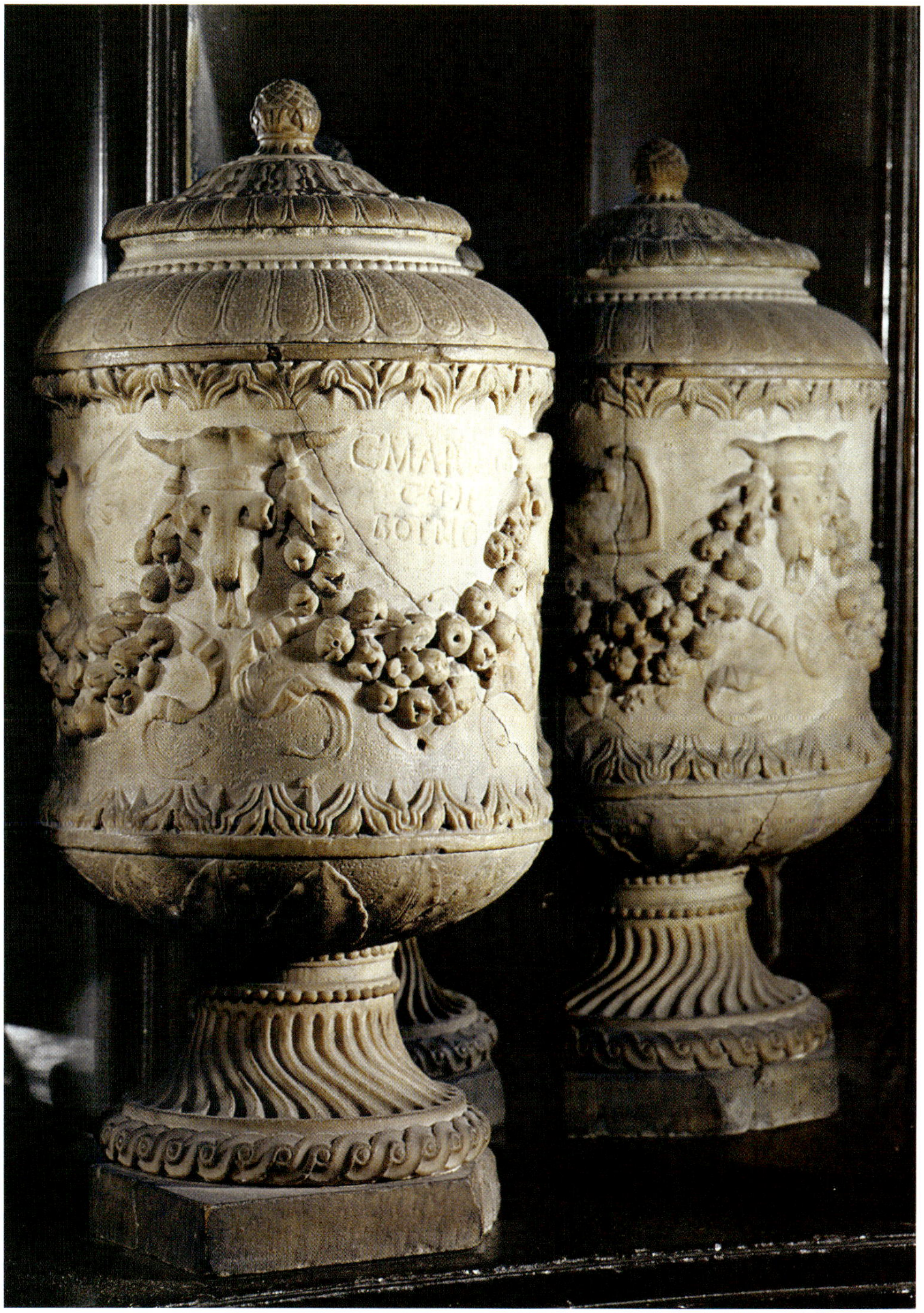

82.
Cylindrical cinerary vase with bucrania and garlands

Marble
Roman with 18th-century additions
Soane Museum A44

The whole piece may perhaps be the product of one of the eighteenth-century workshops in Rome known to Robert and James Adam. Sir John Soane purchased it at the 1818 Adam sale, where it formed part of Lot 96.

James Adam's

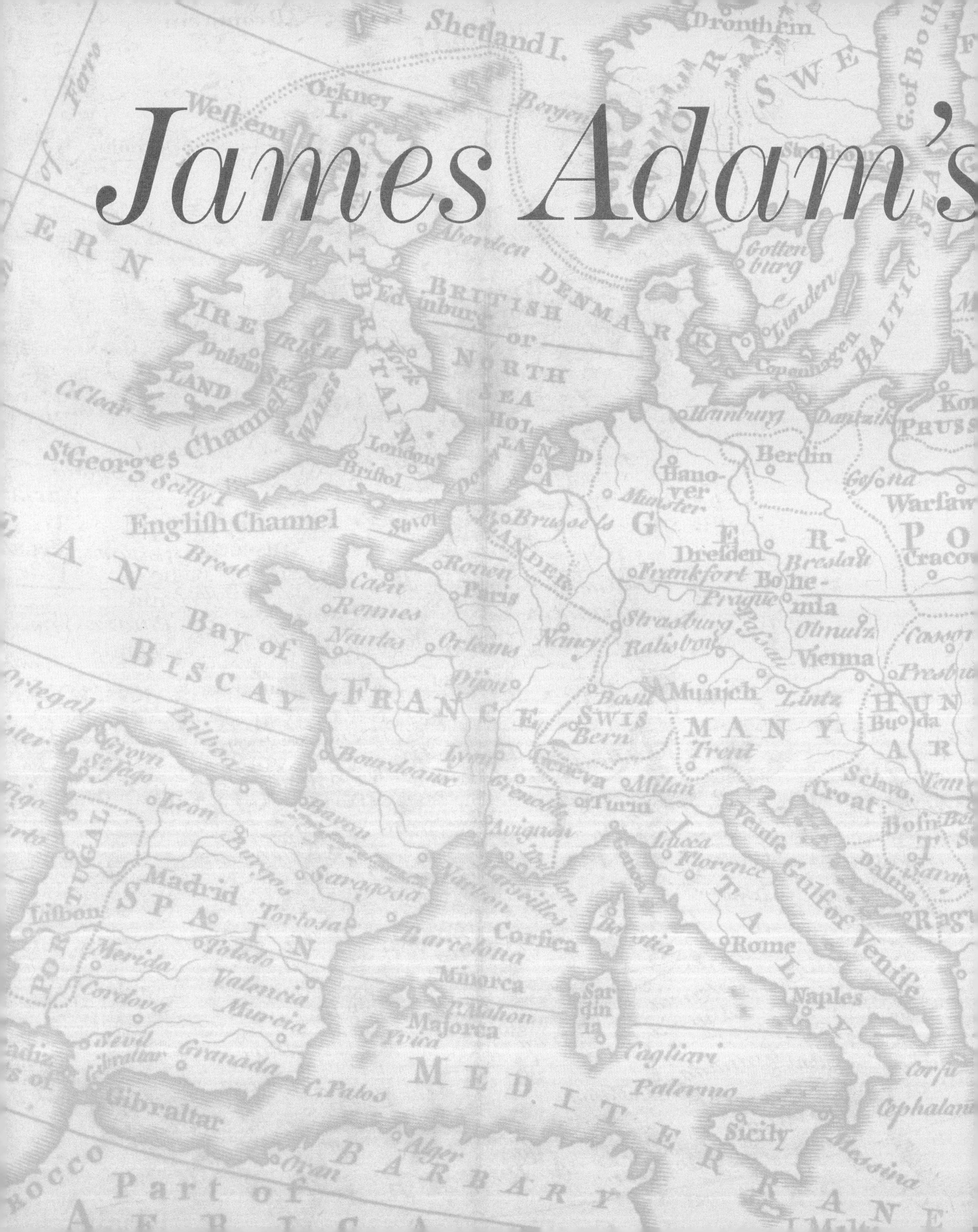

Grand Tour Rome

James Adam arrived in Rome at the end of February 1761. He took two apartments in the Casa Guarnieri after having 'examined Bob's apartment but found it too small for my great family'. This family, apart from his servants, included George Richardson, who had come with him from London, Antonio Zucchi, Domenico Cunego, Giuseppe Sacco and Agostino Scara. On top of this coterie was Clérisseau, who resumed his role as a sort of director of Adam studies, Laurent Pécheux and probably Giuseppe Manocchi. And there was the Abbé Grant, who assumed the same role of guide, philosopher and friend that he had played with Robert. It was he who alerted James to the final sale of the Albani drawings, a plan to buy them having first been mooted by Robert in 1756, but now with the serious prospect that the youthful George III might purchase the vast collection. James described it coolly and critically to his brother as '200 vols in Folio. I am far from saying however that these Vols are all interesting, that is not the case, in such a vast collection much rubbish must be expected, the mosaics, paintings & bas reliefs of the primitive church or first ages of Christianity will entertain you little, tho there is some curiosity even in this subject. But if you look into the volumes of Domenichino you will see several superb designs & there is a collection of Drawings after Antiquity, Bas reliefs, Altars, tripods, cineranii, urns, that I believe you will own to be most valuable.' He had a further opportunity to study them closely after their purchase, for they remained in the Casa from May to July 1762, before being shipped to London.

This purchase encouraged James to see what else there might be for sale in Rome and what might be shaken from the antique tree. To this end, he produced in 1762 a list of 'Good

Antiquitys yet to be procur'd in Rome'. This gave a brief account of the then major collections – Mattei, Albani, Rondanini, Giustiniani, Spada, Lancellotti, Massimi, Furetti and della Valle – as well as his favourite pieces – the Apollo Verospi, the Barberini Faun, a bust of Pompey from the Spada, a vestal from the Lancellotti, and even some antique chairs from San Giovanni Laterano [fig.83]. He also collected a striking drawing on blue washed paper by Ludovico Tesi for Sansovino's 'Marble Frize in the Church of Madonna del Popoli'. This may have been acquired on its own terms as a noteable drawing, or as a record of an object he hoped in his brazen way to acquire [fig.84]. There were also drawings by James and his assistants of the 'freezes' in the Palazzo delle Valle, the fragments of the gigantic Temple of the Sun in the Colonna Gardens and Renaissance candelabra from St Peter's and the Strozzi Chapel in San Andrea delle Valle [figs 85, 86]. These studies are in a range of hands, most conspicuously that of George Richardson, who had come out to Italy with James, and those of Antonio Zucchi and Giuseppe Manocchi, whom James had recruited in Italy. Manocchi was the more important, on account of his understanding of colour and through it an easy and fluid interpretation of the Antique. James referred to him as his 'Arabesque' who 'paints in Oyl and Guazzo but I don't believe he has any practice in fresco, but is very sharp & is a great mechanical man'. He made a series of drawings for James in 1762, some of which have survived, James noting that 'I have just now had three very fine Drawings made of Antique ceilings that still remain in what they call Livia's Baths in the Palace of the Emperors, they are painted & so pretty & so rare that I thought I could have not have them done with too much care. I imagine they must appear fine even to Bob.' [fig.88]

Very different from the style of Manocchi or Zucchi's work is a large group of pencil and red chalk drawings for architectural sculpture [fig.89]. The draughtsmanship is bolder and clearer than that of the other Adams' assistants, with an emphasis on form quite unlike other work James collected. None are signed, apart from several that are initialled with the chalk capital 'L', but some are similar to drawings in the Clérisseau album in the Hermitage and it is likely they are the work of a Clérisseau Roman pupil, Nicolas-François-David Lhuillier [fig.90]. It is possible, too, that Lhuillier, along with the engraver Cunego, Manocchi and even Clérisseau, were all involved with the great scheme for recording the grotesque work from Raphael's Vatican *Loggie*, underway during James' Roman years and finally appearing in three parts between 1772 and 1777 as the *Loggie di Rafaele nel Vaticano*. James would also have been aware that there were versions of the *Loggie* in the Albani Collection and this perhaps stimulated the competitive Adam spirit to have versions executed in pen and watercolour by Manocchi [fig.87]. They were probably the source, too, for the decorated panels in the Casino at 75 Lower Grosvenor Street.

The counterpart to Robert Adam's scheme for recording ancient Rome in his Desgodetz project was his brother's Parliament House design, which occupied James and his draughtsmen throughout their time in Rome. It was less academic and more practical than the Desgodetz project, and in the early 1760s it did have some chance of being built, especially through the sympathetic ear of the Earl of Bute, an Adam patron and the powerful minister of George III. James and his assistants worked on it during the winter of 1762 and 1763 but despite their collective efforts it had not been finished by the time he left Rome in April that year. He relied principally on Zucchi for translating his designs to paper and for delineating the endless relief panels of British history that were to decorate the firmly neoclassical interior of this Roman Capitol, whose circular central hall was remarkable for its severe classicism [fig.92]. The drawings that were entirely his own work were rather cramped and dead, as can be seen in his design for the baldachino over the throne and some of the sculpture for the exterior of the Parliament House [fig.96]. The rest, including the gigantic chariot that was to crown the central portico, were by the familiar team of draughtsmen, and some were better than others [fig.93]. The British order that James designed for the exterior capitals was drawn for him with great vigour by Zucchi, though James composed what he termed the 'Explanation'. Rather pretentiously and ponderously, he described it as 'This British order invented in Rome by JA. Archt. & intended for the principal portico of a parliament house design'd by him at Rome 1762 most humbly presented to H.M. The king by his subject & servt the Author' [figs 94, 95]. To make sure its merits were fully appreciated, he had it included in his grand portrait by Batoni in the following year. He also appears to have allowed himself to be distracted by other equally grandiose projects, of which his Theatre Royal was the most ambitious. Here, once again, his interest in detail seems to have taken control of the design, and the fountains that were to flank the façade received his greatest attention [fig.97]. Though neither the Parliament House nor the Theatre Royal were built, they were taken on by Robert Adam and surfaced in the later Parliament proposal and the design for the Haymarket Theatre. Even the British order was revived to crown the pilasters for the gateway and screen to Carlton House in Pall Mall.

Robert and James Adam succeeded during their Roman years in converting themselves from provincial, and rather green, Scottish architects to cosmopolitan figures of substance and standing. They understood Italy as the centre of historical styles – Antique, Renaissance, Baroque – all of which they studied, not least during their travels beyond Rome. Like all Grand Tourists, they collected, but in their case, with particular ends in view. Uppermost in their minds was their wish that the collection should instruct – themselves, their pupils and even their clients. What is more, it is surely remarkable that despite the wreck of the Adam family fortunes, a vital part of their collection has survived – to teach, as the Adams wanted, in Sir John Soane's Museum.

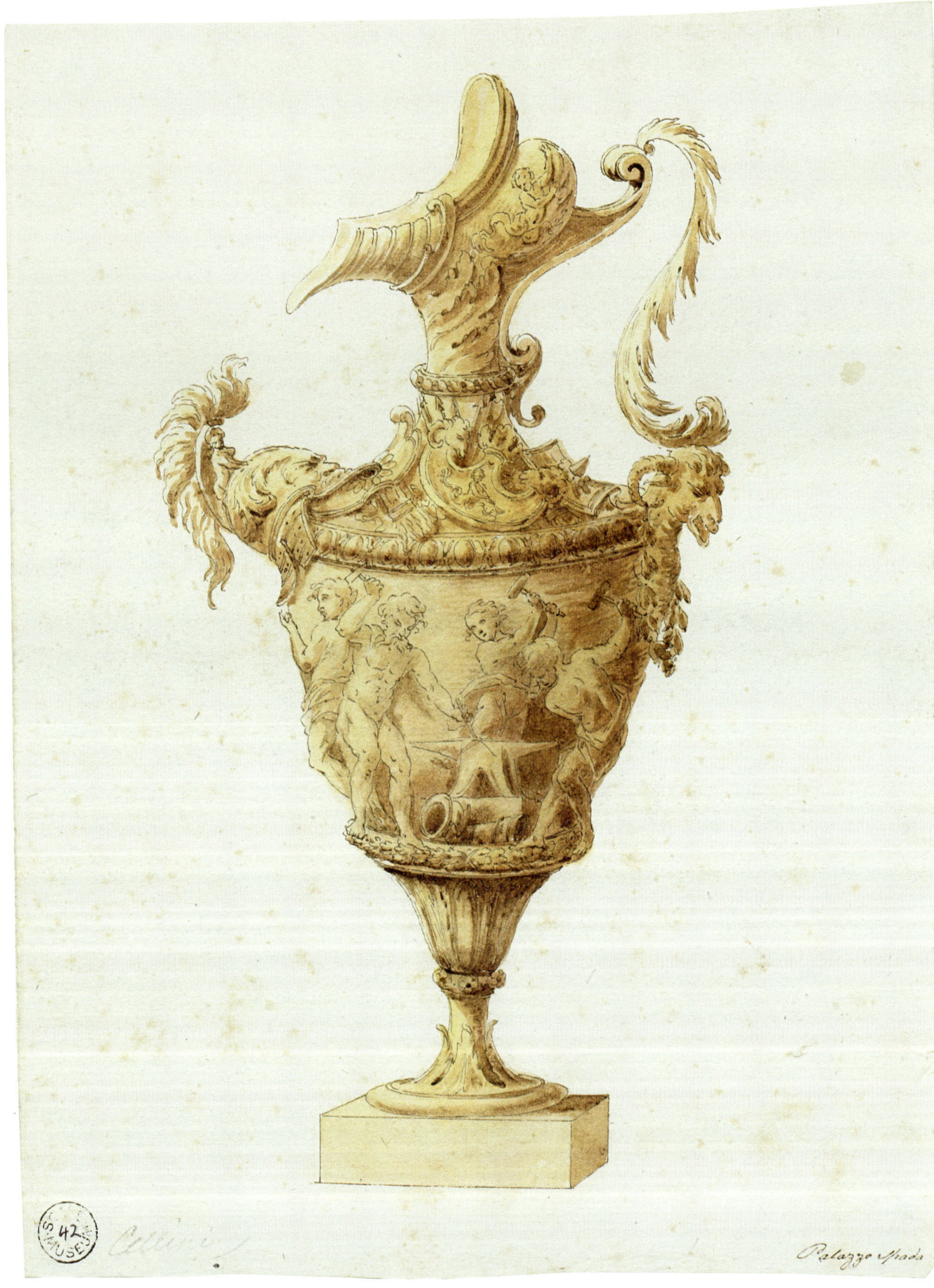
Palazzo Spada

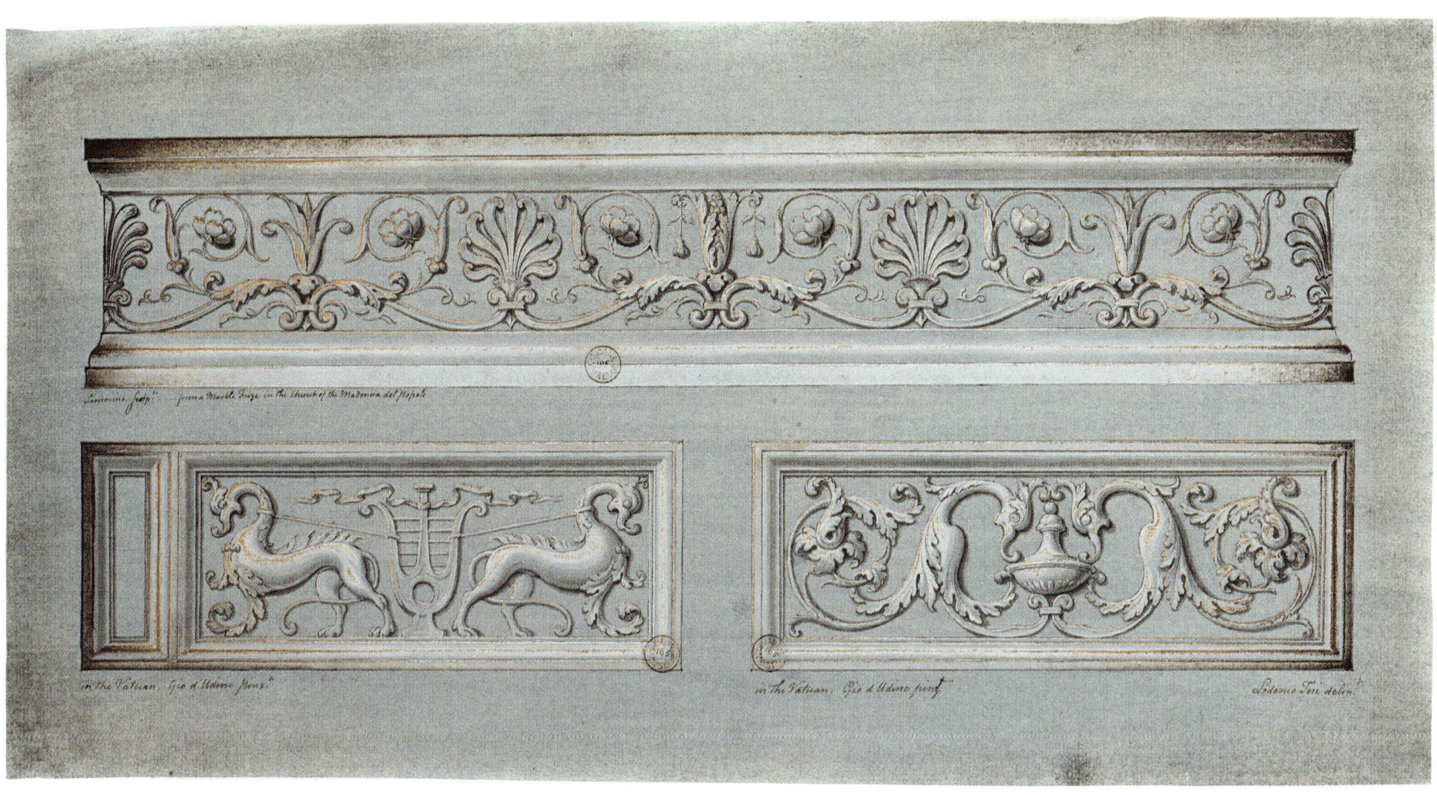

83. Unidentified 18th-century artist
Study of a vase from the Palazzo Spada, Rome

*c.*1761
Pen, and brown and yellow washes
279 x 211 mm
Adam vol. 26/42

This is one of two drawings of vases, owned by James Adam, from the Palazzo Spada. In his list of 'Good Antiquitys to be procur'd at Rome', James included those of the Palazzo Spada but made no mention of such decorative but perhaps minor objects.

84. Ludovico Tesio (1731–82)
Study of three panels of ornament inscribed in ink in a contemporary hand: ... ***from a Marble Frize in the Church of the Madonna del Popoli*** **and** ***in the Vatican***

*c.*1761
Pen with white and gold heightening on blue washed paper
280 x 544 mm
Adam vol. 26/203

This drawing was acquired by James Adam in Rome and shows ornamental panels by two sixteenth-century artists, the sculptor and architect, Sansovino, and the sculptor, Giovanne da Udine.

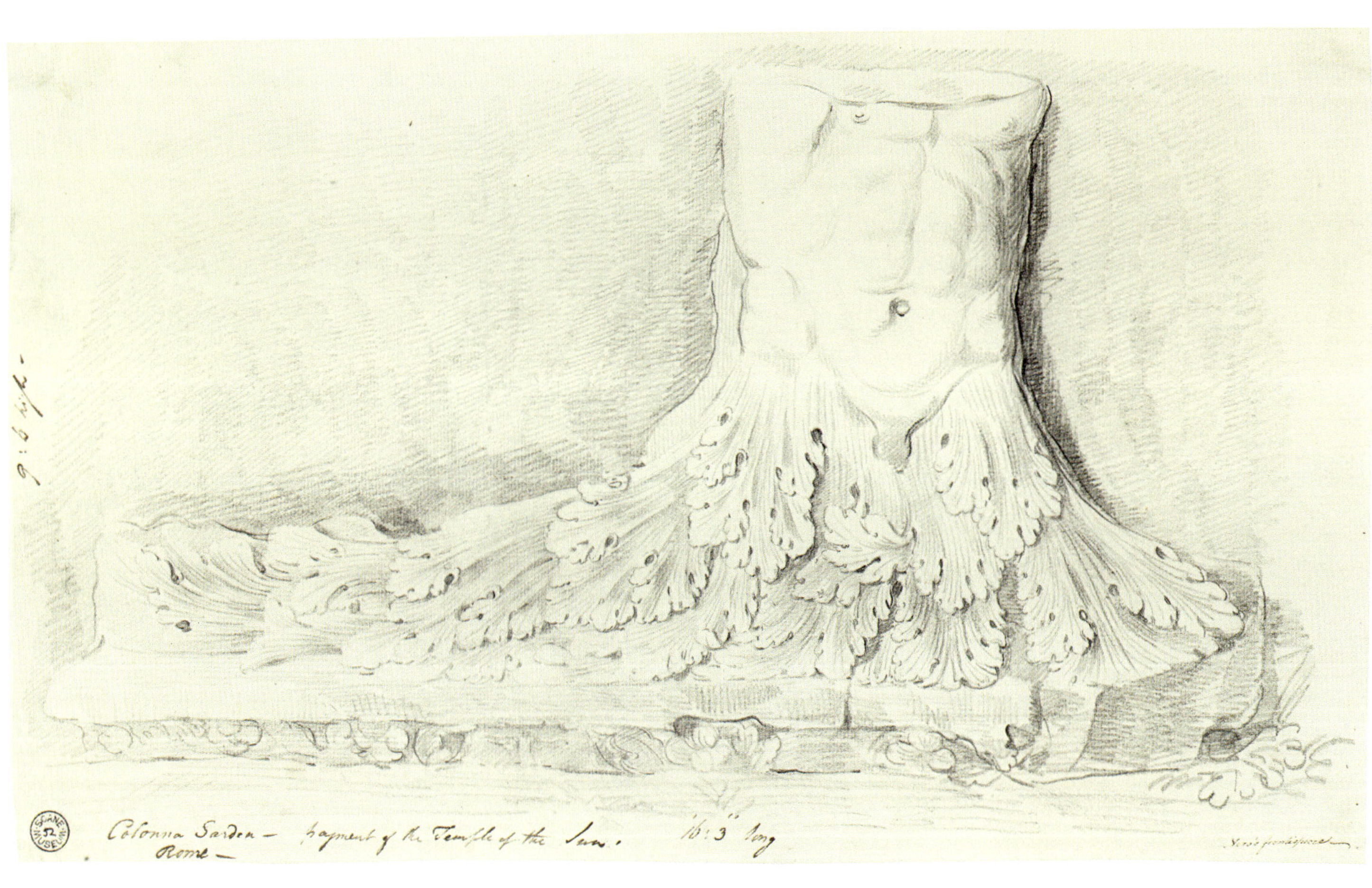

85. George Richardson (?1736–?1813) *Attributed to*
Study of a fragment of sculptural panel

*c.*1761
Black chalk
279 x 467 mm
Adam vol. 26/52

The Temple of the Sun was demolished in 1630 and fragments were built into the walls of the Colonna Gardens in Rome. This is a record drawing, with dimensions in feet and inches, of some fragments from the rear wall of the temple. Both drawing and inscription are probably in the hand of James Adam's Scottish assistant, George Richardson.

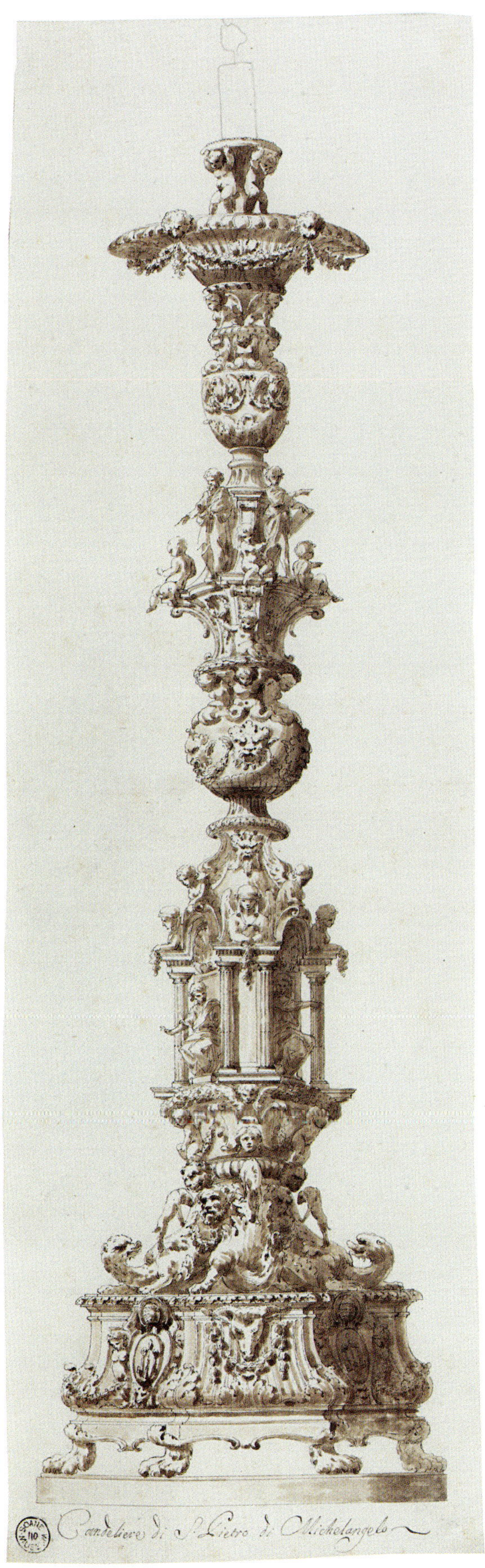

86. Giuseppe Manocchi (*c*.1731–82)
Study of a Renaissance candelabrum, formerly attributed to Michelangelo

c.1761
Pen and brown wash, with later pencil
561 x 183 mm
Adam vol. 26/110

This is a copy of a drawing by Antonio Gentili that probably belonged to the French architect, Henri Marlet, in the late eighteenth century in Rome. The bronze candelabrum shown here was one of six made by Gentili in 1581 and later presented to St Peter's. Robert Adam possibly used drawings such as this, which he described as 'Bronzes executed in Italy in the Style of Mich. Angelo', as a source for his Luton Park candelabra of *c*.1775.

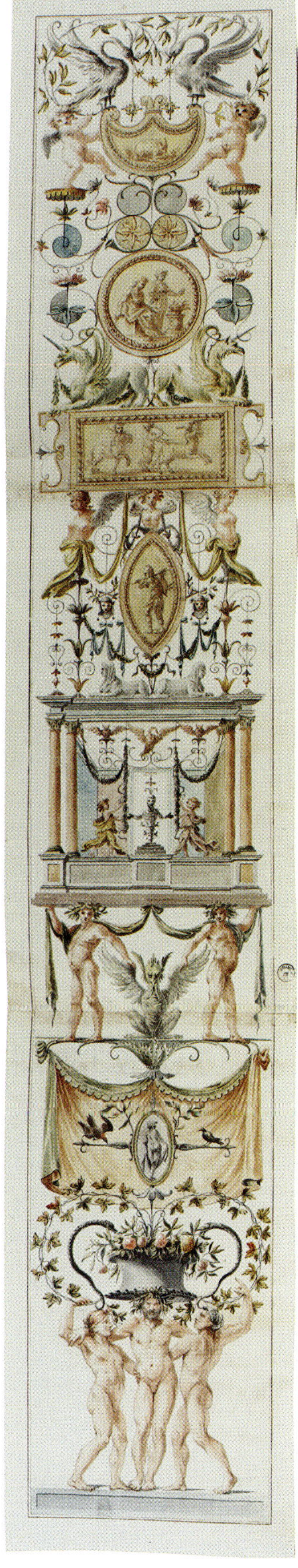

87. Giuseppe Manocchi *Attributed to*
Study of a decorated pilaster

c.1756
Pencil, pen and watercolour
1238 x 236 mm
Adam vol. 26/191

This is one of a series of studies that James Adam commissioned, of the Vatican *Loggie*. He later used versions of them in the proposed decoration of the Adam home at 75 Lower Grosvenor Street.

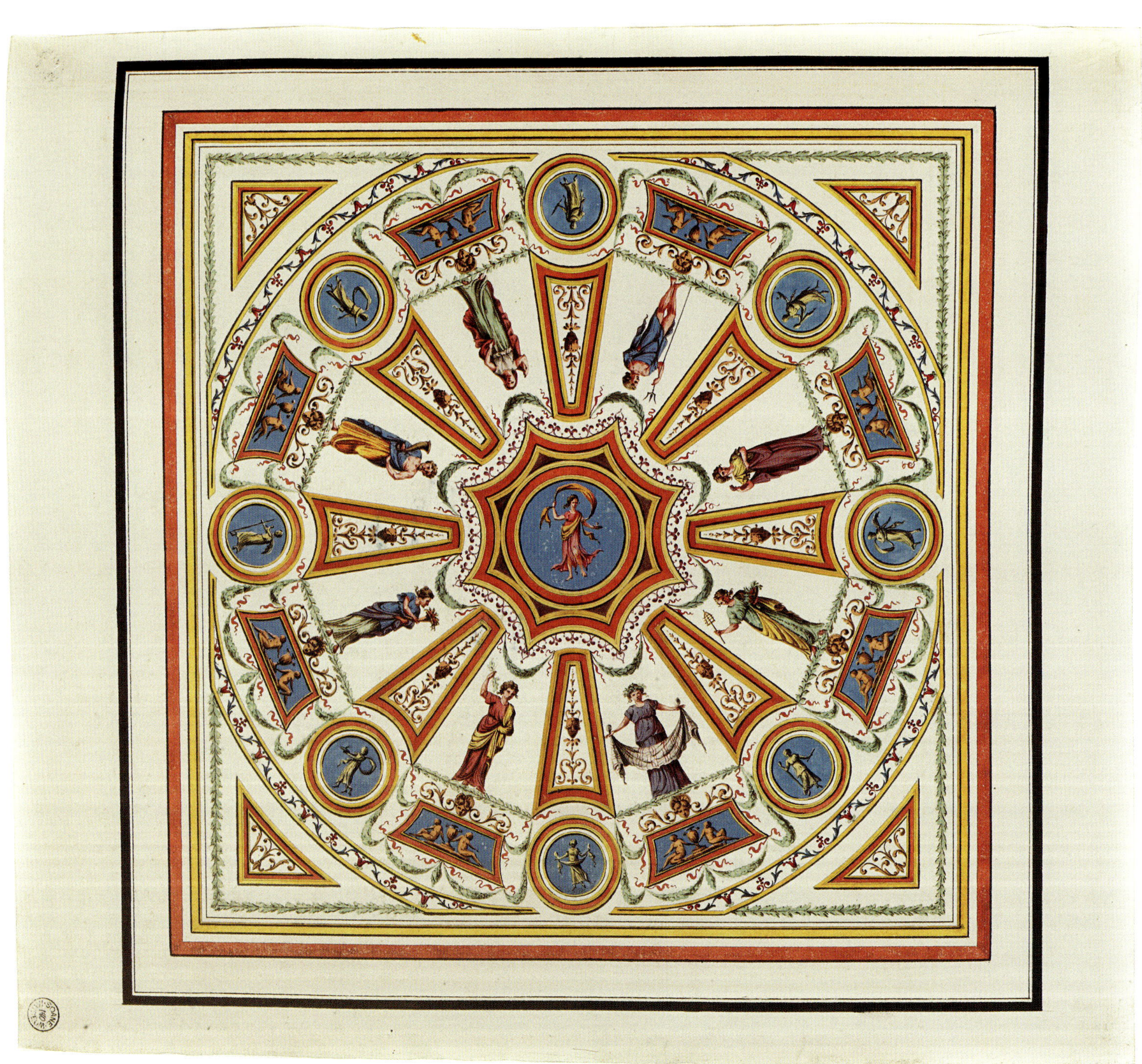

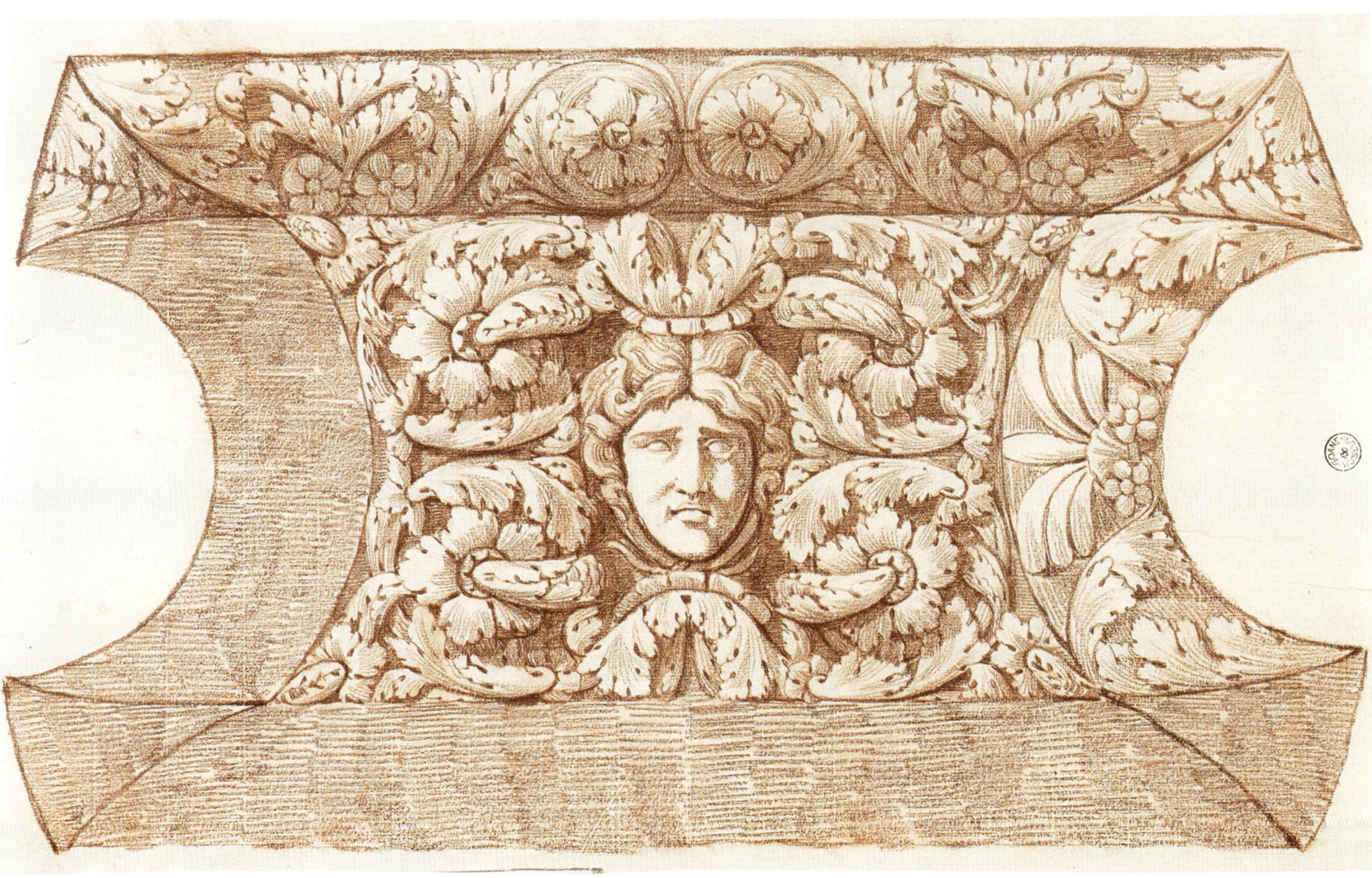

88. Giuseppe Manocchi
Ceiling design after the Antique

c.1762
Pencil, pen, watercolour and bodycolour, with black margins
416 x 464 mm
Adam vol. 26/180

Manocchi's colourful drawings were inspired by classical sources such as this one from James Adam's 1750 copy of Bartoli, *Picturae Antiquae Cryptarum Romanarum*. Manocchi played an important role in both interpreting antiquity and in the introduction of colour into Adam office drawings.

89. Nicolas-François-David Lhuillier (d. 1793) *Attributed to*
Study of the underside of a vault

c.1762
Red chalk
310 x 509 mm
Adam vol. 26/130

There are several similar drawings for antique vaulting in James Adam's collection. Such compositions are not only accurate recordings but are also intended as works of art in their own right.

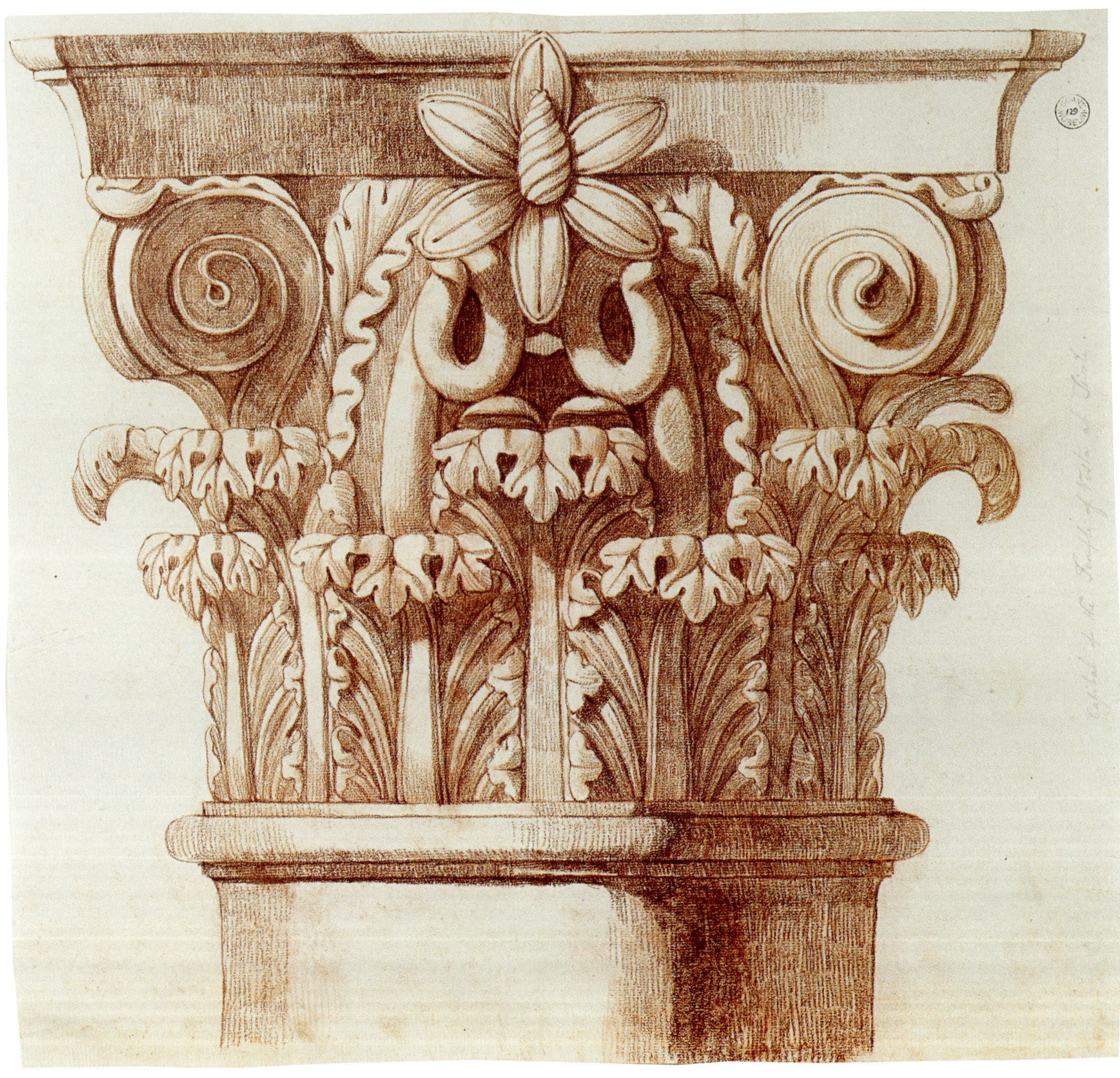

90. Nicolas-François-David Lhuillier *Attributed to*
Drawing of a Corinthian capital

c.1762
Red chalk
411 x 442 mm
Adam vol. 26/129

This would appear to be a drawing of a capital from the Temple of Vesta at Tivoli, a site visited by both Robert and James Adam. The artist has concentrated on the capital, to the exclusion of the fluted column.

91. James Adam (1732–94)
Attributed to
Design for the capital of a Scottish Order composed of entwined thistles on top of a mantling of acanthus leaves above a fluted column

1761 (?)
Pencil and pen
136 x 140 mm
Adam vol. 7/163

Though the capital design is dated 1761 or 1764, it is no doubt the counterpart to James Adam's British Order (fig.94), and, like that one, was intended to decorate his Parliament House. He wrote in 1762 that '...I have taken care that North Britain shall bear its own share in all decorations - so that I will venture to say that posterity would even guess at the architect's being from beyond the Tweed.'

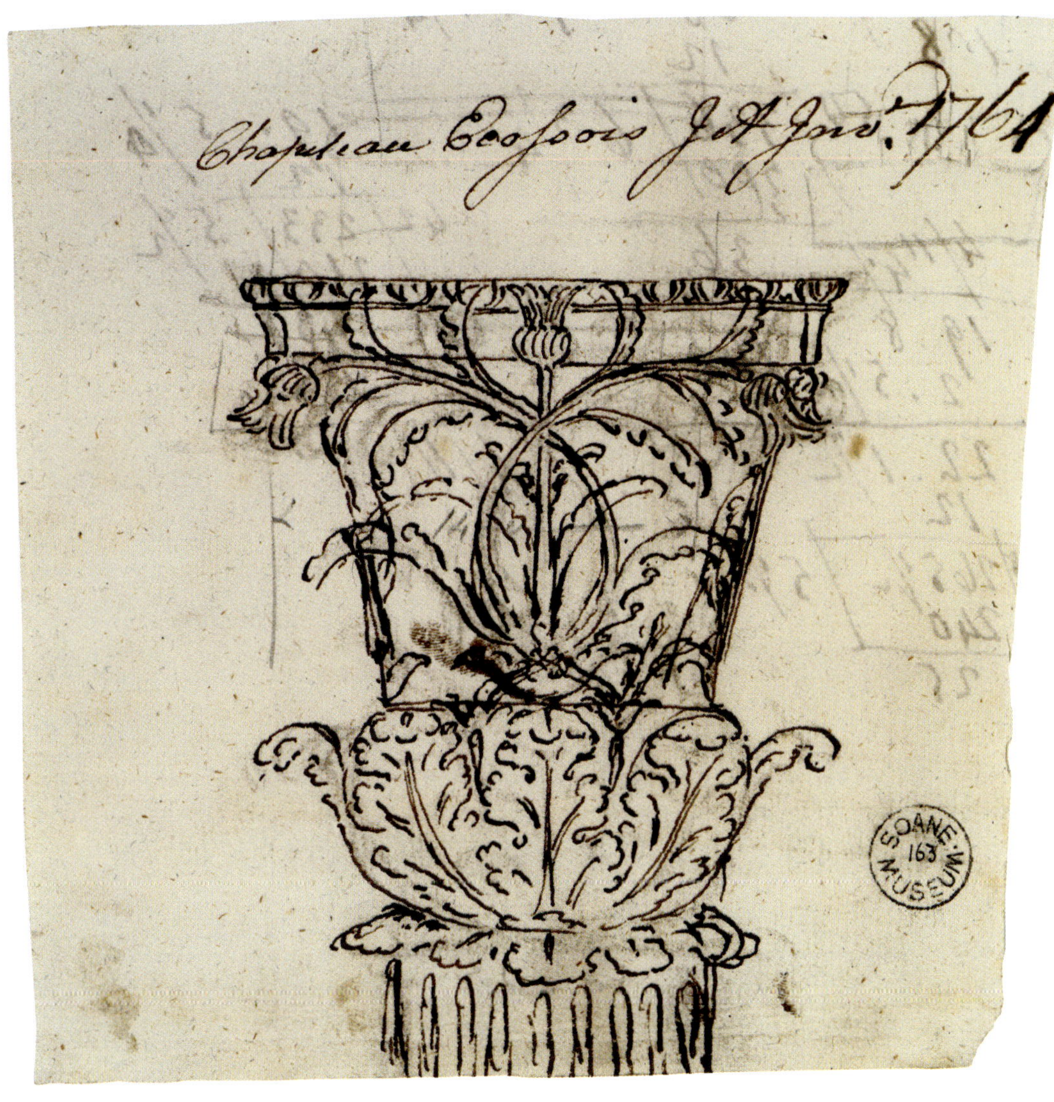

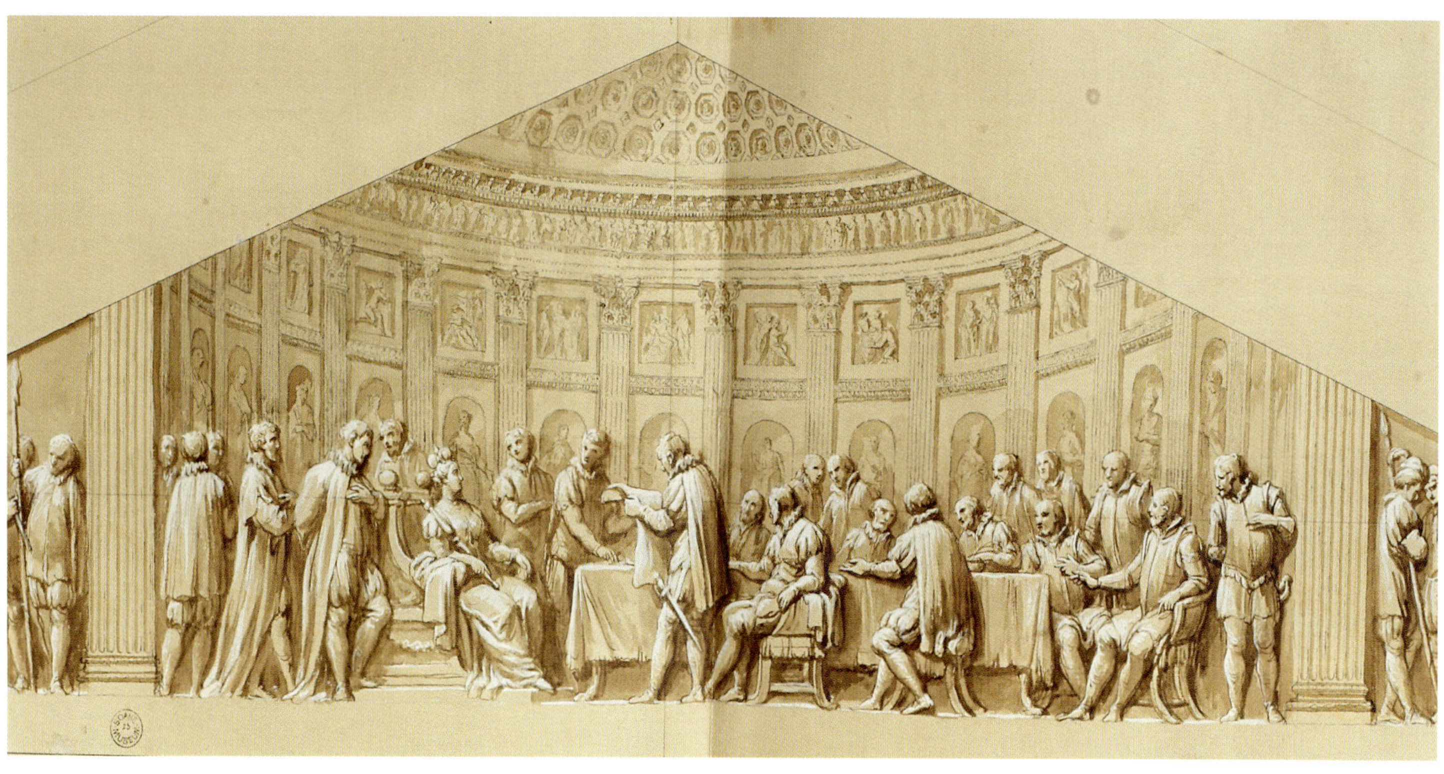

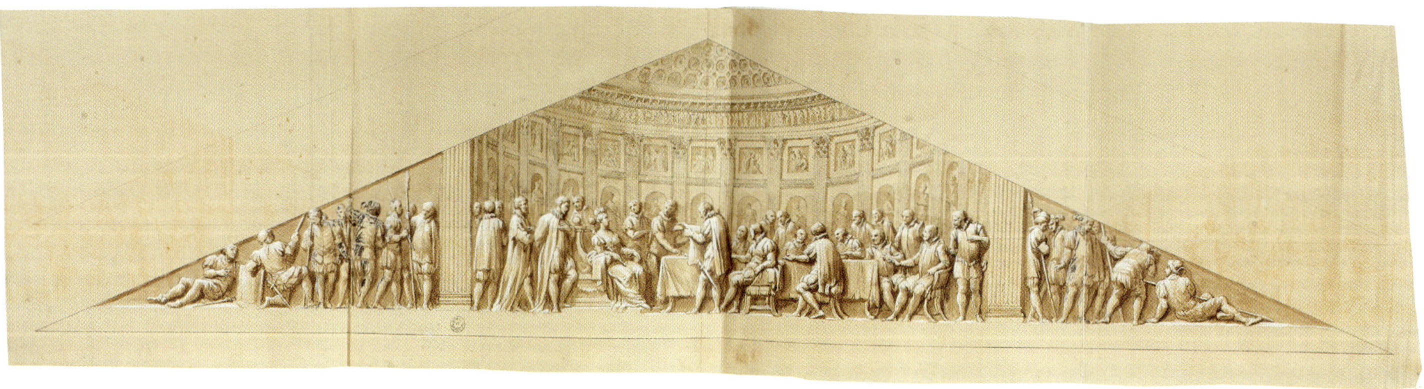

92. Antonio Zucchi (1726–95) *Attributed to*
Design for a sculptural relief for a pediment

1762 or 1763
Pen, brown wash and white heightening, partly oxidised, on brown washed paper
314 x 1278 mm
Adam vol. 7/23

One of many drawings produced for James Adam in Rome for a replacement Parliament building in Westminster. This scene probably depicts the Union of the Parliaments under Queen Anne in 1707. The costume is early seventeenth century, and therefore is anachronistic. The hall in the background is a glimpse of the neoclassical interior James intended for his Parliament scheme, with its great emphasis on sculpture and relief sculpture.

93. Agostino Scara (*fl.*1760s) *Attributed to*
Design for a sculptural group showing a quadriga

1762 or 1763
Pencil, pen and brown wash on grey washed paper
340 x 312 mm
Adam vol. 7/36

Scara was described by James Adam as '...simple and modest, not ambitious, good natured and will soon become skilled in the ornamental way'. In his essay of 1762, discussing the problem of scale, James noted that 'To avoid this in some measure I myself have followed an idea of the ancients and have placed on the top of a high pediment a figure in a triumphal chariot drawn by four horses.' The composition is probably inspired by the quadriga relief of Marcus Aurelius in the Palazzo dei Conservatori, Rome.

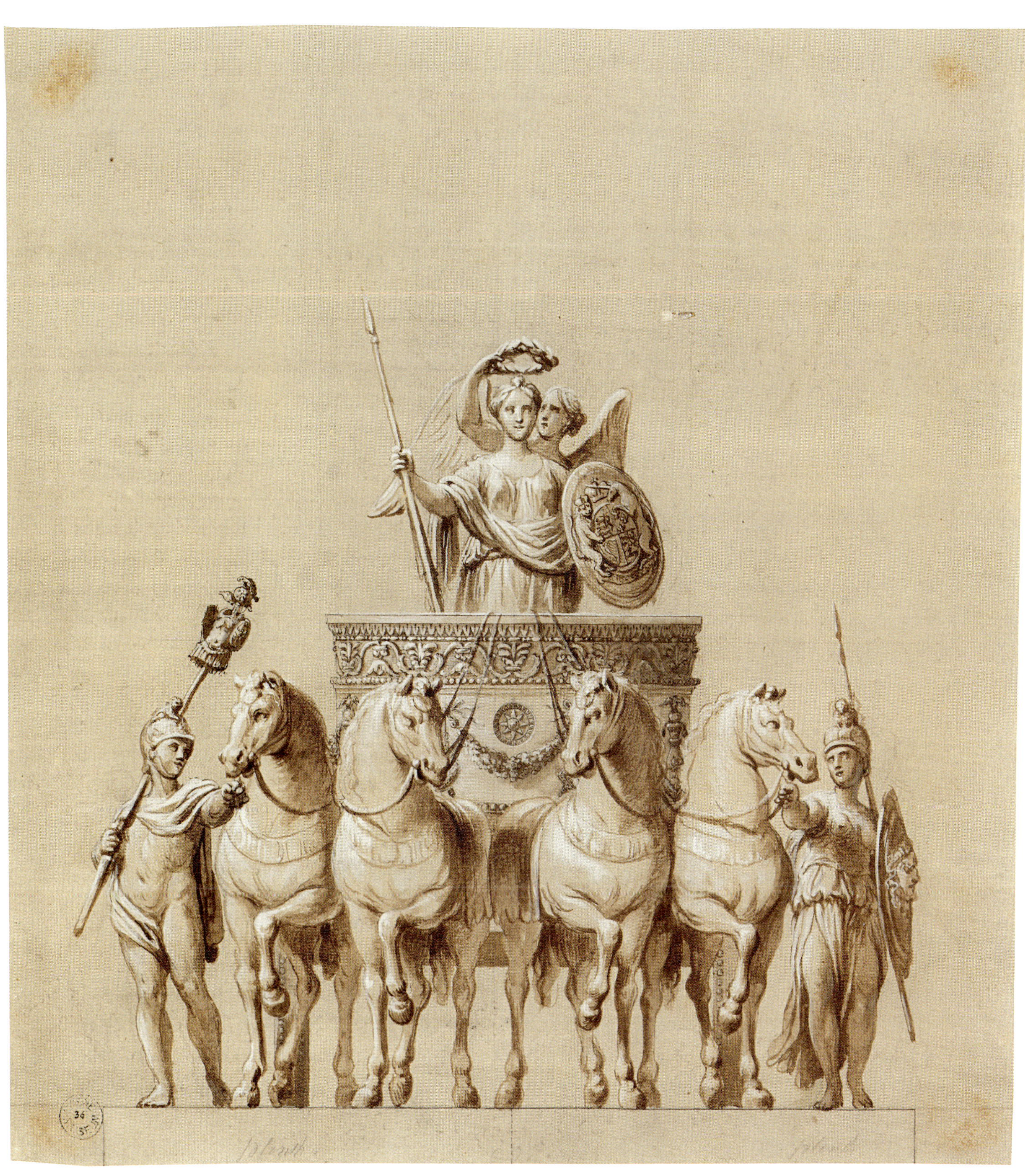
plinth
plinth

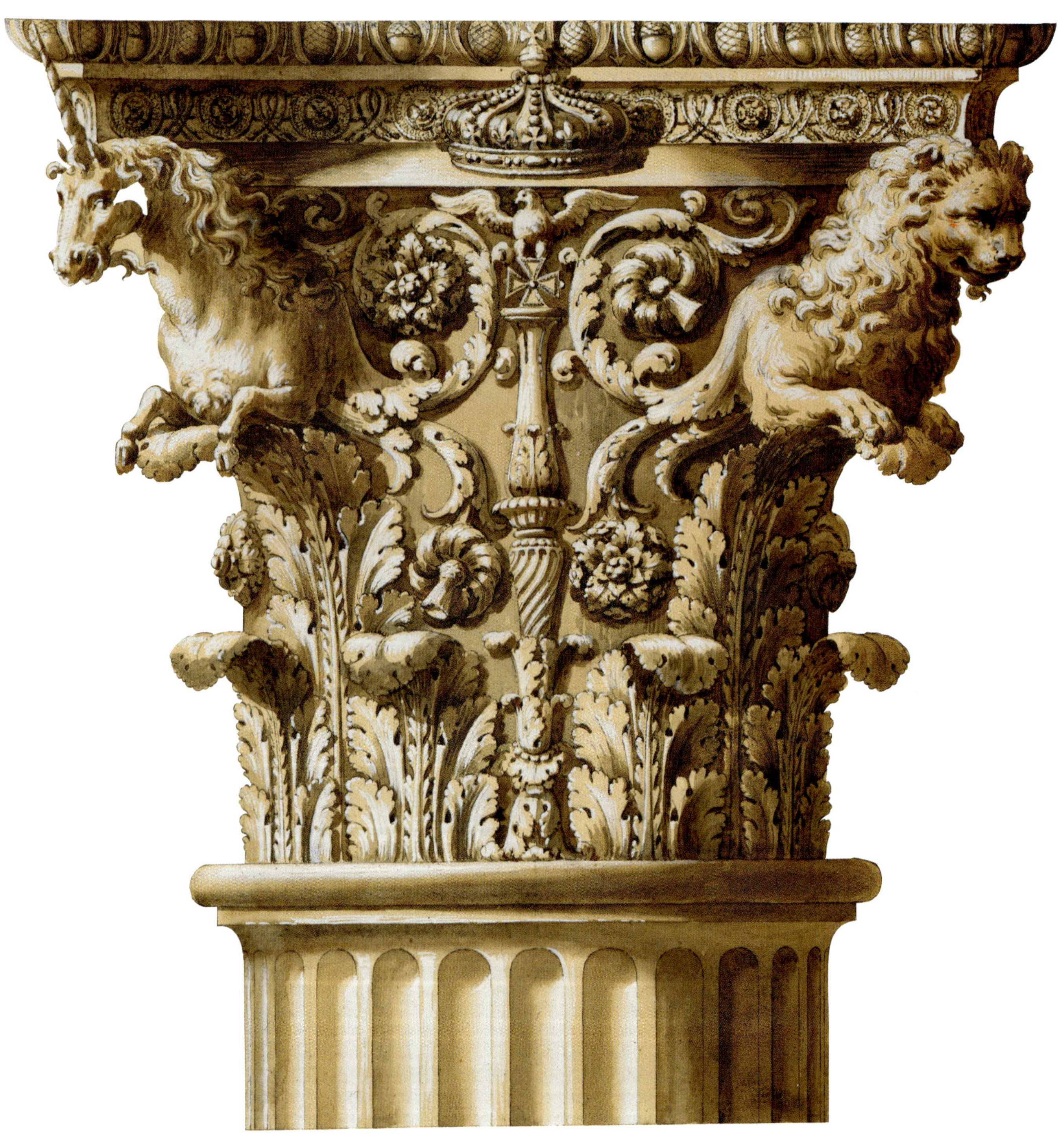

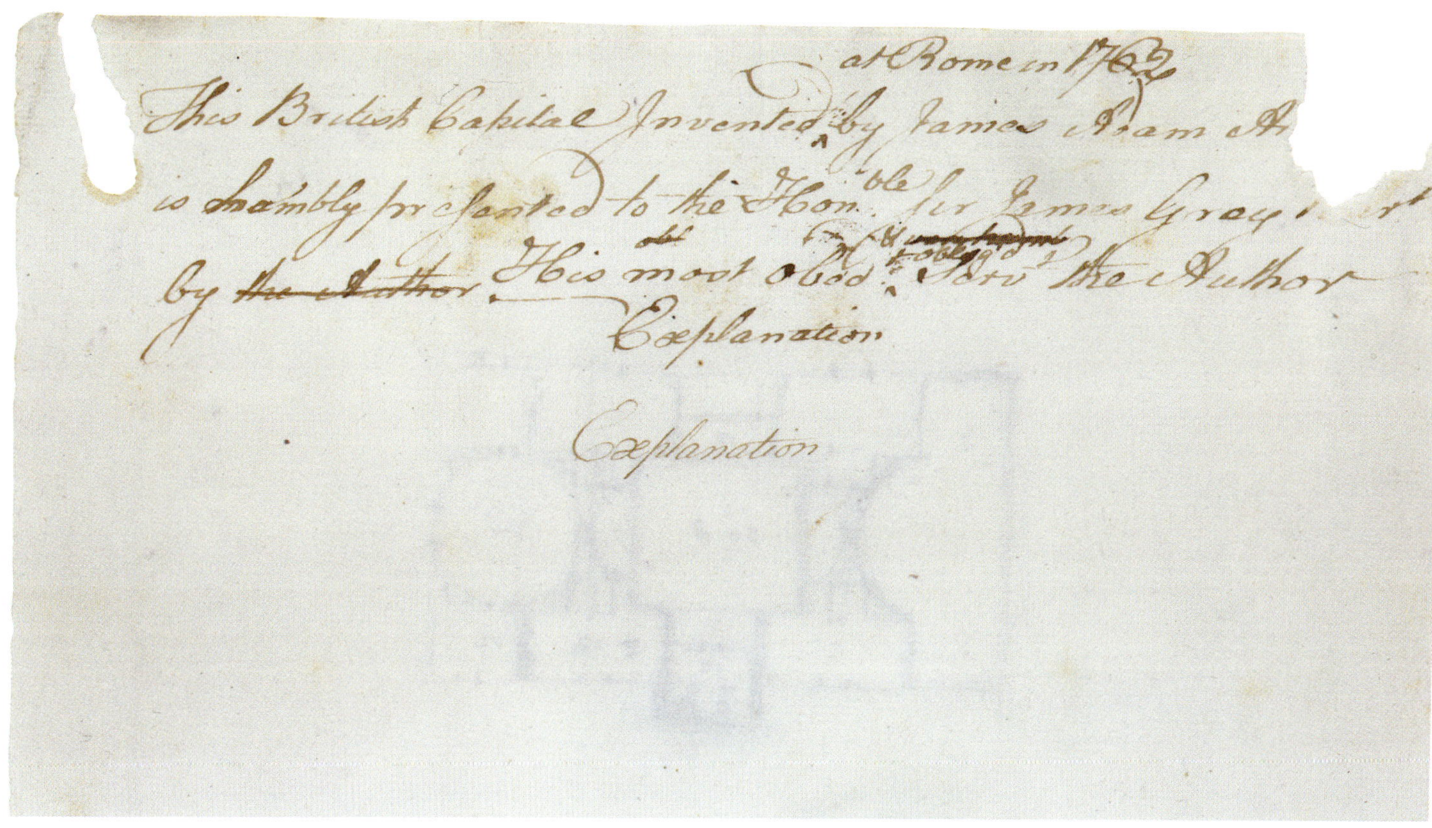

at Rome in 1762
This British Capital Invented by James Adam Ar
is humbly presented to the Hon.ble Sir James Gray
by ~~the Author~~ His most obed.t & obliged Serv the Author
Explanation

Explanation

94. Antonio Zucchi *Attributed to*
James Adam design for a British capital

1762
Pencil, pen and brown wash with white heightening on buff paper
346 x 310 mm
Adam vol. 7/69

This British capital, incorporating a lion and unicorn, was intended for the principal portico of James Adam's Parliament scheme. It also incorporates the British crown, thistles and roses, and the collar of the Order of the Garter. The capital also appears in Batoni's portrait of James Adam of 1763.

95. James Adam
This British Capital Invented at Rome in 1762 by James Adam Architect/ is humbly presented to the Hon'ble Sir James Gray Bart/ by the Author* [deleted] *His most obed't & obliged Serv the Author/ Explanation/ Explanation

1762
Pencil
274 x 200 mm
Adam vol. 7/191 verso

This note appears on the back of a sheet of architectural sketches. Sir James Gray was the British ambassador to Naples at the time of James Adam's visit in 1762, and it was to him and Sir Francis Eyles that James showed his Parliament scheme in Rome, in October 1762. The intended 'explanation' was probably to have been produced on the latter occasion.

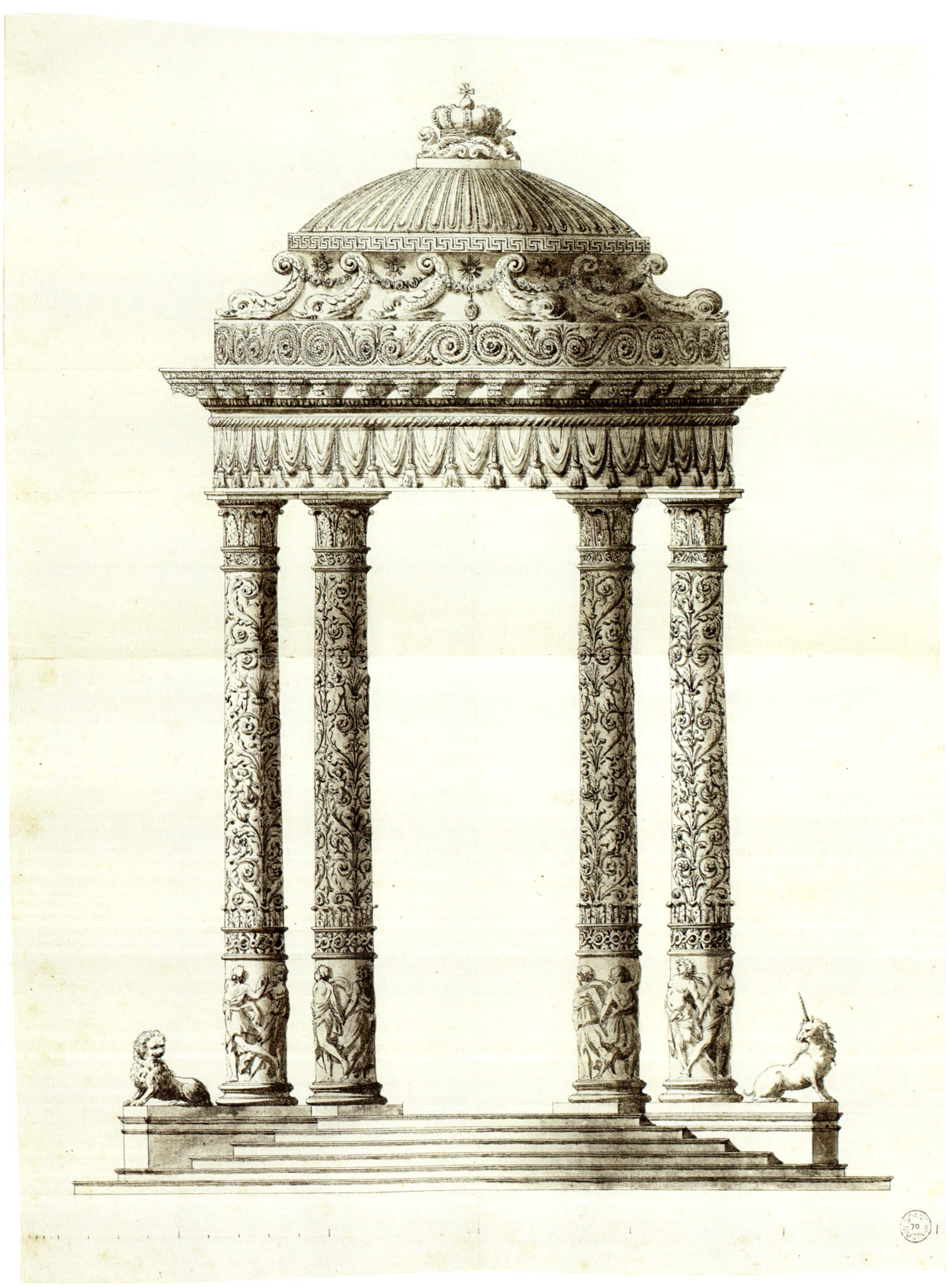

96. James Adam *Attributed to*
Design for a baldachino for the Parliament scheme

1762 or 1763
Pencil, pen and grey wash
533 x 405 mm
Adam vol. 7/70

This baldachino was intended as a grand canopy for the throne in James Adam's scheme for a new Parliament in London. The inspiration for the design came from baldachinos found in numerous Roman churches, of which Bernini's Baroque example for St Peter's was the most notable, and that by Fuga for Santa Maria Maggiore of *c.*1743 the most contemporary.

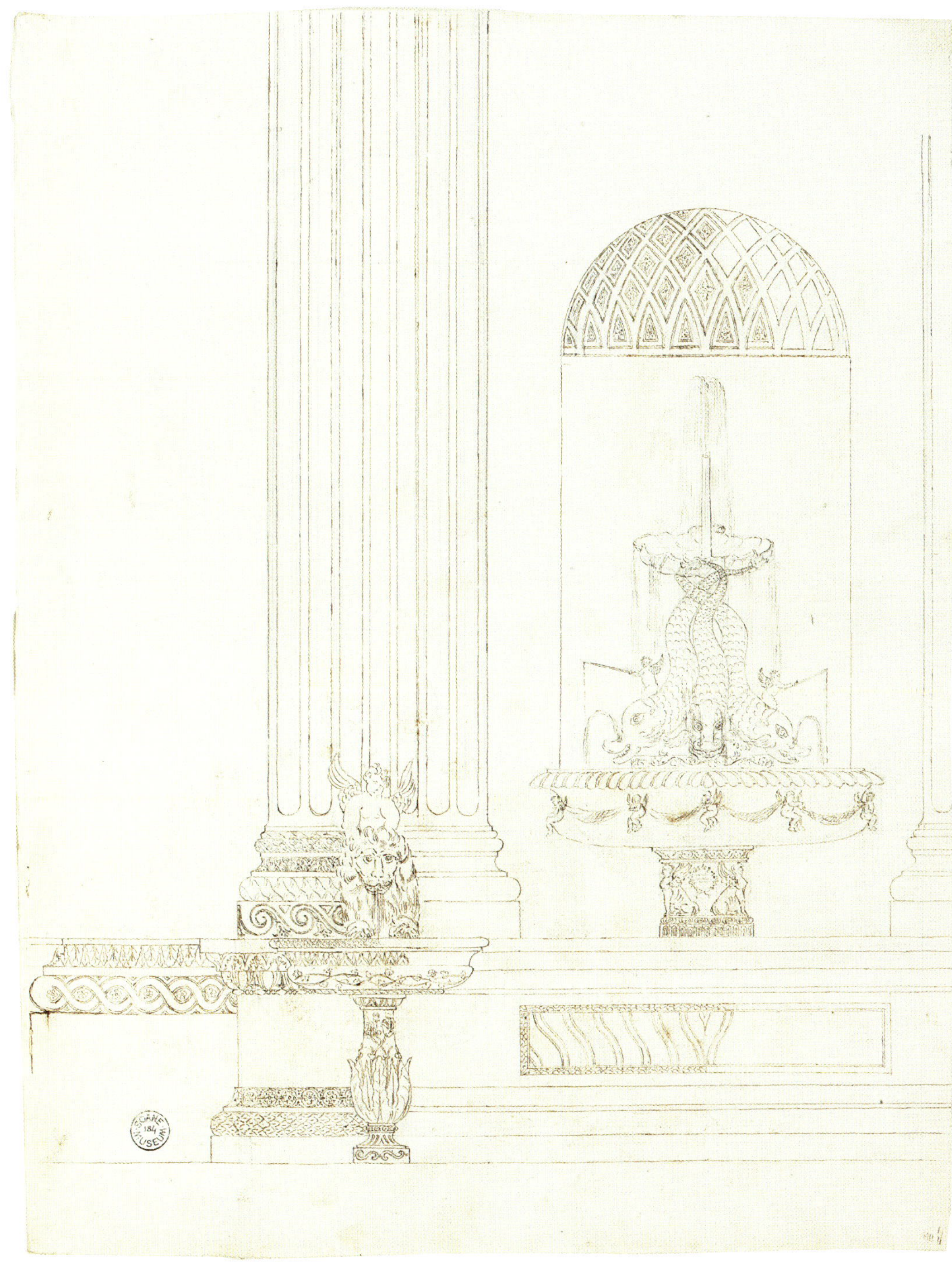

97. James Adam
Unfinished design for a fluted pilaster and fountains

1762
Pencil and pen
420 x 328 mm
Adam vol. 7/184

This drawing is typical of the rather painstaking hand of James Adam in the early 1760s. The fountains and pilaster may have been intended for James' unfinished project for a new Royal Theatre in London.

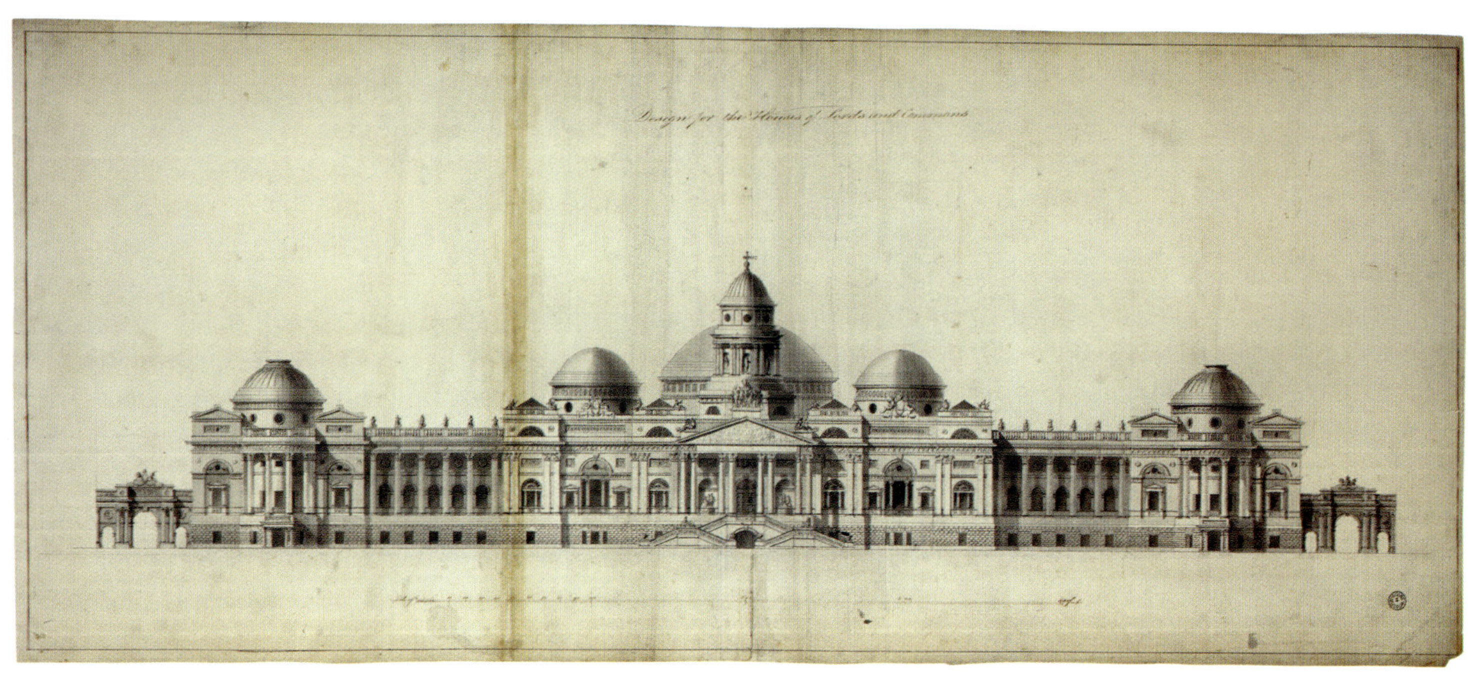

98. James Adam office
Design for the new Houses of Parliament

1762 or 1763 or possibly *c.*1770
Pen and grey wash
467 x 1102 mm
Adam vol. 28/2

This is the elevation, facing the River Thames, of James Adam's scheme for a new Parliament in London. The drawing is a pricked-through copy, possibly of a version of the elevation that he had produced in Rome in 1763. In March of that year, the project was described thus: 'his Plan for a Parliament House is Still improving, creates admiration'; and one of the elevations is described as showing that 'the true Spirit of Antiquity had guided the Architect, as well as in the Building itself, as in the contrivance of every Ornament for it'.

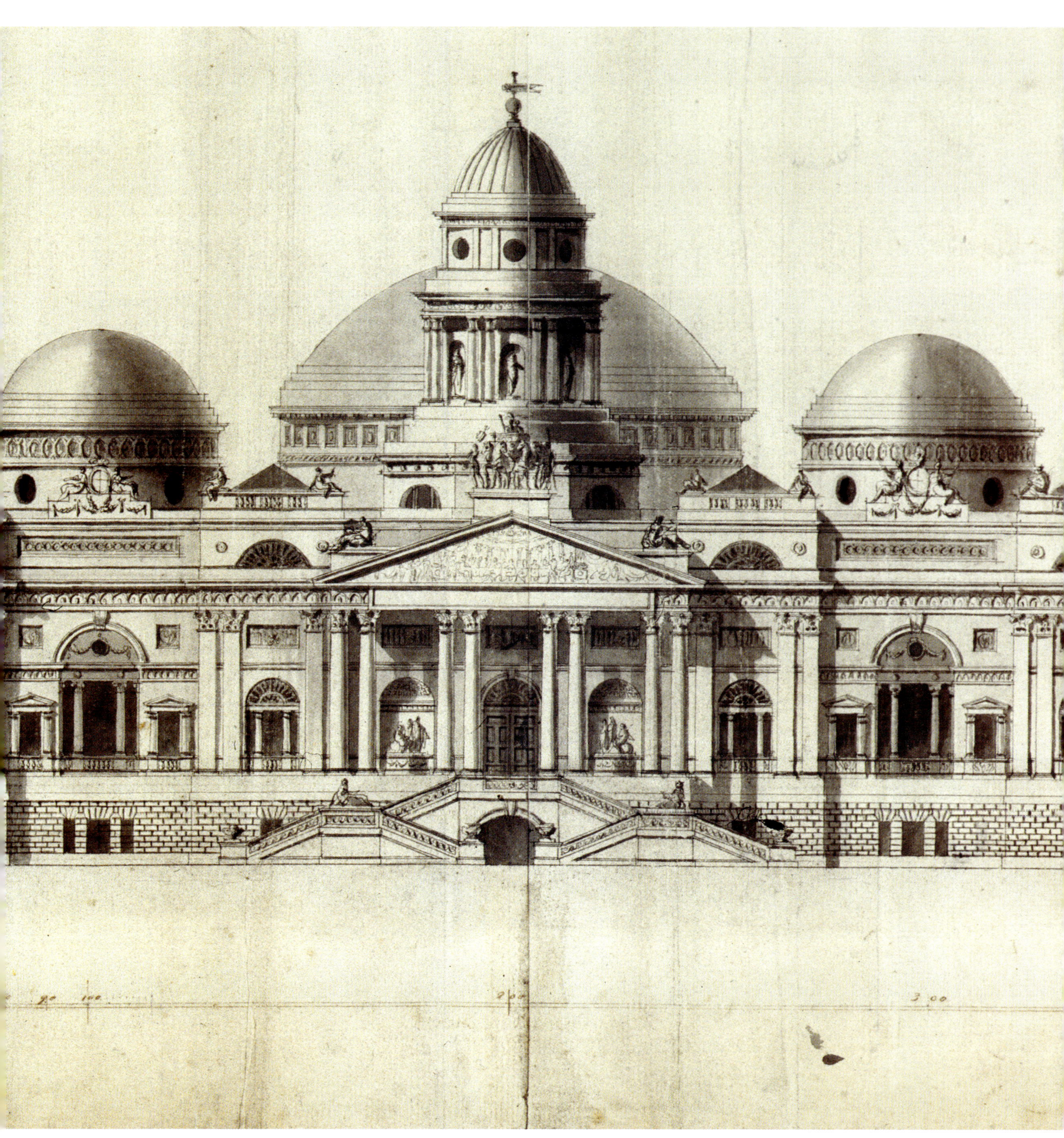

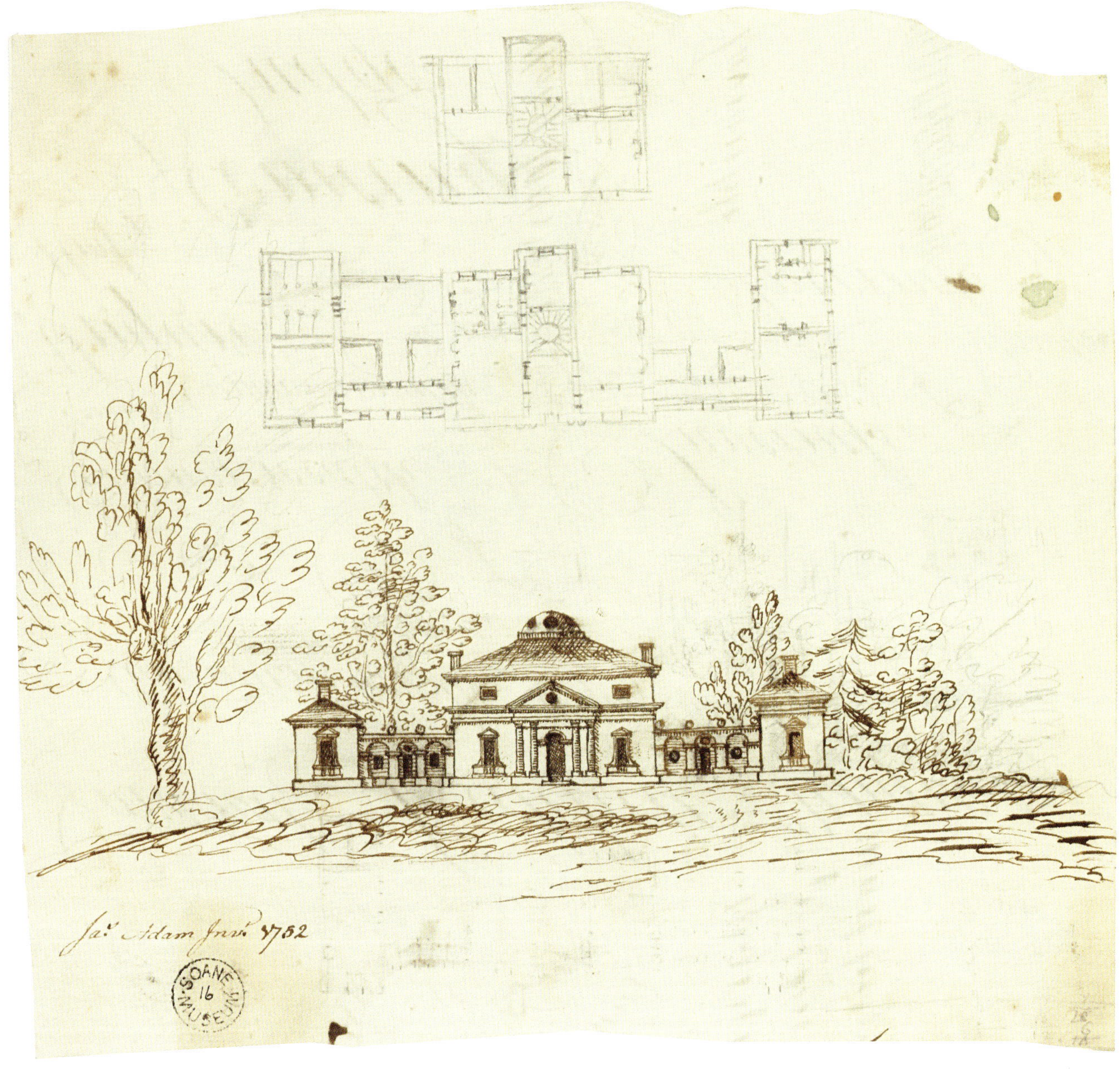

99. James Adam
Design showing two plans and the entrance elevation for a small house of three bays and two storeys

1752
Pencil and pen
187 x 205 mm
Adam vol. 7/16

The small Palladian villa of this sort is characteristic of the work of both Robert and James Adam in the early 1750s. There remain several similar designs dated 1752 in the Blair Adam collection.

100. James Adam
Plan for the Casino at 75 Lower Grosvenor Street

1764
Pen, and grey and brown washes
201 x 317 mm
Adam vol. 7/228

This is a more detailed drawing of the plan at fig.2. It shows particularly the ceiling pattern, as different from the section at fig.4, and the suggested floor pattern.

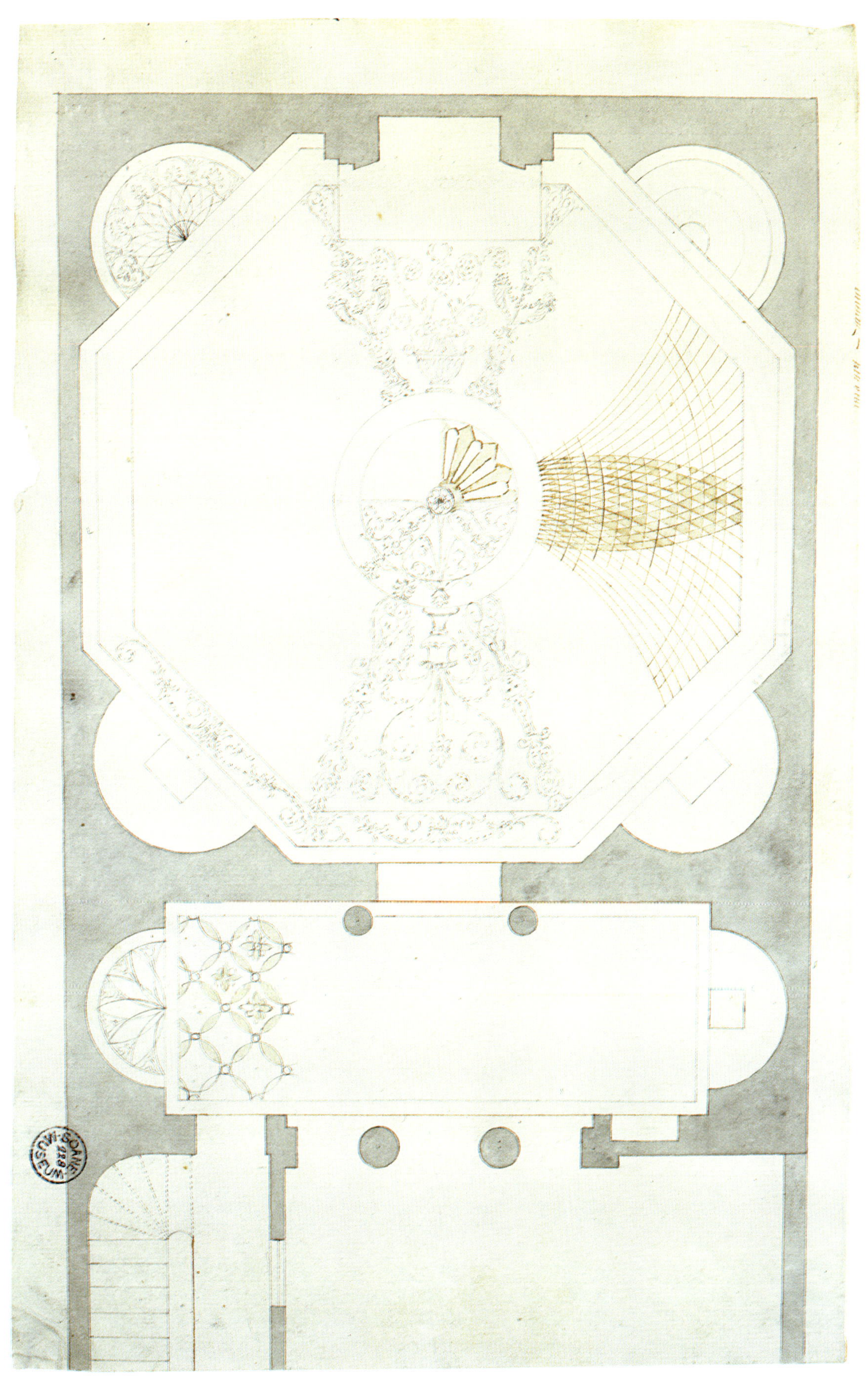

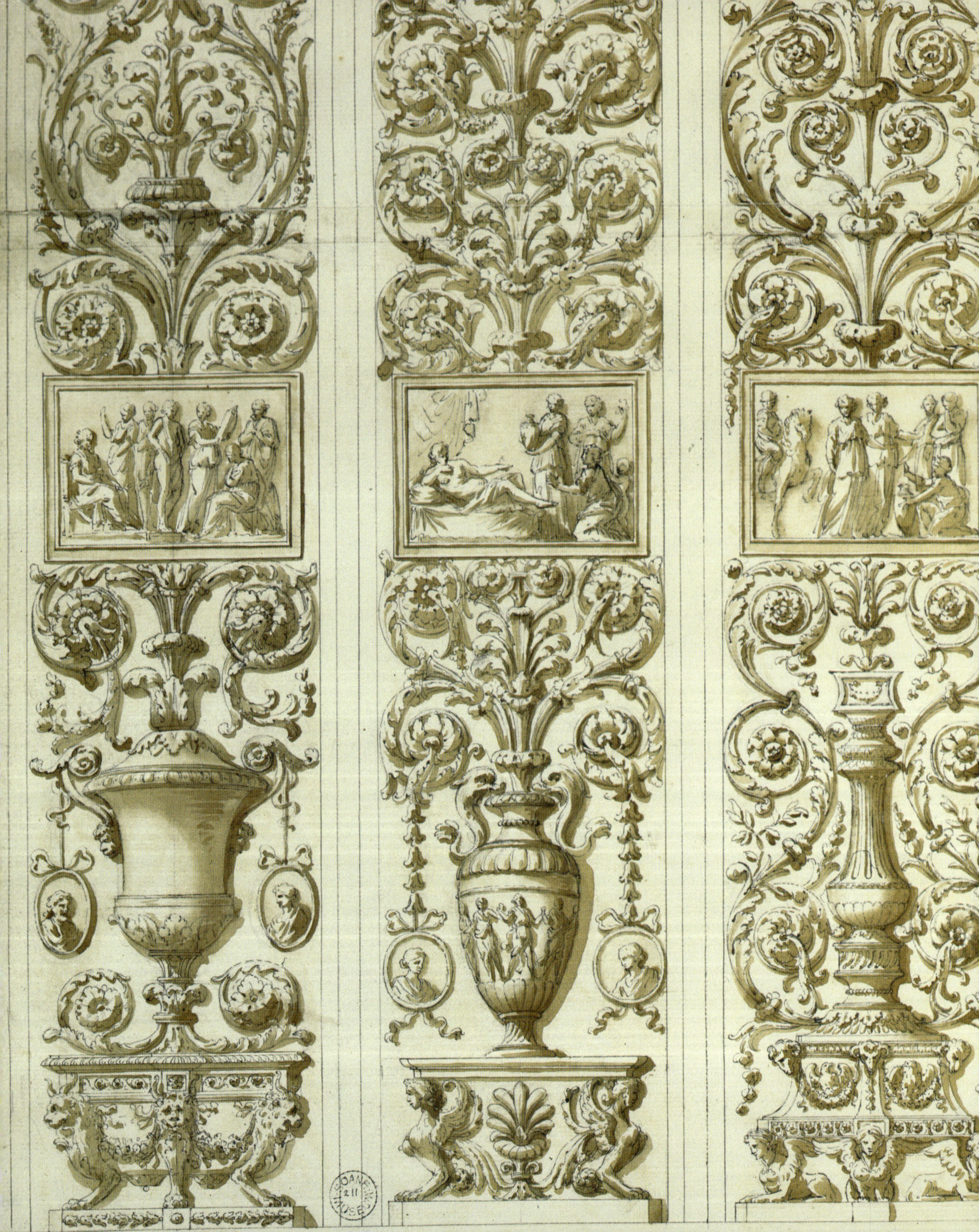

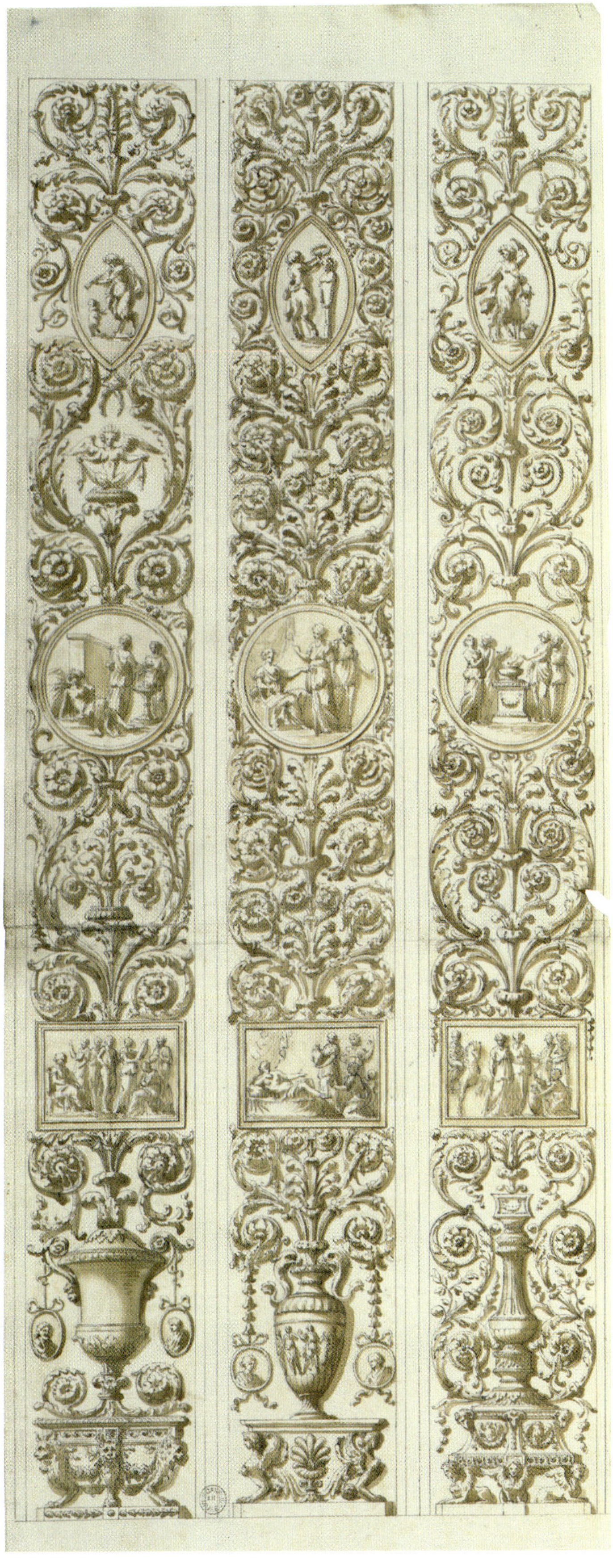

101. James Adam office
Study showing three rectangular grotesque panels, each starting from a vase form with rectangular, circular and oval medallions with relief figures

c.1763
Pencil, pen and brown wash
895 x 298 mm
Adam vol. 7/211

The three panels shown here are derived from the panels in the Vatican *Loggie*, which were also collected for James Adam. There is a further set of twelve such panels, also from an Adam source, in the Soane Museum.

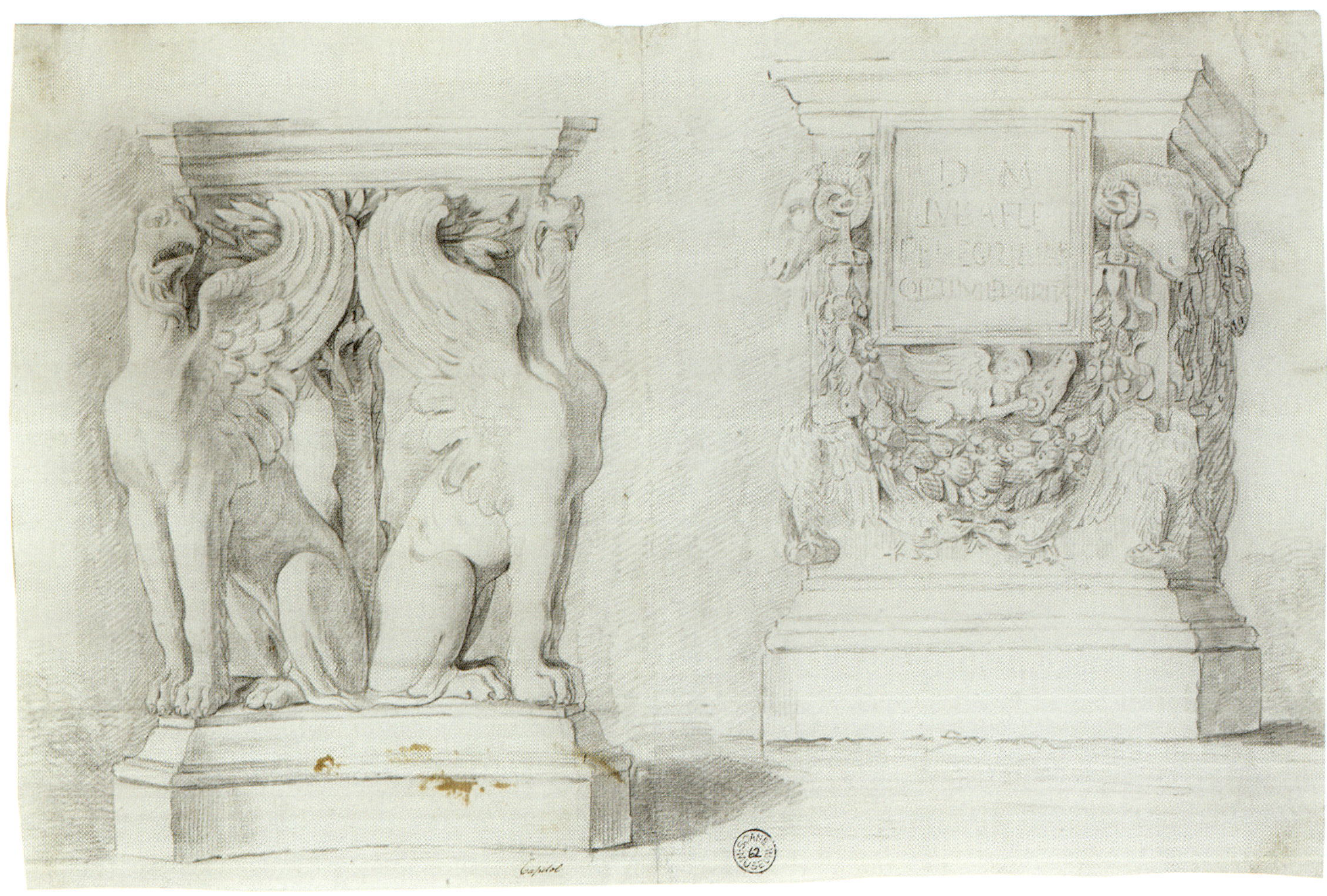

102. Nicolas-François-David Lhuillier *Attributed to*
Two antique studies for a side table, with a concave base and top, the latter supported by two (of three?) griffins beside a funerary altar

1763
Black chalk
274 x 427 mm
Adam vol. 26/62

There are versions of both the table and altar by a similar hand in the Soane Museum. The table may be compared with that from Herculaneum that Robert Adam drew during his Naples tour of 1755 (fig.31), and it is shown as the base for a marble vase in Piranesi's *Vasi, Candelabri, Cippi, Sarcofagi, etc.* [pl. 36].

103. Antonio Zucchi *Attributed to*
Study of one of two marble trophies from the balustrade of the Piazza del Campidoglio

1763
Pen and brown wash on brown washed paper, with black margin
591 x 380 mm
Adam vol. 26/90

This is one of a set of four trophy drawings, all in the same hand and displaying a technique associated with Zucchi. The trophies would have been well known to James Adam through Piranesi's engravings in the *Trofei di Ottaviano Augusto*, and later appear in Adam work at Syon, Osterley and Newby.

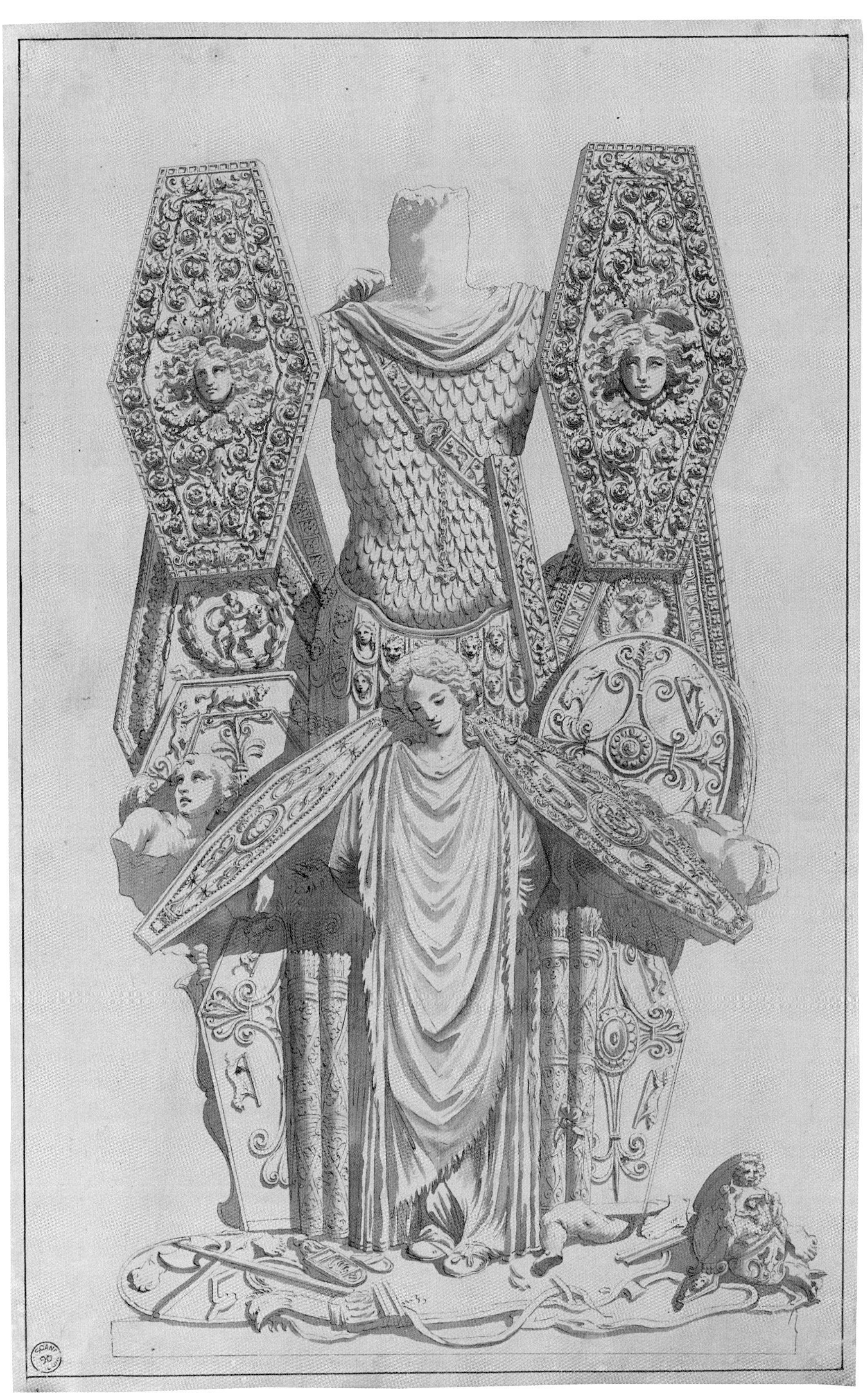

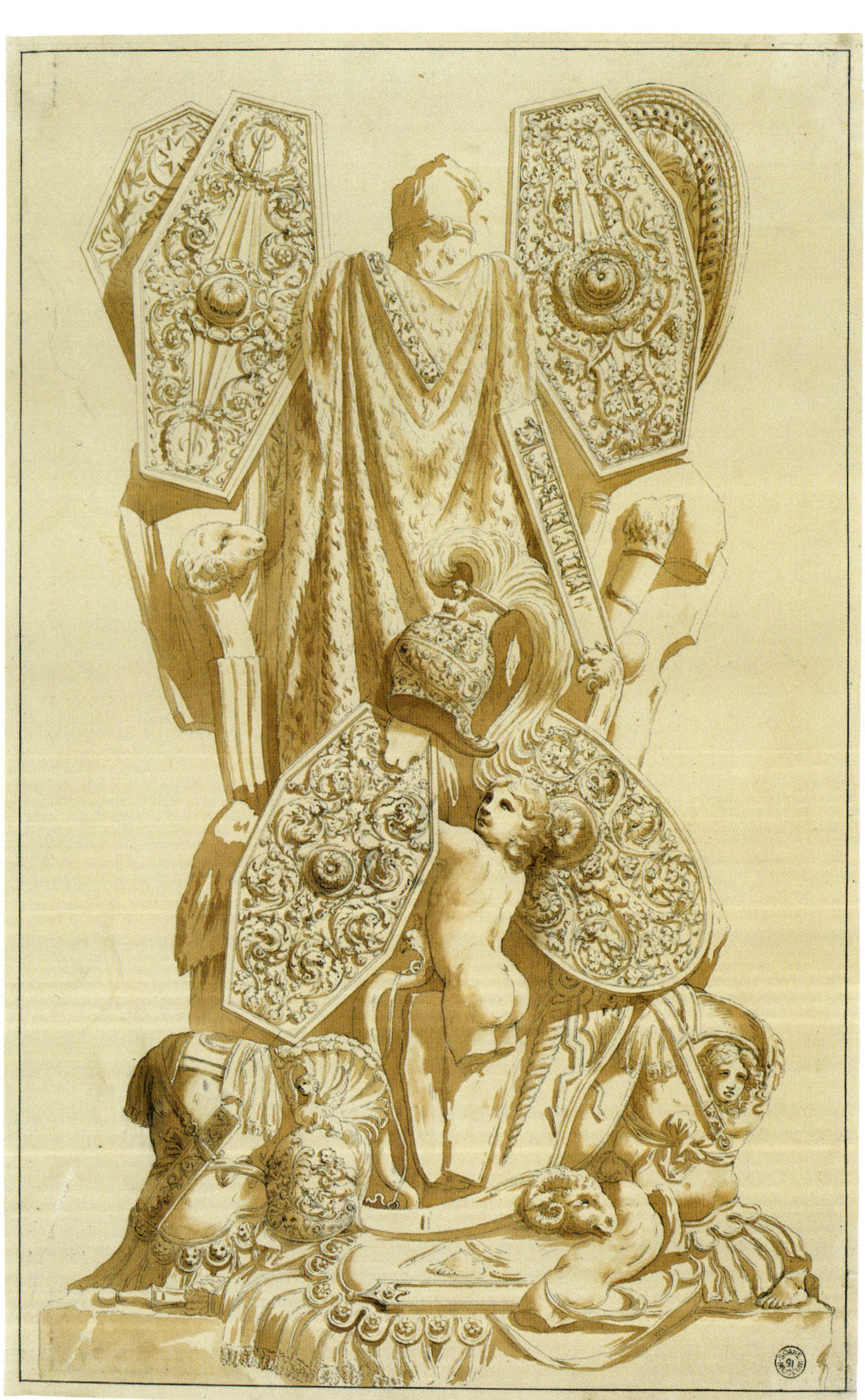

104. Antonio Zucchi *Attributed to*
Study of one of two marble trophies from the balustrade of the Piazza del Campidoglio

1763
Pen and brown wash on brown washed paper, with black margin
590 x 379 mm
Adam vol. 26/91

This drawing is part of a set attributed to Antonio Zucchi, all of which are related to the Trophies of Marius from the Campidoglio, illustrated in Piranesi, *Le Rovine del Castello dell'Acqua Giulia*.

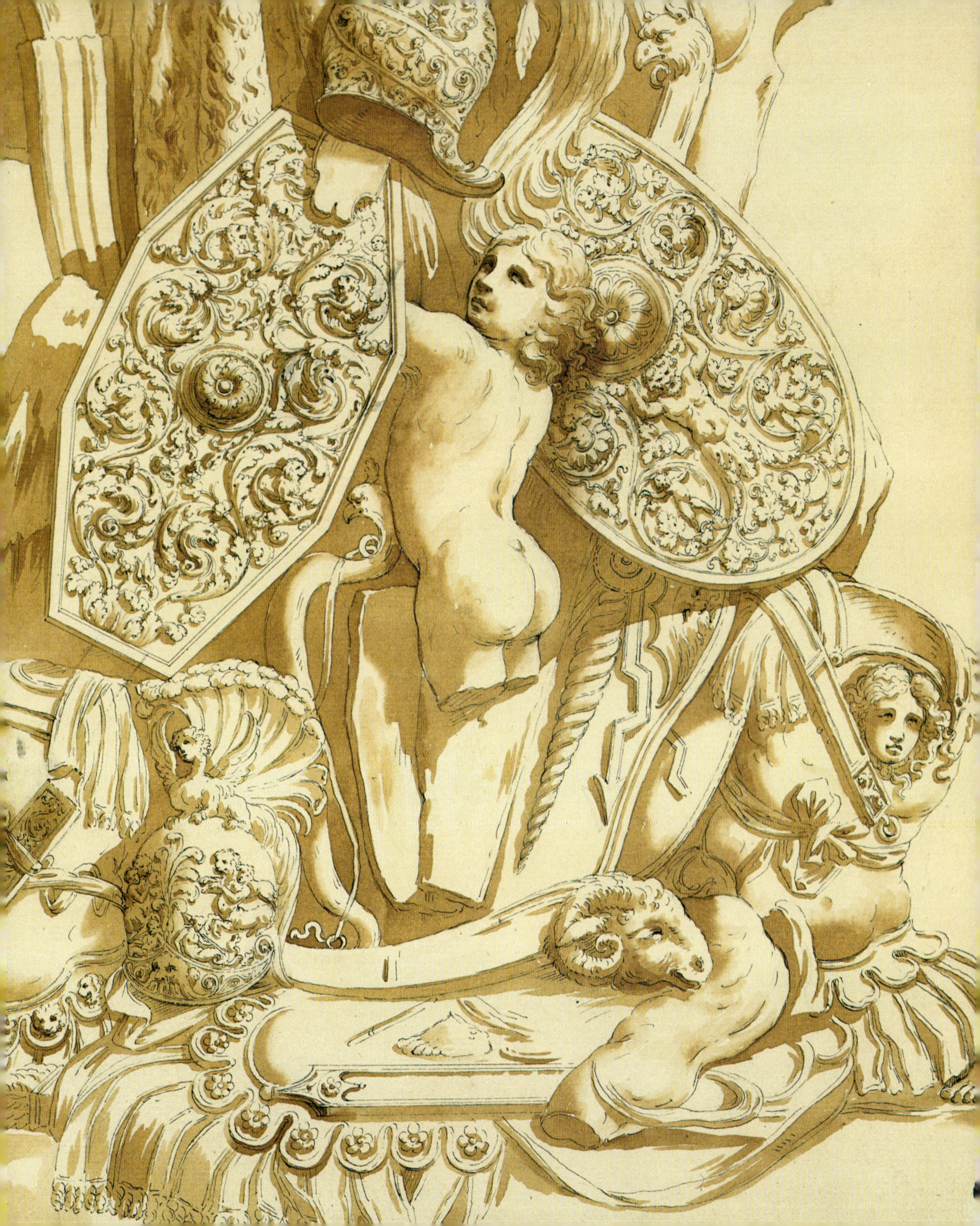

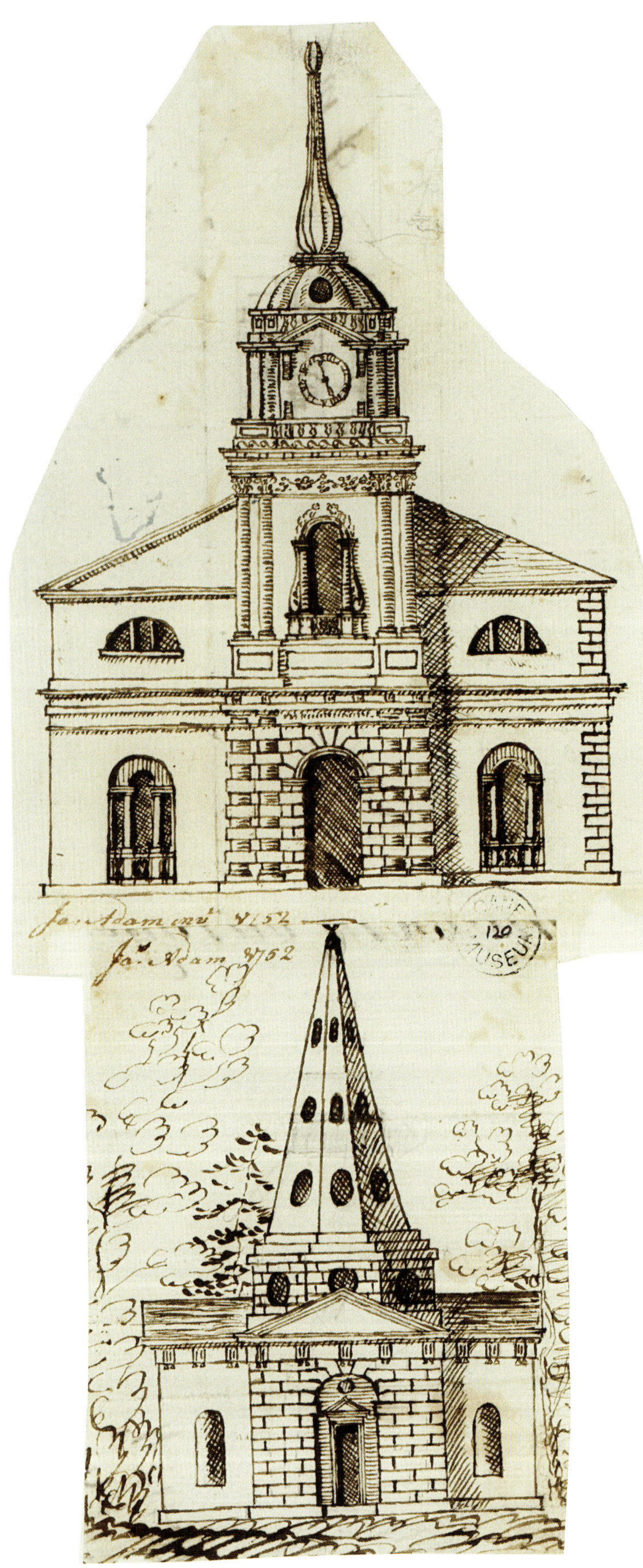

105. James Adam
Study for two façades, each of three bays, the top one for a church, the other an elevation for a mausoleum

1752
Pen
234 x 102 mm
Adam vol. 26/120

This may be compared with several of the Blair Adam drawings that show three-bay buildings in elevation, and belongs to the period of about 1752. The elevations may be connected with James Adam's design of 1753 for Cumnock Church, Ayrshire.

106. Giuseppe Manocchi
Study of a pilaster panel showing grotesque work in a symmetrical composition, after that in the Cesi Chapel of Santa Maria della Pace, Rome

*c.*1762
Pen and brown wash
562 x 200 mm
Adam vol. 26/108

This is a copy of a more elaborate drawing by Clérisseau, now in the Hermitage, which bears the same inscription as this sheet. In the eighteenth century, the Cesi Chapel was attributed to Michelangelo, though it is now regarded as the work of Antonio da Sangallo the younger.

107. Giuseppe Manocchi
Study of a pilaster panel showing grotesque work in a symmetrical composition, after that in the Cesi Chapel of Santa Maria della Pace, Rome

*c.*1762
Pen and brown wash
558 x 205 mm
Adam vol. 26/109

This sheet is a companion to fig.106 and, like that one, is a copy of a Clérisseau drawing held at the Hermitage. The pilaster is now attributed to Simone Mosca.

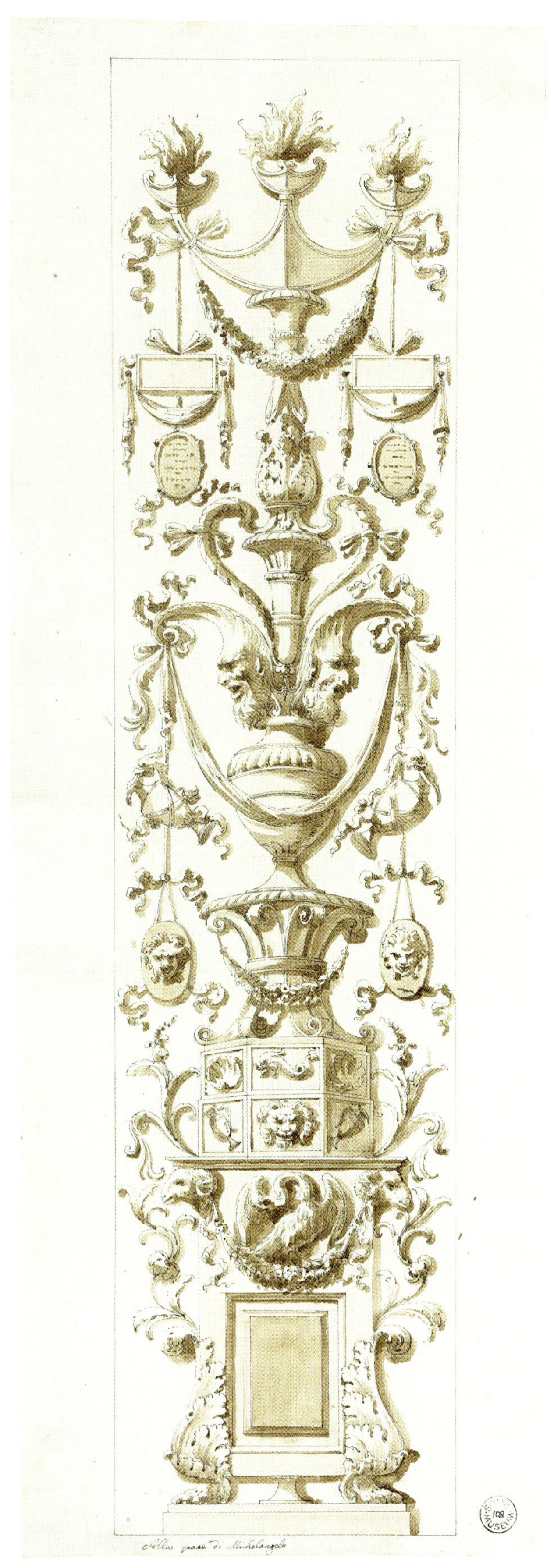

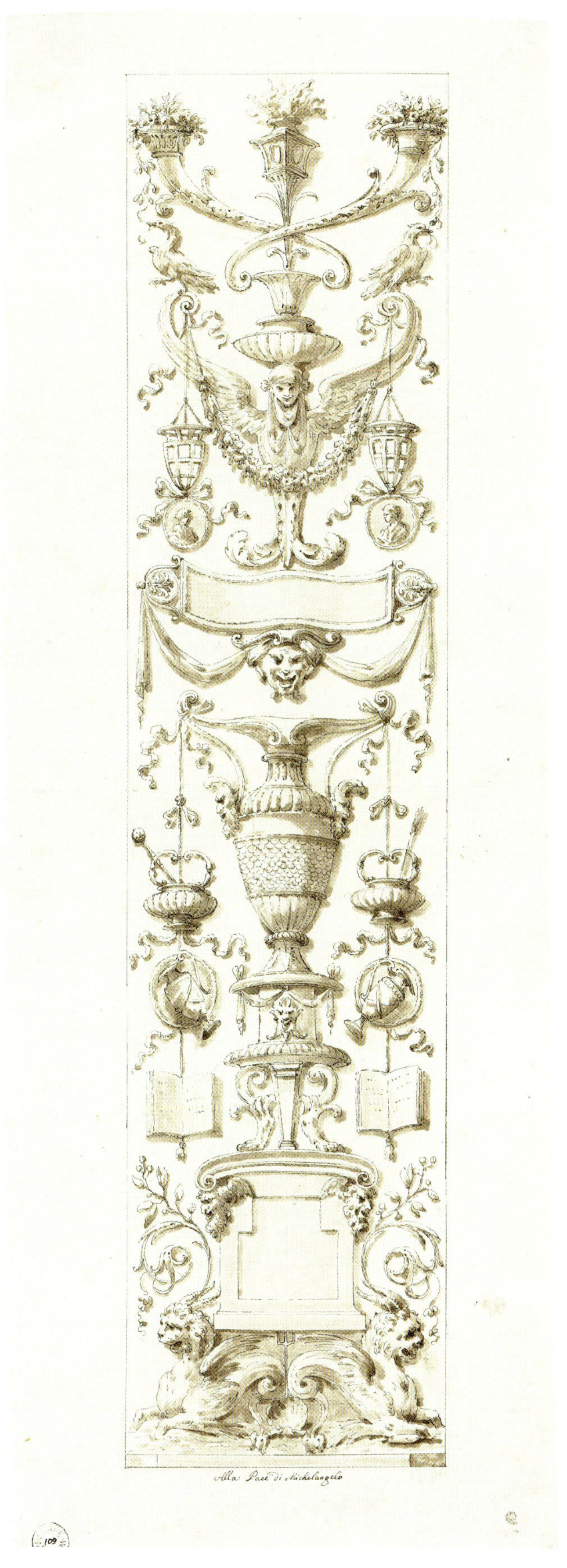

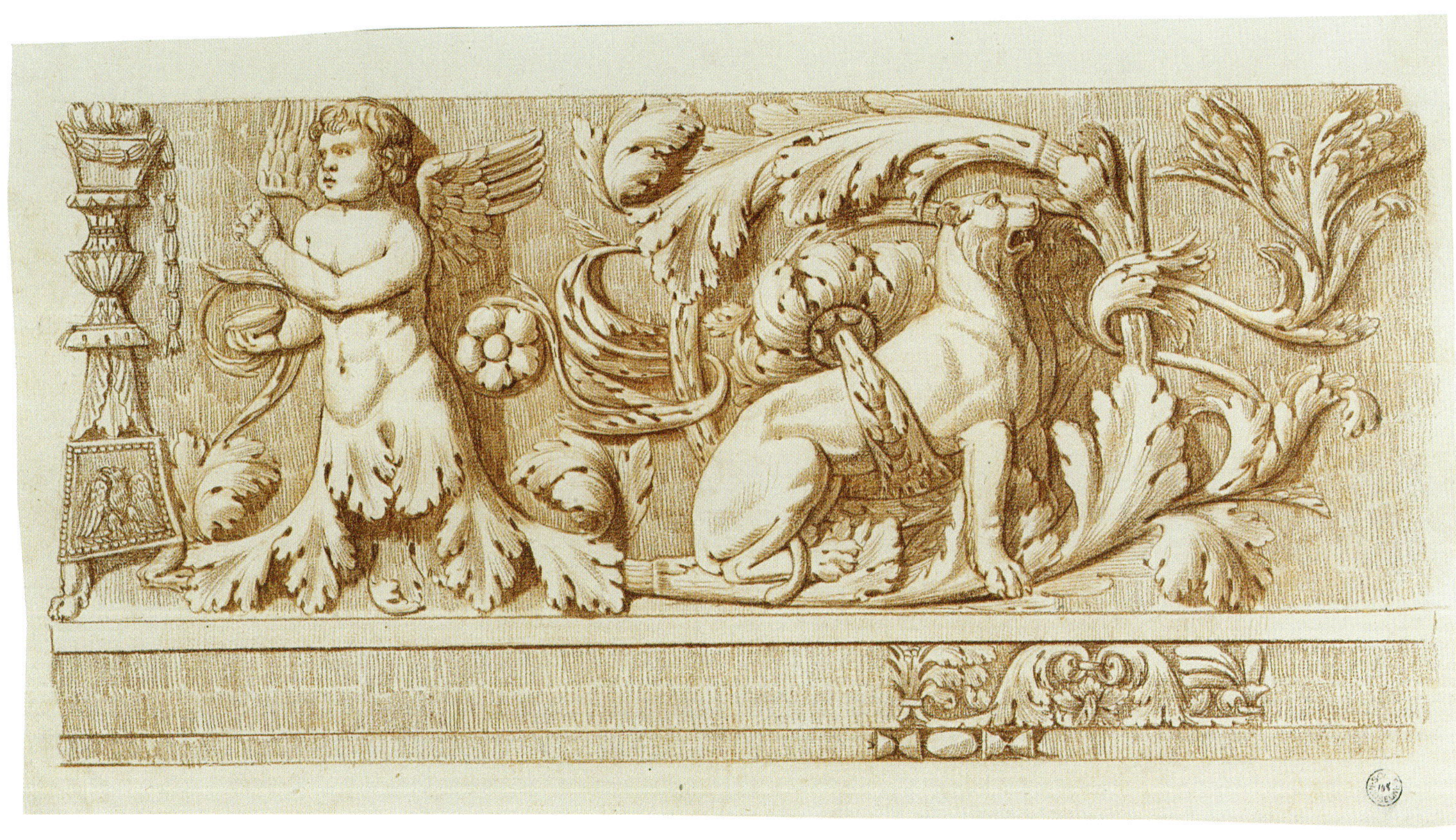

108. Nicolas-François-David Lhuillier *Attributed to*
Study of part of a frieze showing in relief a winged anthropomorphic figure beside a flaming candelabrum

*c.*1763
Red chalk
300 x 550 mm
Adam vol. 26/148

This drawing is part of a large set of Lhuillier compositions of antique subjects that James Adam collected in Rome around 1763.

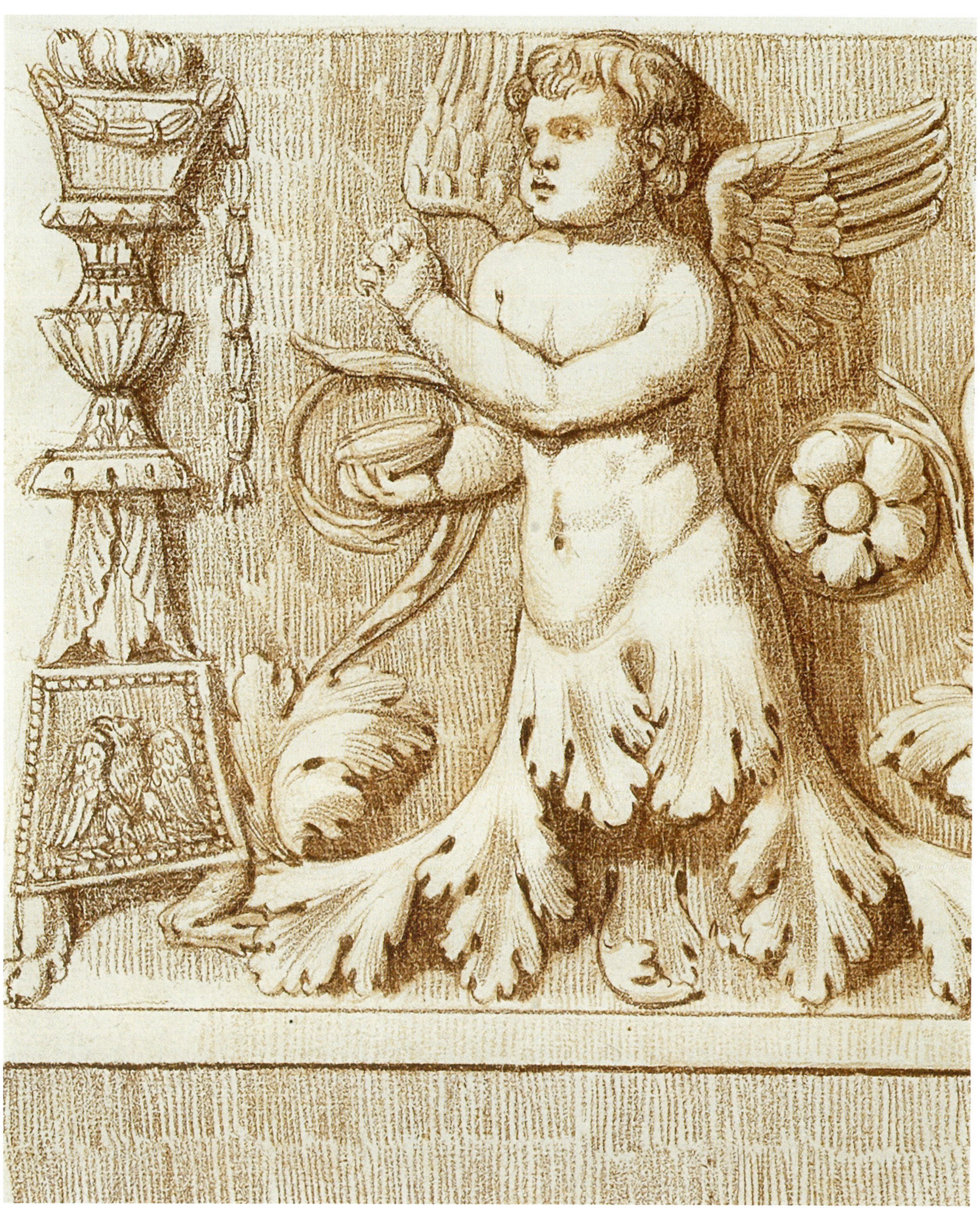

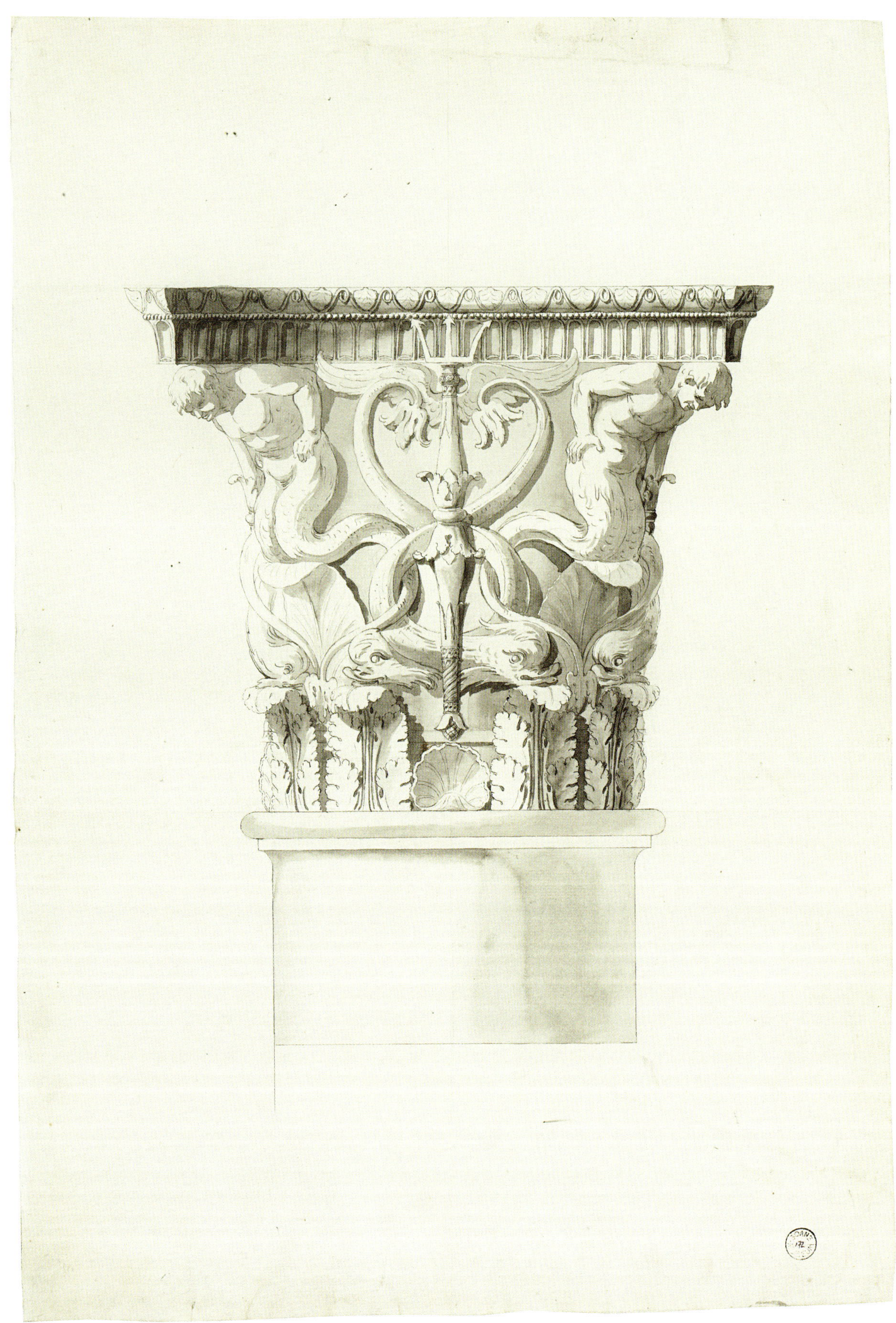

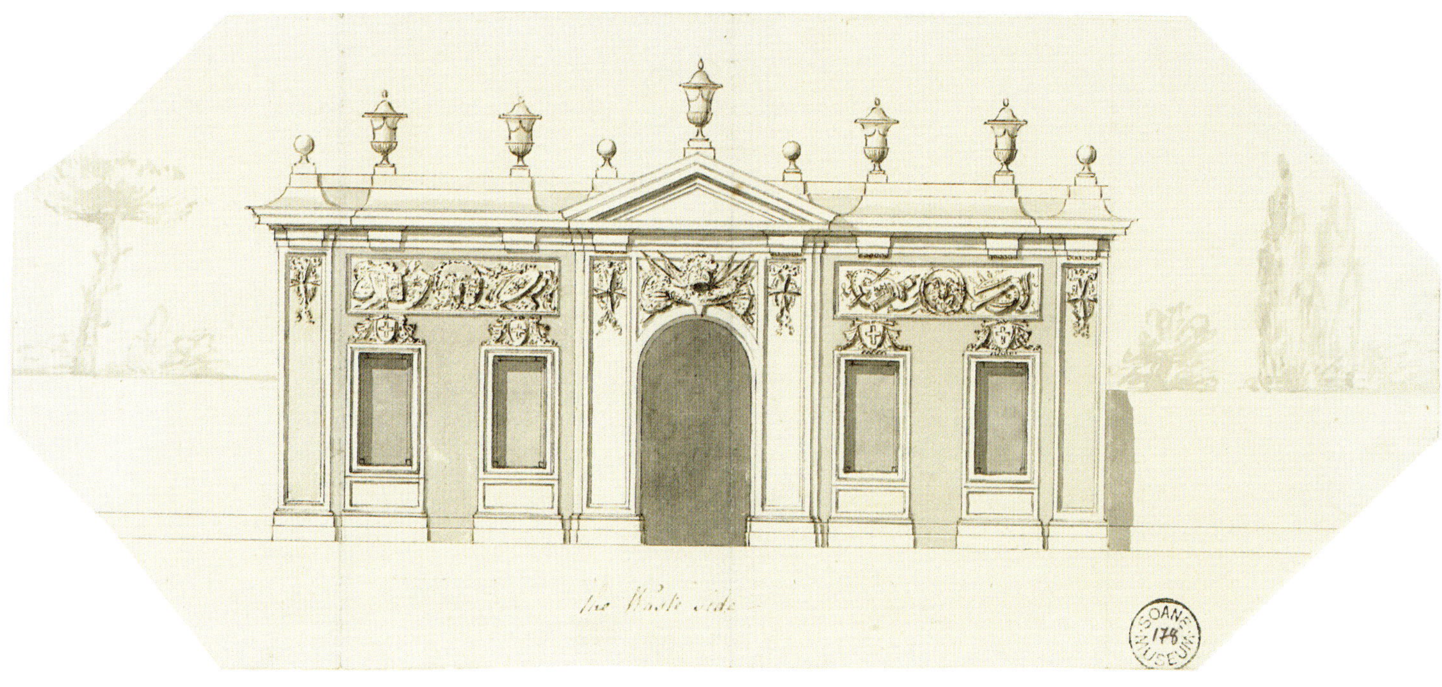

109. Antonio Zucchi *Attributed to*
Study for a nautical capital with two mermen as volutes above a necking of oak and lotus leaves

*c.*1763
Pencil, pen and grey wash
550 x 384 mm
Adam vol. 26/172

This is one of several variants on the classical capital by James Adam, and may also be connected with his Parliament scheme (fig.94). It is possibly inspired by the ancient capitals shown in Piranesi, *Trofei di Ottaviano Augusto*, which first appeared in 1753.

110. Unidentified 18th-century artist
Drawing of a design for the entrance screen or garden front of Santa Maria del Priorato, Rome

*c.*1763
Pen and grey wash
121 x 270 mm
Adam vol. 26/178

This sheet is probably a copy of a drawing of around 1763 and has been trimmed as an octagon. It shows the building as built, apart from the window panels, and can be compared with an early half-elevation in the Kunstbibliothek, Berlin.

Bibliography

Robert and James Adam, *The Works in Architecture,* London, 1773–79

William Adam, *Vitruvius Scoticus*, London, 1811

Geoffrey Beard, *The Work of Robert Adam*, Edinburgh, 1978

Reginald Blomfield, *English Architectural Draughtsmen,* London, 1912

Arthur Bolton, *The Architecture of Robert and James Adam,* 2 vols, London, 1922

Edgar Bowron and Joseph Rishel, editors, *Art in Rome in the Eighteenth Century*, Philadelphia and London, 2000, catalogue of an exhibition at The Philadelphia Museum of Art, and The Museum of Fine Arts, Houston, 2000–2001

Malcolm Campbell, *Piranesi, Rome Recorded,* New York, 1990

Valery Chevtchenko, *Charles-Louis Clérisseau (1721–1820) Dessins du musée de l'Ermitage Saint-Petersbourg*, catalogue of an exhibition held at the Musée du Louvre, Paris, 1995

Howard Colvin, *A Biographical Dictionary of British Architects, 1600–1840*, 3rd edn, London, 1995

Nicole Dacros, *Le Loggie di Raffaello*, Rome, 1986

Antoine Desgodetz, *Les Edifices Antiques de Rome*, Paris, 1697

Lynda Fairbairn, *Italian Renaissance Drawings from the Collection of Sir John Soane's Museum*, 2 vols, London, 1998

John Fleming, 'Cardinal Albani's Drawings at Windsor', *The Connoisseur*, vol. 142, 1958, pp.164–169

John Fleming, 'An Italian Sketchbook by Robert Adam, Clérisseau and others', *The Connoisseur*, 146, 1960, pp.186–194

John Fleming, *Robert Adam and his Circle in Edinburgh & Rome*, London, 1962

Luke Herrmann, *Paul and Thomas Sandby*, London, 1986

James Holloway, *The Discovery of Scotland*, Edinburgh, 1978

John Ingamells, *A Dictionary of British and Irish Travellers in Italy, 1701–1800*, New Haven and London, 1997

David King, *The Complete Works of Robert and James Adam*, London, 2001

James Lees-Milne, *The Age of Adam*, London, 1947

Ian G. Lindsay and Mary Cosh, *Inveraray and the Dukes of Argyll*, Edinburgh, 1973

Ian MacIvor, *Fort George*, Edinburgh, 1996

Thomas McCormick, *Charles-Louis Clérisseau and the Genesis of Neo-Classicism*, Cambridge, Massachusetts and London, 1990

Paolo Antonio Paoli, *Avanzi delle antichita esistenti a Pozzuoli Cuma e Baia*, Naples, 1768

John Pinto, *The Trevi Fountain*, London, 1986

RIBA, *Catalogue of the Drawings Collection of the Royal Institute of British Architects, A*, London, 1969

RIBA, *Catalogue of the Drawings Collection of the Royal Institute of British Architects, L–N*, London, 1973

Margaret Richardson, editor, *Soane: Connoisseur & Collector*, catalogue of an exhibition at Sir John Soane's Museum, London, 1995

Alistair Rowan, *Catalogues of Architectural Drawings in the Victoria and Albert Museum, Robert Adam*, London, 1988

Frank Salmon, *Building on Ruins; The Rediscovery of Rome and English Architecture*, London, 2000

Felice Stampfle, *Giovanni Battista Piranesi, Drawings in the Pierpont Morgan Library*, New York, 1978

Damie Stillman, 'Robert Adam's Grand Tour', *Antiques*, Vol. 83, June 1963, pp.670–674

Damie Stillman, *English Neo-classical Architecture*, 2 vols, London, 1988

A. A. Tait, 'The Sale of Robert Adam's Drawings', *The Burlington Magazine*, 120, July 1978, pp. 444–451

A. A. Tait, *Robert Adam: drawings and imagination*, Cambridge, 1993

A. A. Tait, *Robert Adam, The Creative Mind: from the sketch to the finished drawing*, catalogue of an exhibition at Sir John Soane's Museum, London, 1996

Peter Ward-Jackson, *Victoria and Albert Museum, Italian Drawings*, 2 vols, London, 1979

John Wilton-Ely, *Piranesi as Architect and Designer*, London, 1993

Index

Note: References are to page numbers. Those in *italic* refer to the captions to the illustrations.

A

Adam, James 9, 15, *17*, 26, 107, *148*
  architectural drawings *36*, 127, *141*, *144*, *152*
  at Herculaneum 46–47
  collections 11, 12, *33*, *116*, 125–126, *147*
  Parliament House designs 126–127, *135*, *136*, *139*, *141*, *142*, *157*
  in Rome 63, 125, 127, *139*
Adam, John 9, *36*
Adam, Robert 9, *17*, *20*, *30*, *43*, 127
  architectural plans *23*, *77*, *96*
  Casino 15, *19*
  collections 11, 12, 105–107, *123*, *129*
  dedications 107, *116*
  early influences 25–26, *27*, *28*, *29*, *33*, *34*
  family mausoleum *36*, *70*
  in Florence *90*
  Gothic architecture *88*, *90*, *121*
  journey to Naples *38*, 45–47, *48*, *50*, *55*, *58*
  rebuilding of Lisbon 64, *67*
  in Rome 63–65, *66*, *68*, *72*, *75*, *78*, *80*, *82*, *86*, *87*, *92*, *98*, *100*, *102*, *110*
  Scottish drawings *32*, *93*
  in Venice *119*
Adam, William (brother of James and Robert) 9, 11, 12, 16
Adam, William (father of James and Robert) 25, *36*
Albani, Cardinal 65
  collection 107, 125, 126
Albano, near Rome *86*
Albemarle Street (No. 13) 11, 16
Algardi, Alessandro 105
Amigoni, Jacopo 16
Arch of Titus, Rome *110*
Augsburg, Germany 107
Avignon, France *48*

B

Bagnol, France *48*
Baiae, Italy 46, 47, *52*
Bartoli, Pietro Santi *133*
Batoni, Pompeo 127, *139*
Bernini, Gian Lorenzo *141*
Blair Adam, Kinross 25, *28*, *29*, *43*, *93*, *121*, *144*
Bologna, Italy 16
Bragge, Dr *28*
Bramante, Donato 65
Brunias, Agostino 64, 107
Bute, John Stuart, 3rd Earl of 127

C

Campus Martius, Rome *113*
Capua, Italy 46, *55*
Carlton House, London 127
Caroline, Queen 26, *34*
Casa Guarnieri, Rome 63, 65, *66*, 107, 125
Casino at Lower Grosvenor Street 15, 16, *19*, 126, *144*
Catherine Street, London 16
Cesi Chapel, Santa Maria della Pace *152*
Chatelain, J.-B.-C. *28*
Clérisseau, Charles-Louis 9, *13*
  drawing instruction 63, 64, 65, *72*, *92*, *94*, 106
  with James Adam 125
  journey to Naples 45–47, *51*, *52*, *53*, *55*, *57*, *58*, *60*
  in Rome *78*, *80*, *84*, *85*, *86*, *96*, *113*, *152*
Clerk, John 25, 65, 105, 106
Clerk, Susan 11, 12
Colonna Gardens, Rome *130*
Cortona, Pietro Berrettini da 106
Cumnock Church, Ayrshire *152*
Cunego, Domenico 125, 126
Curzon, Sir Nathaniel 16

D

Desgodetz, Antoine 16, 64, 126
Dewez, Laurent-Benoît 64, 107
  drawing instruction 12, 65, *72*, *77*, *92*, *100*, *102*
Domenichino 16, 125
Domus Augustiana, Rome *85*
Duff House, Banff *36*
Dughet, Gaspard *28*, *29*

E

Elgin Cathedral, Scotland 26, *32*
Eyles, Sir Francis *139*

F

Fano, Italy *87*
Florence 45, *90*
Fontana, Carlo 107
Fort George, Scotland 25–26
Frascati, Italy 47
Fuga, Ferdinando *141*

G

Genoa, Italy 45
Gentili, Antonio *131*
George III 15, 125
Gibson Craig, Wardlaw and Dalziel (lawyers) 11, 12
Grant, Abbé 105, 125
Gray, Sir James *139*
Greyfriars Churchyard, Edinburgh *36*

H

Hadrian's Villa, Tivoli 64
Hawthornden Castle, Midlothian 26, *31*, *39*
Haymarket Theatre, London 127
Herculaneum 45, 46–47, *55*

I

Inverary Castle, Scotland 26

J

Jenkins, Thomas 105

K

Kent, William 26, *34*

L

Lallemand, Jean-Baptiste 9, *60*, *78*, *88*, 106, *110*
  drawing instruction 64–65, *70*, *72*, *75*, *102*
Lerici, Italy 38, 45

Lhuillier, Nicolas-François-David 15, 126, *133*, *134*, *148*, *154*
Ligorio, Pyrro 105
Lisbon, Portugal 64, *67*
Lower Grosvenor Street (No. 75) 15–16, *17*, *20*, *23*, *131*
see also Casino at Lower Grosvenor Street

M
Madonna del Popoli, Rome 126, *129*
Madonna dell'Orto, Rome *118*
Manocchi, Giuseppe *17*, 125, 126, *131*, *133*, *152*
Maratta, Carlo 16
Marlet, Henri *131*
Metella, Cecilia, tomb of *110*
Michelangelo 105
Montano, Giovanni Battista 107
Monte Cassino, Italy 47
Morris, Roger 26
Mosca, Simone *152*

N
Naples 45, *60*, *139*
Natali, Giovanni Battista 45–46
Newby Hall, North Yorkshire *148*
Nîmes, France 45, *48*

O
Osterley Park, London *148*

P
Palace of the Emperors, Rome 126
Palazzo Cancellaria, Rome 65
Palazzo dei Conservatori, Rome *136*
Palazzo delle Valle, Rome 126
Palazzo Lancellotti, Rome 126
Palazzo Spada, Rome 126, *129*
Paoli, Antonio Paolo 46, *48*
Parliament House, London 126–127, *135*, *136*, *139*, *141*, *142*, *157*
Pécheux, Laurent 63, 106, 125
circle of *108*, *109*
Penicuik House, Edinburgh 12
Piazza del Campidoglio, Rome *148*, *150*
Piranesi, Giovanni Battista 9, *57*, 64, 107, *115*, *116*, *150*
Trofei di Ottaviano Augusto *148*, *157*
Vasi, Candelabri, Cippi, Sarcofagi *55*, *148*
Pompeii 45
Pont du Gard, Vers-Pont-du-Gard 45, *48*
Portici, Italy 46, *55*
Porto Fino, Gulf of Genoa 26, *38*
Posilippo, Italy 46, *51*
Poussin, Gaspar 25, *33*
Pozzuoli (Puteoli), Italy 46, *57*, *60*

R
Raphael 105, 126
Rembrandt 106
Reni, Guido 16
Ricci, Marco 25
Richardson, George 125, 126, *130*
Richmond Park, London 26, *34*
Rimini, Italy 65, *87*
Roman Baths *23*, 64, *68*
Rosa, Salvator 25, *33*
Rose, Joseph 15

S
Sacco, Giuseppe 125
St Gereon, Cologne *88*
St Peter's, Rome 126, *131*, *141*
Salvi, Nicola *82*, 106
San Andrea delle Valle, Strozzi Chapel 126
San Giovanni Laterano, Rome 126
San Isidoro, Rome *66*
San Pietro in Montorio, Rome 65
Sandby, Paul 26, *29*, *32*
drawings *31*, *39*, *40*
Sandby, Thomas 26, *40*
Sangallo, Antonio da, the younger *152*
Sansovino, Jacopo 126, *129*
Santa Maria degli Angeli *100*
Santa Maria del Priorato, Rome *157*
Santa Maria della Pace, Rome *152*
Santa Maria della Salute, Venice *119*
Santa Maria Maggiore, Rome *141*
Santi Giovanni e Paolo, Rome *88*, *110*
Scara, Agostino 125, *136*
Soane, Sir John 11, 15, 16, *20*, *22*, *113*, *123*
Sora, Italy 65
Isola di Liri 47, *58*
Spalatro, Dalmatia *119*
Strozzi Chapel, San Andrea delle Valle 126
Syon House, London *148*

T
Temple of the Sun, Rome 126, *130*
Temple of Vesta, Tivoli *134*
Teniers, David 16
Tesio, Ludovico 126, *129*
Theatre Royal, London 127, *141*
Tivoli, near Rome *134*
Tomb of the Plautii, Rome *85*, *110*
Trajan's Column and markets, Rome *68*
Trevi Fountain *82*, 106, *108*, *109*

U
Udine, Giovanne da *129*

V
Vasari, Giorgio 107
Vatican, *Loggie* 15, *17*, *19*, 126, *131*, *147*
Velletri, near Rome 47, *53*
Venice 107, *119*
Via Clivio di Scauro *110*
Vianen, Adam van *121*
Vicenza, Italy 107
Villa Ludovisi, Rome *70*
Virgil's tomb, Mergellina 46, *50*, *51*
Viterbo, Italy 65
Vivares, François *25*, *29*
Volpato, Giovanni 15

Z
Zucchi, Antonio 125, 126, 127, *136*, *139*, *148*, *150*, *157*